Le Cordon Bleu®

The
Chocolate
Bible

First published in 2013 in the United States by

Carroll & Brown Limited

20 Lonsdale Road, London NW6 6RD

© Le Cordon Bleu International BV 2008,
 text and photography

English translation by Robyn Cahill

Previously published as Petit Larousse du Chocolat

© Larousse 2008

M&M's® is a registered trademark of Mars, Inc.

FROSTIES® is a registered trademark of The Kellogg Company

Library of Congress Cataloging-in-Publication Data

Petit Larousse du chocolat.

Le Cordon Bleu chocolate bible / English translation by Robyn Cahill.

pages cm

Translation of: Petit Larousse du chocolat.

Includes index.

ISBN 978-1-909066-13-7 (hardcover : alk. paper)

1. Cooking (Chocolate) 2. Desserts. 3. Cooking, French. I. Cordon bleu (School : Paris, France) II. Title. III. Title: Chocoloate bible.

TX767.C5P47813 2013

641.6'374--dc23

2013016802

ISBN: 978-1-909066-13-7

10 9 8 7 6 5 4 3 2 1

Printed in China

Le Cordon Bleu®

The Chocolate Bible

CARROLL & BROWN LIMITED

Preface

Le Cordon Bleu...

Le Cordon Bleu, the first school of cuisine and pastry founded in Paris in 1895, is an international ambassador for French culinary excellence.

Today, Le Cordon Bleu has a presence in some 20 countries, where more than 40 schools offer not only training in the culinary arts but also in hotel and restaurant management. More than 20,000 students attend the schools annually. Le Cordon Bleu sees itself as the exponent of French culinary expertise serving today's world.

The school welcomes a host of students from around the world wanting to discover French cuisine and pastry expertise, from the very basic techniques to the most advanced.

The teaching chefs at Le Cordon Bleu are all top notch restaurant professionals having gained their experience at the heart of some of the most renowned establishments. They are recipients of prestigious honors and/or winners of competitions including the coveted but rigorous, Meilleur Ouvrier de France challenge. As such, this guarantees the school's commitment to a high level of training adapted to meet the needs of the current professional world.

Le Cordon Bleu's internationally recognized curriculum provides students with all the fundamental tools necessary to attain employment. It also gives them the opportunity to be considered among the best in their profession. The mastery of these tools alone will allow students to express creativity and evolve over the course of their professional lives.

Both the general public and experienced amateurs are welcomed at Le Cordon Bleu. They come from every continent of the world to experience French gastronomy and the art of living, joining regular students (pending availability) to participate in demonstration and practical classes.

Le Cordon Bleu is also involved in numerous related activities including publishing, gourmet products, table arts and decoration, and licensing and consulting services.

Le Cordon Bleu also manages teaching restaurants. For instance in Ottawa, Canada's capital, the school's restaurant was recently named among the 63 best restaurants in North America. In Mexico City, a non-profit restaurant is operated by apprenticed Mexican scholarship holders and is housed in the former French Embassy building.

The partners and students of Le Cordon Bleu constitute a vast network of "ambassadors" – not only of France's gastronomic culture but of the art de vivre. On an international scale, they encourage and promote the dialogue between cultures by making French know-how available and locally accessible.

The book…

Chocolate arouses as much passion among pastry chefs as it does fondness among chocolate lovers. When it comes to taste, chocolate is a powerful ingredient but it can be complicated to implement in the kitchen. Therefore, it seems indispensable to have on hand a reference on chocolate combining the culinary and teaching competences of Le Cordon Bleu.

In this book dedicated to chocolate, the chefs at Le Cordon Bleu wish to share their knowledge and techniques through a variety of recipes able to be reproduced by anyone whatever his or her level of skill and, of course, they are suitable for every occasion.

To gain the knowledge necessary for creating these desserts, step-by-step technique photographs are scattered throughout the book. The reader can visualize at a glance the basics mastered by all great pastry chefs and taught at Le Cordon Bleu.

Le Cordon Bleu is keen to make this book accessible to all. Thus, in spite of the level of excellence of the recipes, they are always presented in a simple and creative manner.

Moreover, we have ensured that the recipes call for easy-to-find ingredients and basic equipment. In order that the best possible results can be obtained, all the recipes were tested by Le Cordon Bleu's pastry chefs and students.

Cakes, tarts, mousses, or candies… Work your way with ease through the entire book of recipes and techniques and you will discover chocolate in all of its forms!

ENJOY!

Patrick Martin Executive chef of Le Cordon Bleu International
Vice President, Education and Development

Le Cordon Bleu around the world

LE CORDON BLEU PARIS
8, rue Léon Delhomme
75015 Paris, France
T: +33 (0)1 53 68 22 50
F: +33 (0)1 48 56 03 96
paris@cordonbleu.edu

LE CORDON BLEU LONDON
15 Bloomsbury Square
London WC1A 2LS, UK
T: +44 (0) 207 400 3900
F: +44 (0) 207 400 3901
london@cordonbleu.edu

LE CORDON BLEU MADRID
Universidad Francisco de Vitoria
Ctra. Pozuelo-Majadahonda,
Km. 1,800
Pozuelo de Alarcón, 28223
Madrid, Spain
T: +34 91 715 10 46
F: +34 91 351 87 33
madrid@cordonbleu.edu

LE CORDON BLEU INTERNATIONAL BV
Herengracht 28
1015 BL Amsterdam

The Netherlands
T: +31 20 661 6592
F: +31 20 661 6593
amsterdam@cordonbleu.edu

LE CORDON BLEU ISTANBUL
Özyegin University
Çekmeköy Campus
Nisantepe Mevkii, Orman Sokak,
No:13, Alemdag, Çekmeköy 34794
Istanbul, Turkey
T: +90 216 564 9000
F: +90 216 564 9372
istanbul@cordonbleu.edu

LE CORDON BLEU LIBAN
Rectorat B.P. 446
USEK University – Kaslik
Jounieh – Lebanon
T: +961 9640 664/665
F: +961 9642 333
liban@cordonbleu.edu

LE CORDON BLEU JAPAN
Le Cordon Bleu Tokyo Campus
Le Cordon Bleu Kobe Campus
Roob-1, 28-13 Sarugaku-Cho,

Daikanyama, Shibuya-Ku, Tokyo 150-
0033, Japan
T : +81 3 5489 0141
F : +81 3 5489 0145
tokyo@cordonbleu.edu

LE CORDON BLEU KOREA
7th Fl., Social Education Bldg.,
Sookmyung Women's University,
Cheongpa-ro 47gil 100, Yongsan-Ku,
Seoul, 140-742 Korea
T: +82 2 719 6961
F: +82 2 719 7569
korea@cordonbleu.edu

LE CORDON BLEU, INC.
Le Cordon Bleu Chicago Campus
Le Cordon Bleu Minneapolis/St Paul
Campus
Le Cordon Bleu Orlando Campus
Le Cordon Bleu Boston Campus
Le Cordon Bleu Los Angeles Campus
Le Cordon Bleu Miami Campus
Le Cordon Bleu CCA - San Francisco
Campus
Le Cordon Bleu Scottsdale Campus
One Bridge Plaza N, Suite 275, Fort

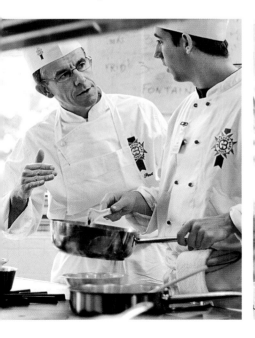

Lee, NJ USA 07024
T: +1 201 490 1067
info@cordonbleu.edu

LE CORDON BLEU OTTAWA
453 Laurier Avenue East
Ottawa, Ontario, K1N 6R4, Canada
T: +1 613 236 CHEF(2433)
Toll free +1 888 289 6302
F: +1 613 236 2460
Restaurant line +1 613 236 2499
ottawa@cordonbleu.edu

LE CORDON BLEU MEXICO
Universidad Anáhuac North Campus
Universidad Anahuac South Campus
Universidad Anáhuac Querétaro
Campus
Universidad Anáhuac Cancún Campus
Universidad Anáhuac Mérida Campus
Universidad Anáhuac Puebla Campus
Universidad Anáhuac Tampico Campus
Universidad Anáhuac Oaxaca Campus
Av. Universidad Anáhuac No. 46, Col.
Lomas Anáhuac
Huixquilucan, Edo. De Mex. C.P. 52786,
México
T: +52 55 5627 0210 EXT. 7132 / 7813
F: +52 55 5627 0210 EXT.8724
mexico@cordonbleu.edu

LE CORDON BLEU PERU
Le Cordon Bleu Peru University
Campus
Le Cordon Bleu Peru Campus
Le Cordon Bleu Cordontec Campus
Av. Nuñez de Balboa 530
Miraflores, Lima 18, Peru
T: +51 1 617 8300
F: +51 1 242 9209
peru@cordonbleu.edu

LE CORDON BLEU AUSTRALIA
Le Cordon Bleu Adelaide Campus
Le Cordon Bleu Sydney Campus
Le Cordon Bleu Melbourne Campus
Le Cordon Bleu Perth Campus
Days Road, Regency Park
South Australia 5010, Australia
Free call (Australia only) : 1 800 064
802
T: +61 8 8346 3000
F: +61 8 8346 3755
australia@cordonbleu.edu

LE CORDON BLEU NEW ZEALAND
Level 2, 48-54 Cuba Street
Wellington, 6142 New Zealand
T: +64 4 4729800
F: +64 4 4729805
info@lecordonbleu.co.nz

LE CORDON BLEU MALAYSIA
Sunway University
No. 5, Jalan Universiti, Bandar Sunway,
46150 Petaling Jaya, Selangor DE,
Malaysia
T: +603 5632 1188
F: +603 5631 1133
malaysia@cordonbleu.edu

LE CORDON BLEU THAILAND
946 The Dusit Thani Building
Rama IV Road, Silom
Bangrak, Bangkok
10500 Thailand
T: +66 2 237 8877
F: +66 2 237 8878
thailand@cordonbleu.edu

LE CORDON BLEU SHANGHAI
No. 1548, South Pudong Road,
Shanghai, China 200122
Tel + 86 136 0166 9198
Fax +86 21 65201011
shanghai@cordonbleu.edu

www.cordonbleu.edu
e-mail : info@cordonbleu.edu

Contents

A few tips before starting…

INGREDIENTS: All the ingredients in this book are the ones used in the testing of the recipes. Most are easily found in your local supermarket; only few will be available in specialty stores. The basic ingredients include all purpose flour, whole milk, baking powder, medium eggs, heavy whipping cream (35% butterfat), and unsalted butter, unless indicated otherwise. Flour has been measured using the "sift and spoon" method: Before measuring, stir or whisk the four to lighten it. Next, sift if required by the recipe. Then, spoon the flour lightly into the measuring cup and level it by sweeping a knife across the top of the cup. Spoon measures indicated are level spoonfuls. Use good-quality dark, bittersweet, milk, or white chocolate. However, when tempering and/or glazing, professional couverture chocolate is the best choice. For this process, always use chocolate containing at least 31% cocoa butter. Couverture chocolate is also known as confectioners' chocolate (and should not be confused with baking chocolate).

SPECIFIC EQUIPMENT: The recipes generally use items found in most kitchens. Some of the recipes, however, require specific items such as: a fine mesh wire strainer, pastry bags fitted with round or fluted tips, dessert or tart rings in different sizes, a candy thermometer (an electronic one with a temperature probe is ideal for tempering chocolate), and a kitchen scale.

OVEN TEMPERATURES: The oven temperatures and cooking times indicated in the recipes can vary slightly depending on your oven. All the recipes were tested in a small electric multi-function oven.

Temptingly rich cakes

The best way to make a basic ganache

In this recipe, equal amounts of chocolate and heavy whipping cream are used to produce a creamy chocolate mixture suitable for filling, glazing, or coating cakes. If the quantity of chocolate is increased, the ganache will become firmer—perfect for preparing truffles and other confections. Some of the recipes in this book use an adapted form of this basic version.

1. Coarsely chop 10½ oz bittersweet chocolate and place in a large bowl.

2. Heat 1¼ cups cream in a saucepan until simmering, and pour it over the chocolate.

3. Stir the cream and chocolate until evenly combined. Continue stirring until the mixture has cooled and is smooth and glossy. Let the ganache rest at room temperature until it can be easily spread.

The best way to make meringue, batter or pastry discs

Prepare the meringue, batter, or pastry, following the recipe of your choice, for example, on p. 36, 44, or 68.

① Place a dessert ring or tart pan of the appropriate size on a sheet of parchment paper and using it as a guide, trace a circle on the paper.

② Turn the marked side of the parchment paper over onto a baking sheet. Fit a pastry bag with a round tip, pushing it right through to the end of the bag to prevent it leaking when piping. Twist the bag just above the tip to seal it. Make a collar by folding the top of the bag over your hand and fill using a spatula.

③ Clear any air pockets by twisting the bag until the mixture is visible in the tip. Start piping in the center of the circle, working outward in a spiral until the circle is filled. Bake according to the directions indicated in the chosen recipe.

The best way to make a rolled sponge

Cook the sponge and prepare the filling as indicated on p.18 or 76.

(1) Put the cooked sponge on piece of parchment paper (or a clean dish towel), crust-side down.

(2) Using a palette knife, spread the filling evenly over the sponge leaving a small border along the outside edges uncovered.

(3) Start rolling on one of the long sides; fold approximately ³/₄ inch of the sponge over tightly. Using the parchment paper as a guide, slowly pull up the edge to form the sponge into a roll. Finish with the seam underneath and cut a small piece off each end to even the roll.

The best way to glaze a cake or tart

Cook the cake or tart. Let cool and prepare the glaze indicated in the recipe of your choice, for example, on p. 24 or 32.

(1) Place the cake on a wire rack over a large bowl.

(2) Pour the glaze over the entire cake including the sides.

(3) Use a palette knife to spread the glaze evenly over the top of the cake and around the sides. To set the glaze, refrigerate for 30 minutes before serving.

Chocolate Delight

SERVES 6

DIFFICULTY ★ ★ ★

PREPARE: 30 minutes

COOK: 25 minutes

$4\frac{1}{2}$ tbsp unsalted butter

1 cup superfine sugar

2 eggs

1 cup flour, sifted

$\frac{1}{4}$ cup unsweetened cocoa
  powder, sifted

1 tsp vanilla extract

Preheat the oven to 350°F. Butter an 8-in round cake pan.

Melt the unsalted butter in a saucepan over low heat.

Place the sugar and the eggs in a heatproof bowl; whisk to combine. Stand the bowl over a bain-marie and whisk continuously for 5–8 minutes, or until the mixture becomes light and doubles in volume. Do not allow it to become too hot. Remove the bowl from the bain-marie and continue whisking quickly by hand, or with an electric mixer on high speed, until the batter is cool and falls in a ribbon from the whisk or mixer. Gently fold in the sifted flour and cocoa powder, adding it in 2 or 3 batches. Quickly add the melted butter and the vanilla extract.

Pour the cake batter into the prepared cake pan, to come $\frac{2}{3}$ of the way up the side. Bake for 25 minutes, or until the surface of the cake is firm but springy to the touch. Turn the cake out onto a wire rack and cool.

CHEF'S TIP: Sprinkle sliced almonds on the bottom and sides of the buttered cake pan before pouring the batter into it and/or dust the cake with confectioners' sugar when cooled. A red fruit coulis would be a delicious accompaniment for this simple dessert.

Chocolate Yule Log

SERVES **10–12**

DIFFICULTY ★ ★ ★

PREPARE: 1 ½ hours

COOK: 8 minutes

REFRIGERATE: 1 hour

Almond Sponge

5½ oz almond paste

½ cup confectioners' sugar

3 egg yolks

2 egg whites

⅓ cup superfine sugar

¾ cup + 1 tbsp flour, sifted

3½ tbsp unsalted butter, melted

Ganache

7 oz bittersweet chocolate

1 cup heavy whipping cream

5 tbsp soft unsalted butter

3½ tbsp rum

Rum Syrup

½ cup water

½ cup superfine sugar

1 tsp coffee extract

3 tbsp rum

Coffee Buttercream

1 egg

2 egg yolks

¼ cup + 1 tbsp superfine sugar

⅓ cup water

1 cup + 2 tbsp soft unsalted butter

Coffee extract, to taste

◇ See p.14: Making a rolled sponge.

Preheat the oven to 350°F. Line a 15 x 12-in jelly-roll pan with parchment paper.

Almond Sponge: Place the almond paste in a bowl and add the confectioners' sugar; beat until the mixture resembles fine breadcrumbs. Whisk in the egg yolks one at a time. In a separate bowl, whisk the egg whites until frothy; add 2 tbsp of the superfine sugar a little at a time, whisking until the egg whites are smooth and shiny. Gradually add the remaining sugar, whisking until stiff peaks form. Fold ⅓ of the whisked egg whites and half the sifted flour into the almond-confectioners' sugar mixture; carefully fold in another ⅓ of the egg whites and the remaining flour. Fold in the rest of the egg whites and the melted butter. Pour a 2-in layer of batter into the prepared pan. Bake about 8 minutes, or until the sponge is firm but springy to the touch. Cool on a wire rack.

Ganache: Coarsely chop the chocolate and place in a bowl. Heat the cream in a saucepan until simmering then pour over the chocolate; stir until smooth. Add the unsalted butter and the rum. Set the ganache aside at room temperature until it can be easily spread.

Rum Syrup: Place the water and sugar in a saucepan over low heat; stir until the sugar is completely dissolved then bring to the boil; cool. When the syrup is cold, add the coffee extract and the rum.

Coffee Buttercream: Beat the whole egg and egg yolks in the bowl of an electric mixer until well combined. Place the sugar and water in a saucepan and stir over low heat until the sugar is completely dissolved. Bring to the boil and cook (do not stir) the syrup until it registers 250°F on a candy thermometer. With the mixer running, gradually pour the syrup in a thin steady stream down the inside of the bowl; continue beating until cool. Add the unsalted butter and coffee extract.

Peel off and discard the parchment paper used to cook the sponge. Place the sponge on another piece. Brush with the rum syrup and spread with a layer of coffee buttercream. Start rolling on one long side and fold approximately ¾ in of the sponge over tightly. Using the parchment as a guide, slowly pull up the edge, forming the sponge into a roll. Finish with the seam underneath; cut a small piece off each end to even the roll. Coat with coffee buttercream and refrigerate for 1 hour. Before serving, spread ganache over the coffee buttercream, using a palette knife.

Fresh Fruit Yule Log

SERVES 10–12

DIFFICULTY ★ ★ ★

PREPARE: 1½ hours

COOK: 8 minutes

REFRIGERATE: 1 hour

Chocolate Sponge

3 egg yolks

6 tbsp superfine sugar

3 egg whites

½ cup + 1 tbsp flour, sifted

3 tbsp unsweetened cocoa
  powder, sifted

Chocolate Cream

1½ oz bittersweet
  chocolate

1 sheet or ¾ tsp powdered
  gelatin

⅔ cup milk

2 egg yolks

¼ cup superfine sugar

2 tbsp cornstarch

¾ cup heavy whipping
  cream

Chocolate Syrup

½ cup water

½ cup superfine sugar

2 tbsp unsweetened cocoa
  powder

Finishing

1 cup strawberries, diced*

1 pear, diced*

¾ cup raspberries*

¾ cup blackberries*

1 kiwi, diced*

*Plus extra for decoration

Confectioners' sugar

Preheat the oven to 350°F. Line a 15 x 12-in jelly-roll pan with parchment paper.

Chocolate Sponge: Combine the egg yolks and 2 tbsp of the sugar; beat until pale yellow and creamy. In a separate bowl, whisk the egg whites, gradually adding the remaining sugar until stiff peaks form; gently incorporate the egg yolk-sugar mixture. Fold in the sifted flour and cocoa powder. Pour the sponge batter into the prepared pan and smooth with a palette knife. Bake for about 8 minutes, or until firm but springy to the touch. Cool on a wire rack.

Chocolate Cream: Chop the chocolate and set aside in a large bowl. Soften the sheet or powdered gelatin in a small bowl of cold water. Bring the milk to the boil and remove from the heat. Whisk the egg yolks and sugar until pale yellow and creamy; add the cornstarch. Slowly whisk in half the hot milk then add the remaining milk; return the mixture to the saucepan and stir continuously over low heat until thickened. Continue stirring and boil for 1 minute; remove from the heat. (Squeeze the excess water from the sheet gelatin.) Add the gelatin to the hot milk mixture. Pour over the chopped chocolate and stir until smooth; cool. Cover the surface with plastic wrap, stir from time to time and set aside to cool. Beat the whipping cream until firm and gently fold into the cooled chocolate cream.

Chocolate Syrup: Place the water, sugar, and cocoa powder in a saucepan and stir over low heat until the sugar is completely dissolved then, bring to the boil; cool.

Finishing: Fold the fruit carefully into the chocolate cream. Line a 14-in log mold with a piece of parchment paper larger than the mold. Cut the chocolate sponge into 2 rectangles— 5 x 14 in and 2 x 14 in. Place the larger rectangle in the mold (it will come up the sides) and brush with chocolate syrup. Fill with the chocolate-fruit cream, mounding the cream toward the top. Brush the smaller rectangle with chocolate syrup and place it on top of the fruit cream. Refrigerate for 1 hour then carefully invert the log and turn it out onto a platter. Decorate with extra fruit and dust with confectioners' sugar.

Fruit and Nut Chocolate Loaf

SERVES 12

DIFFICULTY ★ ★ ★

PREPARE: 25 minutes

COOK: 50 minutes

COOL: 15 minutes

$^2/_3$ cup dried apricots

$^1/_3$ cup dried pears

$^1/_3$ cup blanched
hazelnuts, toasted

3 tbsp pistachios

$^1/_2$ cup candied mixed
fruit

1 cup + 2 tbsp soft unsalted
butter

2 cups confectioners'
sugar

5 eggs

$2^1/_2$ cups flour, sifted

6 tbsp unsweetened cocoa
powder, sifted

2 tsp baking powder,
sifted

Preheat the oven to 350°F. Butter a 10 x 4-in loaf pan.

Cut the dried apricots and pears into small pieces. Combine with the hazelnuts, pistachios, and candied fruit; set aside.

Place the soft unsalted butter in a bowl and beat until creamy. Add the confectioners' sugar and beat until the mixture is soft and light. Beat in the eggs one at a time and add the sifted flour, cocoa, and baking powder. Stir well to combine all the ingredients. Gently fold in the reserved dried fruit and nuts.

Pour the batter into the prepared loaf pan and bake for 50 minutes, or until firm but springy to the touch.. Cool in the loaf pan for 15 minutes before turning out onto a wire rack.

CHEF'S TIP: The cake can be kept refrigerated for several days or wrapped in plastic wrap and frozen for several weeks. If desired, the fruits and nuts can be omitted and a simple chocolate loaf prepared, using the remaining ingredients.

Chocolate-Raspberry Square

SERVES 8–10

DIFFICULTY ★ ★ ★

PREPARE: 1 hour

COOK: 20-25 minutes

REFRIGERATE: 15 minutes

Chocolate Sponge

2³/₄ oz bittersweet
  chocolate

1³/₄ oz unsweetened
  cooking chocolate

¹/₂ cup + 1 tbsp soft
  unsalted butter

3 egg yolks

¹/₂ cup superfine sugar

4 egg whites

¹/₃ cup cornstarch, sifted

¹/₂ tsp baking powder,
  sifted

Chocolate Mousse

6 oz dark (55%) chocolate

1¹/₄ oz unsweetened
  cooking chocolate

1¹/₄ cups heavy whipping
  cream

5 egg yolks

7 tbsp superfine sugar

Raspberry Syrup

¹/₄ cup water

¹/₄ cup superfine sugar

¹/₂ cup raspberry juice

3 tbsp raspberry eau-de-
  vie

Raspberry Glaze

¹/₂ cup raspberries

1 or 2 tsp mild honey

¹/₃ cup superfine sugar

1¹/₄ tsp powdered fruit
  pectin

Preheat the oven to 350°F. Line a 7-in square cake pan with parchment paper.

Chocolate Sponge: Melt the chocolates over a bain-marie. Remove from the heat and stir in the unsalted butter, egg yolks, and ¹/₄ cup of the sugar. In a separate bowl, whisk the egg whites, gradually adding the remaining sugar until the whites are smooth, shiny, and stiff peaks form; gently fold onto the chocolate mixture. Add the sifted cornstarch and baking powder and mix to combine. Pour the batter into the prepared cake pan and smooth with a palette knife. Bake for about 20– 25 minutes, or until firm. Cool on a wire rack.

Chocolate Mousse: Roughly chop the chocolates and melt over a bain-marie. Remove from the heat and cool. Whisk the whipping cream until firm. Combine the egg yolks and sugar and whisk until pale yellow and creamy. Using a spatula, stir in the chocolate a little at a time. Fold in the whipped cream.

Raspberry Syrup: Place the water, sugar, and raspberry juice in a saucepan over low heat, stir until the sugar dissolves then bring to the boil; let cool. Add the raspberry eau-de-vie to the cold syrup.

Raspberry Glaze: Put the raspberries, honey, and 3 tbsp of the sugar into a saucepan and bring to the boil. Combine the pectin with the remaining sugar and add to the raspberry mixture; bring to the boil again. Set aside to cool.

Using a long, serrated knife, cut the sponge horizontally into two even layers. Brush or sprinkle one with the raspberry syrup and coat with the chocolate mousse. Place the other layer on the chocolate mousse and brush it with the syrup. Use a spatula or palette knife to spread the raspberry glaze over the surface of the sponge. Refrigerate for 15 minutes, or until firm. If necessary, even the sides of the chocolate raspberry square with a sharp knife dipped in hot water.

CHEF'S TIP: If desired, other berries, such as blackberries, could be used to prepare the glaze. If you do not have the pectin, replace it with 2 sheets or 1¹/₃ tsp powdered gelatin, softened in cold water before using. If you do not have a 7-in square cake pan, use a jelly-roll pan or cookie sheet. In which case, cook the sponge for 15 minutes then, when cool, cut into 2 even squares.

Genovese Almond Cake

SERVES 4–6

DIFFICULTY ★ ★ ★

PREPARE: 20 minutes

COOK: 25 minutes

Sliced almonds

4 tbsp unsalted butter

4 eggs

7 oz almond paste (33% almonds)

2½ tbsp flour, sifted

2 tbsp unsweetened cocoa powder, sifted

½ tsp baking powder, sifted

Preheat the oven to 350°F. Butter a 7-in square cake pan and sprinkle it with sliced almonds.

Melt the unsalted butter in a saucepan and set aside.

Beat the eggs into the almond paste, one at a time. Continue whisking for 5 minutes, or until the mixture is pale and thick and falls from the whisk in a ribbon without breaking. Fold in the sifted flour, cocoa, and baking powder; add the melted butter.

Pour the cake batter into the prepared cake pan, to come ⅔ up the sides. Bake for 25 minutes, or until firm. Turn out onto a wire wire rack and cool.

Chocolate Heart

SERVES 8–10

DIFFICULTY ★ ★ ★

PREPARE: 1½ hours

COOK: 40 minutes

REFRIGERATE: 50 minutes

Chocolate Cake

8 oz bittersweet
  chocolate, chopped

½ cup + 2 tbsp unsalted
  butter

4 egg yolks

¾ cup superfine sugar

4 egg whites

6½ tbsp flour, sifted

Ganache

9 oz bittersweet chocolate

1 cup heavy whipping
  cream

Decoration

Raspberries, strawberries,
  blackberries, blueberries

◊ See p.15: Glazing
a cake or tart.

Preheat the oven to 350°F. Butter and dust with flour a heart-shaped cake pan (or a 9½-in round cake pan).

Chocolate Cake: Melt the chocolate and the unsalted butter over a bain-marie; stir until smooth. Beat the egg yolks and half the sugar until they are pale and thick. In a separate bowl, whisk the egg whites, gradually adding the remaining sugar until they are smooth, shiny, and stiff peaks form. Fold the sifted flour into the egg yolk-sugar mixture and combine with the melted chocolate-butter mixture. Whisk ⅓ of the egg whites into the chocolate mixture to lighten it; carefully fold in the remainder in two separate batches. Rest the batter for 5 minutes before pouring it into the prepared cake pan. Bake for 40 minutes, or until a knife inserted into the center of the cake comes out clean. Cool on a wire rack before turning the cake out; refrigerate for 20 minutes.

Ganache: Coarsely chop the chocolate and place in a bowl. Heat the cream in a small saucepan until simmering and pour over the chocolate; stir until smooth. Set the ganache aside for about 10 minutes at room temperature, until it can be easily spread.

When the chocolate cake is cold and fairly hard, cut a thin slice from the top to level it; use a long serrated knife and cut in a sawing motion. Spread the ganache evenly over the entire surface of the cake; refrigerate for 30 minutes until firm. Decorate with berries.

CHEF'S TIP: The cake can be kept refrigerated for 2–3 days. It can also be served with a crème anglaise or whipped cream.

Meringues and Spiced Pears in a Chocolate and Wine Sauce

SERVES **6**

DIFFICULTY ★ ★ ★

PREPARE: 1½ hours

COOK: 35 minutes approx

Meringues

4 egg whites

¼ cup superfine sugar

¾ cup almond meal/flour, sifted

⅔ cup confectioners' sugar, sifted

¼ cup flour, sifted

Ganache

3¼ oz bittersweet chocolate

6½ tbsp heavy whipping cream

2 tsp mild honey

2½ tbsp soft unsalted butter

Spiced Pears

6 pears

½ lemon

2 tbsp unsalted butter

2 tbsp mild honey

Spices: ground cinnamon, nutmeg, and pepper and cloves

Chocolate and Wine Sauce

3½ oz bittersweet chocolate

1½ cups red wine

3 star anise

2½ tbsp superfine sugar

Preheat the oven to 325°F. Trace six 3¼-in circles on parchment paper and turn the marked side over onto one or more baking sheets, depending on the oven size.

Meringues: Whisk the egg whites, gradually adding the sugar until stiff peaks form. Carefully fold in the sifted almond meal/flour, confectioners' sugar, and flour. Fit a pastry bag with a medium-size round tip and fill with the meringue mixture. Start piping in the center of the circles, working outward in a spiral until filled. Pipe a raised border on the edge of each circle to form a nest. Bake for 20 minutes. Remove the nests from the hot baking sheets; cool on a wire rack.

Ganache: Coarsely chop the chocolate and place in a bowl. Heat the cream and the honey in a small saucepan until simmering and pour over the chocolate; stir until smooth. Add the unsalted butter and stir until well combined. Divide the ganache evenly between the cooled meringue nests; set aside to harden.

Spiced Pears: Peel and cut the pears in half and core, leaving the stalks in place for presentation, if preferred. Rub with the lemon to prevent discoloration. Place the unsalted butter, honey, and spices in a large frying or sauté pan and bring to the boil. Lower the heat, arrange the pear halves in a single layer and cook gently for 15 minutes; turning the pears over after approximately 7 minutes.

Chocolate and Wine Sauce: Coarsely chop the chocolate. In a medium saucepan, heat the wine and the star anise over medium heat. Then raise the heat and boil until the liquid is reduced by one-half. Add the chopped chocolate, 4 tsp water, and sugar, bring to the boil again. Cook until the chocolate is completely melted. Using a fine-meshed strainer, strain the sauce; cool.

Warm 6 dessert plates. Spoon a pool of sauce onto each plate, place a meringue nest in the center and top with 2 pear halves.

CHEF'S TIP: If desired, decorate with spices such as cinnamon sticks, vanilla pods, and star anise.

Chocolate Hazelnut Square

Cake

4 tbsp unsalted butter

6 egg yolks

$^2/_3$ cup superfine sugar

4 egg whites

$^1/_2$ cup flour, sifted

6 tbsp unsweetened cocoa
  powder, sifted

$^1/_2$ cup hazelnut or almond
meal/flour

Glaze

$3^1/_2$ oz bittersweet
  chocolate

$6^1/_2$ tbsp heavy whipping
  cream

1 tbsp mild honey

Decoration

$5^1/_2$ oz chocolate sprinkles

Preheat the oven to 350°F. Butter a 7-in square cake pan and dust it with flour.

Cake: Melt the unsalted butter; set aside. Beat the egg yolks and $^1/_2$ cup of the sugar until pale and thick. In a separate bowl whisk the egg whites, gradually adding the remaining sugar, until they are smooth and shiny and stiff peaks form. Gently fold into the egg yolk-sugar mixture. Combine the sifted flour and cocoa powder in a bowl; add the hazelnut meal/flour. Fold one-third of this mixture into the egg white mixture; carefully fold in the remainder in 2 separate batches; add the melted butter. Pour the batter into the prepared cake pan. Bake for 20 minutes, or until a knife inserted into the center of the cake comes out clean. Cool before turning out onto a wire rack.

Chocolate Glaze: Finely chop the chocolate and place in a bowl. Heat the cream and the honey in a small saucepan until simmering and pour over the chocolate; stir gently until smooth. Set aside to cool. Use a palette knife or spatula to spread the glaze evenly over the entire surface of the cake; press the chocolate sprinkles around the sides. Refrigerate for 1 hour, or until the glaze is firm.

CHEF'S TIP: This cake is even more delicious when served with an orange sorbet.

Chocolate Walnut Cake

SERVES 8–10

DIFFICULTY ★ ★ ★

PREPARE: 1¼ hours

COOK: 40 minutes approx

COOL: 2 hours

REFRIGERATE: 1 hour

Chocolate Cake

6½ oz bittersweet chocolate

½ cup + 2 tbsp soft unsalted butter

½ cup (packed) dark brown sugar

2 egg yolks

¾ cup chopped walnuts

7 tbsp almond meal/flour

2 egg whites

3 tbsp superfine sugar

Chocolate Glaze

3½ oz bittersweet chocolate

6½ tbsp heavy whipping cream

1 tbsp mild honey

Decoration

1¾ oz white chocolate

Walnut halves

◊ See p.15: Glazing a cake or tart.

◊ See p.318: Making a paper pastry bag.

Preheat the oven to 325°F. Butter an 8-in round cake pan.

Chocolate Cake: Finely chop the chocolate and set aside. Place the soft unsalted butter in a bowl and beat until smooth. Add the dark brown sugar and continue beating until creamy. Blend in the egg yolks, then the chopped chocolate, walnuts, and ground almonds; set the mixture aside. In a separate bowl, whisk the egg whites until frothy. Add 1 tbsp of the sugar a little at a time and continue whisking until the egg whites are smooth and shiny. Add the remaining sugar, whisking until stiff peaks form. Whisk ⅓ of the egg whites into the chocolate mixture to lighten it; carefully fold in the remainder in 2 separate batches. Pour the batter into the prepared cake pan and bake for approximately 40 minutes, or until a knife inserted into the center of the cake comes out clean. Cool for at least 2 hours before turning the cake out onto a wire rack.

Chocolate Glaze: Finely chop the chocolate and place in a bowl. Heat the cream and honey in a small saucepan until simmering and pour over the chocolate; stir gently until smooth. Set aside to cool. Use a palette knife or spatula to spread the glaze evenly over the entire surface of the cake. Refrigerate for 1 hour, or until the glaze is firm.

Decoration: Make a small paper pastry bag. Melt the white chocolate, cool and pour it into the pastry bag; snip off the tip. Decorate the surface of the cake with geometric designs and walnut halves.

CHEF'S TIP: The cake can be kept refrigerated for 2–3 days or, if carefully wrapped in plastic wrap, it can be frozen for several weeks.

Autumn Leaf Gateau

SERVES **6**

DIFFICULTY ★ ★ ★

PREPARE: 1½ hours

COOK: 1 hour

REFRIGERATE: 2 hours

Almond Meringue

4 egg whites

$^2/_3$ cup superfine sugar

1 $^1/_3$ cups almond meal/flour

Chocolate Mousse

9 oz bittersweet (55%)
  chocolate

4 egg whites

$^3/_4$ cup superfine sugar

$^1/_3$ cup heavy whipping
  cream

Decoration

9 oz bittersweet chocolate

$^1/_3$ cup confectioners'
  sugar or unsweetened
  cocoa powder, sifted

◇ See p.13: Shaping
meringue, batter, or pastry
discs.

Preheat the oven to 210°F. Trace three 8-in circles on parchment paper and turn the marked side over onto one or more baking sheets, depending on oven size.

Almond Meringue: Whisk the egg whites, gradually adding the sugar, until the whites are smooth and shiny and stiff peaks form; gently fold in the ground almonds a little at a time. Fit a pastry bag with a plain round tip and fill it with the almond meringue. Start piping in the center of each traced circle, working outward in a spiral until filled. Bake for 1 hour. Cool on a wire rack until required.

Chocolate Mousse: Chop the chocolate and melt in a bain-marie over low heat. Remove from the heat and stir until smooth; cool. Whisk the egg whites, gradually adding the sugar, until they are smooth and shiny and stiff peaks form. Whisk the whipping cream until firm and clinging to the whisk. Quickly whisk $^1/_3$ of the egg whites into the chocolate mixture to lighten it. Use a spatula and carefully fold in the remainder in 2 separate batches; fold in the whipped cream. Refrigerate until firm.

Heat the oven to 125°F and put two baking sheets into it. Chop the chocolate for decoration and melt over a bain-marie; set aside.

Put a meringue disc on a plate and spread it with a layer of chocolate mousse. Place the second meringue disc on top and spread it with a layer of chocolate mousse, reserving some mousse for later use. Finish with the remaining meringue disc and refrigerate for 30 minutes.

Remove the pastry sheets from the oven and spread with a thin layer of melted chocolate. Place in the bottom of the refrigerator for 10 minutes. Spread the top of the cake with the reserved chocolate mousse and smooth the surface using a palette knife; refrigerate for 30 minutes. When the chocolate on the pastry sheets begins to harden, remove from the refrigerator and bring to room temperature. Use a broad flat scraper to scrape up a wide rectangle of chocolate. Wrap it around the gateau, carefully folding it over the top. Scrape the remainder, in smaller rectangles, bending them gently until wavy; use to decorate the top of the cake (see photo opposite). Dust lightly with confectioners' sugar or cocoa powder.

Chocolate Strawberry Cake

SERVES 6–8

DIFFICULTY ★ ★ ★

PREPARE: 2 hours

COOK: 25 minutes approx

REFRIGERATE: 1½ hours approx.

Sponge

4 eggs

²/₃ cup superfine sugar

1 cup flour, sifted

Kirsch Syrup

²/₃ cup water

³/₄ cup superfine sugar

4 tsp Kirsch

Chocolate Mousseline Cream

5³/₄ oz milk chocolate

3 egg yolks

6 tbsp superfine sugar

3 tbsp cornstarch

2 cups milk

1 cup soft unsalted butter

1 lb 2 oz strawberries, cut in halves

Decoration

Confectioners' sugar

7 oz pink almond paste (refrigerated 1 hour)

Strawberry halves (optional)

Bittersweet chocolate, melted (optional)

Preheat the oven to 350°F. Butter an 8-in round cake pan.

Sponge: Place the eggs and sugar in a heatproof bowl; whisk to combine. Stand the bowl over a bain-marie and whisk continuously for 5–8 minutes, or until the mixture becomes light and doubles in volume. Do not allow it to become too hot. Remove from the bain-marie and continue whisking quickly by hand, or with an electric mixer on high speed, until cool and the batter falls in a ribbon from the whisk or mixer. Gently fold in the sifted flour, adding it in 2 or 3 batches. Pour the mixture into the prepared cake pan, to come ²/₃ up the side. Bake for 25 minutes, or until the surface is firm but springy to the touch. Turn out onto a wire rack and cool.

Kirsch Syrup: Place the water and sugar in a saucepan over low heat, stir until the sugar dissolves then bring to the boil; cool. Add the Kirsch.

Chocolate Mousseline Cream: Chop the chocolate and place in a large bowl. Combine the egg yolks, 4 tbsp of the sugar and the cornstarch in another bowl; whisk until pale yellow and creamy. Bring the milk and the remaining sugar to the boil. Slowly whisk ¹/₂ of the hot milk-sugar mixture into the egg yolk mixture and add the remaining milk; return to the saucepan. Stir continuously over medium heat until the mixture is thickened and comes to the boil. Pour over the chopped chocolate and stir until smooth. Cover the surface of the chocolate cream with plastic wrap; cool. Beat the unsalted butter until creamy. When the chocolate cream is cold, blend in the creamed butter using an electric mixer; refrigerate the chocolate mousseline cream for 20 minutes.

Line an 8¹/₂-in dessert ring with strawberry halves. Use a long serrated knife to cut the sponge horizontally in 2 even layers. Place one layer in the bottom of the ring and brush with Kirsch syrup. Spread with ¹/₃ of the chocolate mousseline cream. Place the remaining strawberries on the cream and cover with ¹/₂ of the remaining mousseline cream. Top with the other sponge layer, brush with syrup and spread with a thin layer of the remaining mousseline cream, saving the rest for decoration, if desired. Refrigerate for 1 hour before removing the ring.

Roll out a thin 8¹/₂-in disc of almond paste; place it on top of the filled cake. Decorate with strawberries, leftover mousseline cream, and melted chocolate.

Chocolate Almond Kugelhopf

SERVES 8

DIFFICULTY ★ ★ ★

PREPARE: 30 minutes

COOK: 40 minutes

REFRIGERATE: 30 minutes

Cake

5$\frac{1}{2}$ oz bittersweet
   chocolate

$\frac{3}{4}$ cup soft unsalted
   butter

$\frac{1}{2}$ cup (packed) soft dark or
   light brown sugar

3 egg yolks

2 cups almond flour/meal

3 egg whites

3 tbsp superfine sugar

Chantilly Cream

1 cup heavy whipping
   cream

2 or 3 drops vanilla extract

3$\frac{1}{2}$ tbsp confectioners'
   sugar

Decoration

2 tbsp sliced almonds

Preheat the oven to 300°F. Butter an 8$\frac{1}{2}$-in diameter bundt pan or kugelhopf mold.

Cake: Chop the chocolate and melt in a bain-marie over low heat. Remove from the heat and cool. Place the unsalted butter in a bowl and beat until smooth. Blend in the brown sugar and continue beating until creamy. Add the yolks, one at a time, to the butter-sugar mixture, beating well after each addition. Fold in the almond flour/meal and the melted chocolate; set aside. Whisk the egg whites, gradually adding the sugar, until they are smooth and shiny and stiff peaks form. Add $\frac{1}{3}$ of the egg whites to the chocolate mixture to lighten it then gently fold in the remainder. Pour the batter into the prepared mold and bake for 40 minutes, or until a knife inserted into the center of the cake comes out clean. Cool before turning out onto a wire rack.

Chantilly Cream: Combine the cream and vanilla extract and whisk until the cream begins to stiffen. Add the confectioners' sugar and continue whisking until the cream is firm and clings to the whisk. Fit a pastry bag with a star tip, fill it with the Chantilly cream and decorate the top of the cake; sprinkle with sliced almonds.

CHEF'S TIP: Instead of soft brown sugar, Demerara sugar could be used. When making Chantilly cream, use a deep bowl; chill it and the cream 15 minutes before whisking or beating.

Bitter Chocolate Cake

SERVES 8

DIFFICULTY ★ ★ ★

PREPARE: 35 minutes

COOK: 45 minutes

REFRIGERATE: 30 minutes

Cake

$1/2$ cup + 1 tbsp soft
unsalted butter

1 cup superfine sugar

4 eggs

$1 1/4$ cups flour, sifted

$1/2$ cup unsweetened cocoa
powder, sifted

Ganache

$6 1/2$ oz dark (55– 70%)
chocolate

$3/4$ cup heavy whipping
cream

Decoration

$5 1/2$ oz chocolate sprinkles

◊ See p.12: Making a basic
ganache.

Preheat the oven to 350°F. Butter an 8-in round cake pan.

Cake: Place the unsalted butter in a bowl and beat until smooth. Blend in the sugar and beat until creamy. Add the eggs, one at a time, being careful not to over mix. Gently fold in the sifted flour and cocoa powder. Pour the batter into the prepared pan and bake for 45 minutes, or until a knife inserted into the center of the cake comes out clean. Turn out onto a wire rack and cool.

Ganache: Coarsely chop the chocolate and place in a bowl. Heat the cream in a saucepan until simmering and pour it over the chocolate; stir until smooth.

Use a long serrated knife to cut the cake horizontally into two even layers. Place one layer on a wire rack and spread it with a thin layer of ganache, using a palette knife. Top with the remaining layer and refrigerate for 30 minutes.

Glaze the entire surface of the cake with the remaining ganache; press the chocolate sprinkles around the side using a palette knife. To decorate, dip a serrated knife (or a fork) in hot water and make wavy lines in the top.

CHEF'S TIP: If the cake is too dry, brush or sprinkle with the syrup of your choice, before applying the ganache. It could also be decorated with Chantilly cream rosettes.

Chocolate-Cherry Cake

SERVES 8

DIFFICULTY ★ ★ ★

PREPARE: 2 hours

COOK: 30 minutes approx

REFRIGERATE: 1½ hours

Sponge

4 tsp unsalted butter

²/₃ cup superfine sugar

4 eggs

³/₄ cup flour, sifted

6 tbsp unsweetened cocoa
  powder, sifted

Syrup

¹/₂ cup water

6 tbsp superfine sugar

Chocolate Mousse

7 oz dark (55%) chocolate

1²/₃ cups heavy whipping
  cream

25 bottled cherries, pitted

Preheat the oven to 350°F. Butter an 8-in round cake pan.

Sponge: Melt the unsalted butter in a saucepan over low heat; set aside. Place the sugar and the eggs in a heatproof bowl; whisk to combine. Stand the bowl over a bain-marie and whisk continuously for 5–8 minutes, or until the mixture becomes light and doubles in volume. Do not allow it to become too hot. Remove the bowl from the bain-marie and continue whisking quickly by hand, or with an electric mixer on high speed, until cool and the batter falls in a ribbon from the whisk or mixer. Gently fold in the sifted flour and cocoa powder, adding it in 2 or 3 batches. Quickly add the melted butter. Pour the batter into the prepared pan, bake for about 25 minutes, or until the surface is firm but springy to the touch.

Syrup: Place the water and sugar in a saucepan over low heat, stirring until the sugar dissolves, bring to the boil; cool.

Chocolate Mousse: Roughly chop the chocolate and place it in a bowl; melt over a slowly simmering bain-marie until the temperature reaches approximately 115°F on a candy thermometer. Beat the cream until firm peaks cling to the whisk. Whisking quickly, add about one-third of the whipped cream to the hot chocolate. Pour the mixture over the remaining cream and gently fold in using the whisk or a spatula to evenly blend the ingredients.

Use a long serrated knife to cut the sponge horizontally into two layers of equal thickness. Place one layer on a wire rack, brush or sprinkle with syrup and spread with a thick layer of chocolate mousse. Reserve some bottled cherries for decoration and scatter the remainder over the mousse. Brush the other sponge layer with syrup and place it on top of the cherries; refrigerate for 1 hour. Decorate with the remaining chocolate mousse and cherries.

CHEF'S TIP: For a professional touch, fit a pastry bag with a star tip, fill with the chocolate mousse and decorate the cake.

Chocolate-Raspberry Cake

SERVES 8–10

DIFFICULTY ★ ★ ★

PREPARE: 2½ hours

COOK: 8 minutes

REFRIGERATE: 1 hour 10 minutes

Sponge

4 egg yolks

²/₃ cup superfine sugar

4 egg whites

³/₄ cup flour, sifted

6 tbsp unsweetened cocoa powder, sifted

Raspberry Syrup

¹/₂ cup water

¹/₄ cup superfine sugar

3¹/₂ tbsp raspberry liqueur

Chocolate Mousse

9 oz dark (55%) chocolate

2 cups heavy whipping cream

Chocolate Glaze

5¹/₂ oz bittersweet chocolate

1 cup heavy whipping cream

5 tsp mild honey

Decoration

3 cups fresh raspberries

◊ See p.13 Making pastry, batter, or meringue discs.
◊ See p.15 Glazing a cake or tart.

Preheat the oven to 350°F. Prepare one or more baking sheets, depending on the oven size. Trace three 8-in circles on parchment paper and turn the marked side over onto the baking sheet(s).

Sponge: Combine the egg yolks and ¹/₃ cup of the sugar; beat until the mixture is pale yellow and creamy. In a separate bowl, whisk the egg whites, gradually adding the remaining sugar, until the whites are smooth and shiny and stiff peaks form. Gently fold in the egg yolk-sugar mixture, then the sifted flour and cocoa powder. Fit a pastry bag with a plain round tip and fill it with the sponge batter. Start piping in the center of the traced circles, working outward in a spiral until filled. Bake approximately 8 minutes, or until firm; set the discs aside.

Raspberry Syrup: Place the water and sugar in a saucepan over low heat, stirring until the sugar is dissolved then bring to the boil. Remove from the heat; cool. Add the raspberry liqueur to the cold syrup.

Chocolate Mousse: Roughly chop the chocolate and place it in a bowl and melt over a slowly simmering bain-marie until the temperature reaches approximately 115°F on a candy thermometer. Beat the cream until firm peaks cling to the whisk. Whisking quickly, add about one-third of the whipped cream to the hot chocolate. Pour the mixture over the remaining cream and fold in gently with the whisk or a spatula to evenly blend the ingredients.

Chocolate Glaze: Finely chop the chocolate and place in a bowl. Heat the cream and honey in a small saucepan until simmering and pour over the chocolate, stirring gently until evenly combined.

Place one of the sponge discs on a wire rack and brush with raspberry syrup. Spread with ¹/₃ of the chocolate mousse, and arrange ¹/₃ of the raspberries on top. Place the second disc on the wire rack, brush with the raspberry syrup then place it on top of the first layer. Spread it with another ¹/₃ of the chocolate mousse, and arrange another ¹/₃ of the raspberries on top. Place the remaining sponge disc on top. Cover the entire surface of the cake with the rest of the chocolate mousse and refrigerate for 20 minutes. Reheat the chocolate glaze and pour it over the cake; use a palette knife to spread it evenly over the top and around the side. Refrigerate for 50 minutes to set the glaze. Before serving, decorate with the remaining raspberries.

Chocolate and Hazelnut Cake

SERVES 6–8

DIFFICULTY ★ ★ ★

PREPARE: 20 minutes

COOK: 35 minutes

$^{1}/_{2}$ cup milk

$^{1}/_{2}$ cup superfine sugar

1 vanilla pod, split

$3^{1}/_{2}$ oz dark (55– 70%) chocolate

3 tbsp chocolate-hazelnut spread

2 tbsp soft unsalted butter

2 eggs

$^{3}/_{4}$ cup flour, sifted

1 tsp baking powder, sifted

3 tbsp hazelnut flour/meal

Preheat the oven to 350°F. Butter an 8-in round cake pan.

Place the milk and 2 tbsp of the sugar in a saucepan. Using the point of a knife, scrape the seeds from the vanilla pod into the milk, add the pod and bring to the boil. Set aside to infuse.

Coarsely chop the chocolate and combine with the chocolate hazelnut spread; melt over a bain-marie.

Cream the unsalted butter and the remaining sugar. Add the eggs, one at a time, mixing well after each addition. Blend in the melted chocolate and chocolate-hazelnut spread; add one-third of the sifted flour and baking powder.

Remove the vanilla pod from the milk. Add the milk and the remaining sifted flour and baking powder in 2 batches to the chocolate mixture; fold in the hazelnut flour/meal.

Pour the batter into the prepared cake pan and bake for 35 minutes, or until only the center of the cake wobbles. Cool completely before turning out onto a wire rack.

CHEF'S TIP: Instead of ground hazelnuts, whole hazelnuts could be used. Chop or crush, place on a baking sheet lined with parchment paper and toast lightly in a 320°F oven for 5 minutes.

Mom's Cake

SERVES 10–12
DIFFICULTY ★ ★ ★
PREPARE: 20 minutes
COOK: 30–35 minutes

6½ oz bittersweet
  chocolate
½ cup + 3 tbsp unsalted
  butter
6 eggs
1½ cups superfine sugar
¾ cup flour, sifted
1 tbsp coffee extract

Preheat the oven to 325°F. Butter a 2½ quart round gratin dish.

Coarsely chop the chocolate, combine with the unsalted butter and melt over a bain-marie. Remove from the heat and stir until smooth.

Separate the yolks and whites of 3 eggs. Place the 3 yolks and the remaining whole eggs in a bowl; add 1¼ cups of the sugar and beat until pale yellow and creamy. In a separate bowl, whisk the 3 egg whites, gradually adding the remaining sugar, until the whites are smooth and shiny and stiff peaks form.

Carefully, stir the melted chocolate-butter mixture into the egg yolk-sugar mixture. Whisk in one-third of the egg whites to lighten the mixture and gently fold in the remainder. Add the sifted flour and coffee extract. Pour the batter into the gratin dish.

Prepare a roasting pan large enough to hold the gratin dish and add hot water to come halfway up the sides. Place the gratin dish in the pan, transfer to the oven and bake for 30–35 minutes, or until only the center of the cake wobbles. Remove from the oven; cool slightly before serving.

CHEF'S TIP: To prepare your own coffee extract, infuse ⅓ cup of ground coffee in ⅔ cup of hot water. If necessary, add 1 tsp of instant coffee; strain before using. This cake is also excellent served with seasonal fruits, such as apples, pears, or strawberries.

Creamy Chocolate-Fig Cake

SERVES 8

DIFFICULTY ★ ★ ★

MACERATE: 12 hours (overnight)

PREPARE: 1 hour

COOK: 45 minutes

1 ¹/₃ cups dried figs

1 ¹/₂ cups sweet dessert wine (such as Muscat)

¹/₂ cup milk

¹/₂ cup superfine sugar

¹/₂ split vanilla pod

3 ¹/₂ oz dark (55–70%) chocolate

2 tbsp soft unsalted butter

2 eggs

³/₄ cup flour, sifted

¹/₂ tsp baking powder, sifted

◊ This recipe must be started a day ahead.

The day before, place the figs in a bowl, cover with the wine and macerate for at least 12 hours.

Preheat the oven to 350°F. Butter and flour an 8-in round cake pan.

Place the milk and 2 tbsp sugar in a saucepan. Using the point of a knife, scrape the seeds from the vanilla pod into the milk, add the pod and bring to the boil. Set aside to infuse.

Drain the figs and cut in small pieces.

Coarsely chop the chocolate and melt over a bain-marie; cool.

Cream the unsalted butter and the remaining sugar. Mix in the melted chocolate and add the eggs, one by one, beating well after each addition; fold in one-third of the sifted flour and baking powder. Discard the vanilla pod and add one-half of the cooled milk. Fold in another one-third of the sifted flour and baking powder then add the remaining milk. Mix in the rest of the sifted flour and baking powder; add the fig pieces. Pour the batter into the cake pan to come about ³/₄ up the side. Bake for about 45 minutes, or until a knife inserted into the center of the cake comes out clean. Cool for several minutes before turning out onto a wire rack.

CHEF'S TIP: You can replace the figs in this recipe with other dried fruits such as pears, peaches, or apricots.

Chocolate-Apricot Semolina Cake

SERVES 6

DIFFICULTY ★ ★ ★

PREPARE: 45 minutes

COOK: 50–55 minutes

COOL: 2 hours

Cake

2 cups milk

$1/3$ cup superfine sugar

1 vanilla pod, split

$1/2$ cup dried apricots

$1/2$ cup semolina

3 eggs

$1/3$ cup chocolate chips

Decoration

Raspberries

Apricots

Mint leaves

Raspberry coulis (optional)

Preheat the oven to 325°F. Butter an 8-in round cake pan. Place it on a sheet of parchment paper and using it as a guide, cut out a round of parchment. Line the cake pan and brush it with butter.

Put the milk and 2 tbsp of the sugar into a saucepan. Using the point of a knife, scrape the seeds from the vanilla pod into the milk; add the pod. Dice the apricots and add to the milk; bring to the boil. When the milk reaches boiling point, discard the vanilla pod. Stirring continuously, add the semolina in a thin, steady stream. Cook over low heat for 20–25 minutes, or until the semolina thickens and absorbs some, but not all, of the milk. Set aside to cool slightly.

Beat the eggs with the remaining sugar and stir into the cooled semolina. Pour the mixture into the prepared cake pan and sprinkle with chocolate chips; bake for 30 minutes, or until firm. Cool for at least 2 hours before turning out.

Cut the cake into individual portions, serve with fresh raspberries, apricots, and/or a raspberry coulis; decorate with mint leaves.

CHEF'S TIP: Instead of buttering and lining the cake pan with parchment, coat it with caramel and allow it to set, as if you were preparing the mold for a crème caramel. Then, pour in the semolina cake mixture and chocolate chips. Once the cake has cooled and been turned out, it will have a crunchy caramel coating.

Raspberry-Filled Chocolate Sponge

SERVES 8

DIFFICULTY ★ ★ ★

PREPARE: 30 minutes

COOK: 25 minutes

Sponge

4 tsp unsalted butter

4 eggs

$^2/_3$ cup superfine sugar

$^3/_4$ cup flour, sifted

6 tbsp unsweetened cocoa powder, sifted

$^1/_2$ cup raspberry jam

Confectioners' sugar, sifted

Preheat the oven to 350°F. Butter an 8-in round cake pan.

Sponge: Melt the unsalted butter in a saucepan over low heat; set aside. Place the eggs and sugar in a heatproof bowl; whisk to combine. Stand the bowl over a bain-marie and whisk continuously for 5–8 minutes, until the mixture becomes light and doubles in volume. Do not allow it to become too hot. Remove the bowl from the bain-marie and continue whisking quickly by hand, or with an electric mixer on high speed, until cool and the batter falls in a ribbon from the whisk or mixer. Gently fold in the sifted flour and cocoa powder, adding it in 2 or 3 batches. Quickly add the melted butter. Pour the batter into the prepared pan and bake for about 25 minutes, or until the surface is firm but springy to the touch. Cool for several minutes before turning it out onto a wire rack.

Using a long, serrated knife, cut the sponge horizontally into two layers of equal thickness. Spread one with the raspberry jam and place the other layer on top; dust with confectioners' sugar.

CHEF'S TIP: When preparing this type of sponge, the water in the bain-marie must not be too hot. This helps the sponge retain its volume and lightness.

Marbled Chocolate Loaf

SERVES 8

DIFFICULTY ★ ★ ★

PREPARE: 30 minutes

COOK: 50 minutes

COOL: 5 minutes

1 cup + 2 tbsp soft unsalted butter

2¼ cups confectioners' sugar

6 eggs

3½ tbsp rum

2½ cups flour, sifted

2 tsp baking powder, sifted

3 tbsp milk

⅓ cup unsweetened cocoa powder, sifted

Preheat the oven to 350°F. Butter and flour an 11 x 4-in loaf pan.

Cream the unsalted butter and confectioners' sugar. Add the eggs, one at a time, beating well after each addition. Add the rum and fold in the sifted flour and baking powder. Pour half of the batter into a separate bowl. Place the cocoa powder in a small bowl and pour over the milk; stir well to combine. Stir the chocolate mixture into one of the bowls of batter.

Fill the loaf pan with the batter. To obtain a marbled effect, alternate spoonfuls of the plain and chocolate batters. Bake for 50 minutes, or until the point of a knife inserted in the center of the cake comes out clean. Cool for 5 minutes before turning out onto a wire rack.

CHEF'S TIP: You could also use 2 small loaf pans, 7 in long, but you must reduce the baking time to 20 minutes.

Marbled Chocolate-Pistachio Loaf

SERVES 15

DIFFICULTY ★ ★ ★

PREPARE: 40 minutes

COOK: 1 hour

COOL: 10 minutes

Chocolate Batter

4 tbsp unsalted butter

3 eggs

1 cup superfine sugar

6 tbsp heavy whipping cream

1 pinch salt

1 cup + 2 tbsp flour, sifted

6 tbsp unsweetened cocoa powder, sifted

1 tsp baking powder, sifted

Pistachio Batter

4 tbsp unsalted butter

1 tbsp water

1 cup superfine sugar

1 tsp mild honey

1/4 cup shelled pistachios

3 eggs

6 tbsp heavy whipping cream

1 pinch salt

1 1/3 cups flour, sifted

1 tsp baking powder, sifted

Preheat the oven to 325°F. Butter a 11 x 4-in loaf pan.

Chocolate Batter: Melt the unsalted butter in a saucepan over low heat without letting it color; set aside to cool. Combine the eggs and sugar and beat until the mixture is light and creamy. Stir in the cream, melted butter, and salt. Then fold in the sifted flour and cocoa and baking powders.

Pistachio Batter: Melt the unsalted butter in a saucepan over low heat without letting it color; set aside to cool. Heat the water, 2 tbsp of the sugar and the honey in a small saucepan, stirring until the sugar is completely dissolved; bring to the boil. Remove the syrup from the heat. Place the pistachios in a blender and grind to a fine powder. Pour the honey syrup into the blender and mix to obtain a soft paste. Combine the eggs and the pistachio paste in a bowl, add the remaining sugar and beat until the mixture is light and creamy. Stir in the cream, melted butter, and salt then fold in the sifted flour and baking powder.

To obtain a marbled effect, alternate spoonfuls of the batters when filling the prepared loaf pan. Start with the pistachio batter and then drop in the chocolate. Bake for 1 hour, or until the point of a knife inserted in the center of the cake comes out clean. Cool for 10 minutes before turning the cake out onto a wire rack.

CHEF'S TIP: Wrap the cake carefully in plastic wrap and freeze it for several weeks or keep refrigerated for 2–3 days.

The Marvel

SERVES **8–10**

DIFFICULTY ★ ★ ★

PREPARE: 1½ hours

COOK: 30 minutes approx

REFRIGERATE: 25 minutes

Sponge

4 tsp unsalted butter

4 eggs

²/₃ cup superfine sugar

½ cup flour, sifted

6 tbsp unsweetened cocoa
  powder, sifted

Caramelized Walnut Cream

⅓ cup heavy whipping
  cream

1 tbsp honey

½ cup superfine sugar

²/₃ cup chopped walnuts

Chocolate Praline Mousse

5½ oz bittersweet
  chocolate

5 tbsp praline paste (p.314)

2 tbsp heavy whipping
  cream

Decoration

1⅓ cup chopped walnuts

Chocolate shavings (p.209)

Preheat the oven to 350°F. Butter an 8-in round cake pan.

Sponge: Melt the unsalted butter in a saucepan over low heat; set aside. Place the sugar and eggs in a heatproof bowl; whisk to combine. Stand the bowl over a bain-marie and whisk continuously for 5–8 minutes, or until the mixture becomes light and doubles in volume. Do not allow it to become too hot. Remove the bowl from the bain-marie and continue whisking quickly by hand, or with an electric mixer on high speed, until cool and the batter falls in a ribbon from the whisk or mixer. Gently fold in the sifted flour and cocoa powder, adding it in 2 or 3 batches. Quickly add the melted butter. Pour the batter into the prepared pan and bake for about 25 minutes, or until the surface is firm but springy to the touch. Cool for several minutes before turning out onto a wire rack.

Caramelized Walnut Cream: Heat the whipping cream and honey until simmering; set aside. Place the sugar in a separate saucepan and cook slowly until it melts and becomes a golden caramel. Do not stir during the cooking process but gently shake the saucepan occasionally to move the melted sugar off the bottom. Carefully stir in the whipping cream-honey mixture (it will spit violently when the liquid is added); stir until smooth then remove from the heat and immediately add the chopped walnuts. Pour the caramelized walnut cream into a bowl; leave to cool to room temperature.

Chocolate Praline Mousse: Roughly chop the chocolate; place it and the praline paste in a bowl and melt over a slowly simmering bain-marie until the temperature reaches approximately 115°F on a candy thermometer. Beat the cream until firm peaks cling to the whisk. Whisking quickly, add about ⅓ of the whipped cream to the melted chocolate. Pour the mixture over the remaining cream and gently fold in with the whisk or a spatula to evenly blend the ingredients.

Using a long, serrated knife, cut the cooled sponge horizontally into two layers of equal thickness. Spread one with the caramelized walnut cream then add a layer of the chocolate praline mousse. Top with the other sponge layer; refrigerate 15 minutes. Coat the entire surface with the remaining mousse and press the chopped walnuts onto the side of the cake; decorate with chocolate curls.

Molten Chocolate Cakes with Pistachio Cream

SERVES **4**

DIFFICULTY ★ ★ ★

PREPARE: 20 minutes

COOK: 12 minutes

Pistachio Cream

3 tbsp shelled, unsalted pistachios

1 cup milk

3 egg yolks

$^1/_3$ cup superfine sugar

1 or 2 drops vanilla extract

Cake

$4^1/_2$ oz dark (55–70%) chocolate

$^1/_2$ cup + 1 tbsp unsalted butter

3 eggs

$^2/_3$ cup superfine sugar

$^1/_3$ cup flour, sifted

Pistachio Cream: Preheat the oven to 350°F. Put the chopped pistachios on a baking sheet and toast in the oven for 2 minutes; stir to avoid burning. Place in a food processor and grind to a powder. Bring the milk slowly to the boil. Beat the egg yolks and sugar until pale yellow and creamy. Stir in one-third of the hot milk and mix well to combine; pour the mixture into the remaining hot milk. Stirring constantly with a wooden spoon, cook over low heat until the cream is thickened and coats the back of a spoon. (Do not allow to boil!) Remove from the heat immediately and strain into a bowl. Add the vanilla extract and the powdered pistachios. Cool the pistachio cream; refrigerate until required.

Cake: Melt the chocolate and the unsalted butter over a bain-marie; stir until smooth. Beat the eggs and sugar until pale yellow and creamy. Stir in the melted chocolate-butter mixture then fold in the sifted flour. Divide the batter equally between 4 small gratin or baking dishes then bake at 350°F for 12 minutes, until the top is firm.

Serve while still warm accompanied by the pistachio cream.

CHEF'S TIP: If you prefer a more elegant presentation, bake the cakes in 3-in tart rings then turn out onto individual dessert plates before removing the rings. Cover a baking sheet with parchment paper. Butter 4 tart rings and place on the sheet then bake as above. To serve, spoon the pistachio cream around each one. This dessert is also delicious served with thinly sliced fresh, or canned, pears.

King's Cake

SERVES 6

DIFFICULTY ★ ★ ★

PREPARE: 35 minutes

COOK: 12 minutes

REFRIGERATE: 30 minutes

Sponge

1 1/4 cups almonds flour/meal

1 1/4 cups confectioners'
  sugar

2 eggs

4 egg yolks

1/4 cup flour, sifted

5 tbsp unsweetened cocoa
  powder, sifted

5 egg whites

1/3 cup superfine sugar

Ganache

10 1/2 oz bittersweet
  chocolate

1 1/4 cups heavy whipping
  cream

Rum Syrup

1/2 cup water

1/2 cup superfine sugar

2 tsp rum

◊ See page 12: Making
a basic ganache.

Preheat the oven to 350°F. Line a 12 x 15-in jelly-roll pan with parchment paper.

Sponge: Combine the ground almonds, confectioners' sugar, whole eggs, and egg yolks in a bowl and beat for about 5 minutes until light and creamy. Fold in the sifted flour and cocoa powder. Whisk the egg whites in a large bowl, gradually adding the sugar, until the egg whites are smooth and shiny and stiff peaks form. Whisk one-third of the egg whites into the chocolate mixture. Carefully fold in the remainder in 2 or 3 batches. Pour the batter into the prepared pan and bake for 12 minutes, or until firm but springy to the touch.

Chocolate Ganache: Finely chop the chocolate and place in a bowl. Heat the cream in a saucepan until simmering and pour it over the chocolate; stir until smooth. Set aside until the ganache can be easily spread.

Rum Syrup: Place the water and sugar in a saucepan over low heat, stirring until the sugar dissolves then, bring to the boil; remove the pan from the heat and cool. When the syrup is cold, add the rum.

Cut the sponge into three equal 4 x 15-in rectangles. Brush or sprinkle the first piece with rum syrup and spread with a thin layer of ganache; place the second sponge piece on top and add some syrup and ganache. Top with the remaining sponge and add some syrup and ganache, setting some ganache aside for the final decoration; refrigerate 30 minutes.

Spread all the remaining ganache over the top of the cake. Dip a serrated knife (or a fork) in hot water; use to make wavy lines to decorate the top of the cake.

CHEF'S TIP: If you remove the cake from the refrigerator 30 minutes before serving it will be soft and moist.

Florentine-topped Chocolate Mousse-Meringue Pyramids

SERVES 4

DIFFICULTY ★ ★ ★

PREPARE: 1½ hours

COOK: 30 minutes approx

REFRIGERATE: 15 minutes

Almond Meringue

4 egg whites

¼ cup superfine sugar

1¼ cups confectioners' sugar, sifted

1⅔ cups almond flour/meal, sifted

Florentines

6½ tbsp heavy whipping cream

3½ tbsp unsalted butter

2½ tbsp mild honey

6 tbsp superfine sugar

⅓ cup candied cherries

⅓ cup candied orange peel

1½ cup sliced almonds

3 tbsp flour

Milk Chocolate Mousse

7 oz milk chocolate

1¼ cups whipping cream

◇ See p.13: Shaping meringue, batter, or pastry discs.

Preheat the oven to 400°F. Trace 16 circles on parchment paper: 4 x 3¼ in, 4 x 2¾ in, 4 x 2½ in and 4 x 2 in; turn the marked sides over onto 2 baking sheets.

Almond Meringue: Whisk the egg whites in a bowl, gradually adding the sugar, until the whites are smooth and shiny and stiff peaks form. Carefully fold in the sifted confectioners' sugar and ground almonds. Fit a pastry bag with a medium-sized round tip and fill with the meringue. Start piping in the center of each traced circle, working outward in a spiral until filled. Bake for 12 minutes. Remove the meringues from the hot baking sheets to avoid drying.

Florentines: Lower the oven temperature to 350°F. Cover a jelly roll pan with parchment paper. Put the cream, unsalted butter, honey, and sugar in a small saucepan over low heat and cook until the mixture registers 225°F on a candy thermometer. Dice the candied cherries and orange peel and place in a bowl with the sliced almonds and flour; stir to combine. Add the cooked cream mixture, stirring carefully to avoid breaking the almonds. Pour a 1¼-in layer of the mixture onto the prepared jelly roll pan. Bake for 15 minutes, or until the Florentine is lightly golden. Remove from the oven and cool for a few minutes before cutting into small squares or triangles.

Milk Chocolate Mousse: Roughly chop the chocolate and place it in a bowl; melt over a slowly simmering bain-marie until the temperature reaches approximately 115°F on a candy thermometer. Beat the cream until firm peaks cling to the whisk. Whisking quickly, add about one-third of the whipped cream to the hot chocolate. Pour the mixture over the remaining cream and fold in gently with the whisk or a spatula to evenly blend the ingredients.

Fit a pastry bag with a round tip and fill with the milk-chocolate mousse. Pipe balls of mousse onto the 3¼-in meringue discs. Top with the 2¾-in discs and repeat the piping. Add the 2½-in discs and piped mousse then finish with the 2-in discs, to form 4 pyramids. Refrigerate for 15 minutes. Before serving, place a Florentine on top of each pyramid.

Chocolate Pound Cake

SERVES 12

DIFFICULTY ★ ★ ★

PREPARE: 15 minutes

COOK: 45 minutes

1 cup + 2 tbsp soft unsalted
 butter
1 1/4 cups superfine sugar
5 eggs
1 2/3 cup flour, sifted
1 tsp baking powder,
 sifted
2/3 cup unsweetened cocoa
 powder, sifted

Preheat the oven to 350°F. Butter and flour a 10 x 3-in loaf pan.

Beat the unsalted butter until creamy. Add the sugar and continue beating until the mixture is light and fluffy. Add the eggs, one at a time, beating well after each addition. Fold in the sifted flour and baking and cocoa powders; stir to combine.

Pour the batter into the prepared loaf pan to come about 3/4 of the way up the side. Bake for 45 minutes, or until the point of a knife inserted into the center of the cake comes out clean. Turn out onto a wire rack. Serve warm or cold.

CHEF'S TIP: Creaming the unsalted butter instead of melting it makes the cake much lighter.

Chocolate Chip Pound Cake

SERVES 12
DIFFICULTY ★ ★ ★
PREPARE: 15 minutes
COOK: 45 minutes

1 cup + 2 tbsp soft unsalted
  butter
1¼ cups superfine sugar
5 eggs
1⅔ cup flour, sifted
¼ cup chocolate chips
3½ tbsp rum

Preheat the oven to 350°F. Butter and flour a 10 x 3-in loaf pan.

Beat the butter until creamy. Add the sugar and continue beating until the mixture is light and fluffy. Add the eggs, one at a time, beating well after each addition. Fold in the sifted flour and chocolate chips; stir well to combine.

Pour the batter into the prepared loaf pan to come about ¾ up the side. Bake for 45 minutes, or until the point of a knife inserted into the center of the cake comes out clean. Turn out onto a wire rack and, while the chocolate-chip pound cake is still warm, sprinkle or brush with the rum. Serve warm or cold.

CHEF'S TIP: If you like, add the rum to the cake batter before baking.

Queen of Sheba Cake

SERVES 6–8

DIFFICULTY ★ ★ ★

PREPARE: 20 minutes

COOK: 20 minutes

COOL: 15 minutes

3¹/₂ oz almond paste

4 egg yolks

7 tbsp confectioners' sugar

3 egg whites

3 tbsp superfine sugar

¹/₂ scant cup flour, sifted

3 tbsp unsweetened cocoa powder, sifted

2 tbsp unsalted butter

Preheat the oven to 325°F. Butter and flour an 8-in round cake pan.

Place the almond paste and egg yolks in a bowl and beat to combine. Add the confectioners' sugar and continue beating until the mixture is smooth and light. Whisk the egg whites in a separate bowl, gradually adding the sugar, until the whites are smooth and shiny and stiff peaks form. Then blend in the almond paste mixture. Carefully, fold in the sifted flour and cocoa powder. Melt the unsalted butter over low heat without letting it color and mix it into the batter.

Pour the batter into the prepared cake pan and bake for 20 minutes, or until the top is firm but the cnter wobbles slightly. Cool for 15 minutes before turning the cake out onto a wire rack.

CHEF'S TIP: Accompany this moist cake with assorted fresh berries such as blueberries, blackberries, raspberries, or strawberries.

Chocolate-Cointreau Roulade

SERVES 12

DIFFICULTY ★ ★ ★

PREPARE: 1½ hours

COOK: 8 minutes

REFRIGERATE: 20 minutes

Sponge

3 egg yolks

6 tbsp superfine sugar

3 egg whites

²/₃ scant cup flour, sifted

3 tbsp unsweetened cocoa
  powder, sifted

Cointreau Cream

1 sheet or ³/₄ tsp gelatine

1¹/₃ cups milk

3 egg yolks

6 tbsp superfine sugar

3 tbsp flour, sifted

2 tbsp cornstarch

4 tsp Cointreau

3¹/₂ tbsp heavy whipping
  cream

Cointreau Syrup

²/₃ cup water

6 tbsp superfine sugar

4 tsp Cointreau

Chocolate Whipped Cream

3 oz bittersweet chocolate

1¹/₄ cups heavy whipping
  cream

Raspberry Jam

◊ See p.14: Rolling a sponge.

Preheat the oven to 400°F. Line a 15 x 12-in jelly roll pan with parchment paper.

Sponge: Whisk the egg yolks and 2 tbsp of the sugar until pale yellow and creamy. Whisk the egg whites in a separate bowl, gradually adding the remaining sugar until the whites are smooth and shiny and stiff peaks form. Gently fold in the egg yolk-sugar mixture and the sifted flour and cocoa powder. Pour the batter onto the prepared baking sheet and smooth with a palette knife. Bake approximately 8 minutes, or until firm but springy to the touch. Cool on a wire rack.

Cointreau Cream: Soften the sheet or powdered gelatin in cold water. Bring the milk to the boil and remove from the heat. Whisk the egg yolks and sugar until pale yellow and creamy. Add the sifted flour and cornstarch and gradually whisk in some of the hot milk. Return the mixture to the saucepan; stir continuously over low heat until thickened. Stirring continuously, boil for 1 minute, remove from heat, then add the gelatin; remove from the heat. Pour the mixture into a bowl and cover the surface with plastic wrap; cool. Add the Cointreau. Beat the whipping cream until firm and clinging to the whisk; gently fold into the cooled Cointreau cream.

Cointreau Syrup: Place the water and sugar in a saucepan over low heat, stirring until the sugar is completely dissolved then bring to the boil; cool. Add the Cointreau to the cold syrup.

Chocolate Whipped Cream: Chop the chocolate and melt over a bain-marie. Beat the whipping cream until firm peaks cling to the whisk. Whisking quickly, blend in the warm melted chocolate.

Brush or sprinkle the sponge with the Cointreau syrup and spread with a layer of raspberry jam and the Cointreau cream. Start rolling on one of the long sides and fold ³/₄ inch of the sponge over tightly. Using the parchment paper as a guide, slowly pull up the edge to form the sponge into a roll. Finish with the seam underneath and cut a small piece off each end to even it; refrigerate for 20 minutes. Fit a pastry bag with a plain tip, fill with the chocolate whipped cream and pipe the surface of the roll with it.

Chocolate-Raspberry Roll

SERVES 8–10

DIFFICULTY ★ ★ ★

PREPARE: 25 minutes

COOK: 8 minutes

REFRIGERATE: 20 minutes

Sponge

4 tsp unsalted butter

4 eggs

$^2/_3$ cup superfine sugar

$^3/_4$ cup flour, sifted

6 tbsp unsweetened cocoa powder, sifted

Filling

$^2/_3$ cup heavy whipping cream

$6^1/_2$ tbsp confectioners' sugar

$1^2/_3$ cup raspberries

Decoration

Unsweetened cocoa powder and/or confectioners' sugar, sifted

◇ See p.14: Rolling a sponge.

Preheat the oven to 400°F. Line a 12 x 15-in jelly roll pan with parchment paper.

Sponge: Melt the unsalted butter in a saucepan over low heat; set aside. In a heatproof bowl place the sugar and the eggs; whisk to combine. Stand the bowl over a bain-marie and whisk continuously for 5–8 minutes, or until the mixture becomes light and doubles in volume. Do not allow it to become too hot. Remove the bowl from the bain-marie and continue whisking quickly by hand, or with an electric mixer on high speed, until cool and the batter falls in a ribbon from the whisk or mixer. Gently fold in the sifted flour and cocoa powder, adding it in 2 or 3 batches. Quickly add the melted butter.

Pour the batter onto the prepared jelly roll pan and smooth with a palette knife. Bake about 8 minutes, or until the surface is firm but springy to the touch. Cool on a wire rack. Slide the cooked sponge, with the parchment attached, onto a wire rack. Place a sheet of parchment paper and another wire rack on top of the cooked sponge and turn everything over. Remove the top wire rack; peel off the parchment used during cooking. Set aside to cool.

Filling: Whisk the whipping cream and the confectioners' sugar until firm and clinging to the whisk. Spread the sponge with the whipped cream and scatter the raspberries over the surface. Start rolling on one of the long sides and fold $^3/_4$ inch of the sponge over tightly. Using the parchment paper as a guide, slowly pull up the edge to form a roll. Finish with the seam underneath and cut a small piece off each end to even it; refrigerate for 20 minutes. Before serving, dust with sifted cocoa powder and/or confectioners' sugar.

Sachertorte

SERVES **8–10**

DIFFICULTY ★ ★ ★

PREPARE: 35 minutes

COOK: 40 minutes

REFRIGERATE : 40 minutes

Sponge

6¼ oz bittersweet
  chocolate

2 tbsp unsalted butter

7 egg whites

6½ tbsp superfine sugar

3 egg yolks

⅓ cup flour, sifted

¼ cup almond flour/meal,
  sifted

Kirsch Syrup

⅔ cup water

½ cup superfine sugar

1 tbsp Kirsch

Ganache

5½ oz bittersweet
  chocolate

⅔ cup heavy whipping
  cream

Filling

¾ cup apricot jam

Decoration

3½ oz milk chocolate

◊ See p. 319: Making a
paper pastry bag.
◊ See p.15: Glazing
a cake or tart.

Preheat the oven to 350°F. Butter an 8½-in round cake pan.

Sponge: Melt the chocolate and the butter over a bain-marie; stir until smooth. In a separate bowl, whisk the egg whites until frothy. Add 2 tbsp of the sugar, a little at a time, and continue whisking until the egg whites are smooth and shiny. Gradually add the remaining sugar, whisking until stiff peaks form. Mix in the egg yolks, sifted flour, and ground almonds. Add the melted chocolate-butter mixture to the batter. Pour the batter into the prepared cake pan and bake for 40 minutes, or until the top of the sponge is firm but springy to the touch. Cool before turning out.

Kirsch Syrup: Place the water and sugar in a saucepan over low heat, stirring until the sugar is completely dissolved then bring to the boil; cool. Add the Kirsch to the cold syrup.

Ganache: Coarsely chop the chocolate and place in a bowl. Heat the cream until simmering and pour it over the chocolate; stir until smooth. Set the ganache aside until it can be spread easily.

Using a long, serrated knife, cut the cooled sponge horizontally into two layers of equal thickness. Sprinkle or brush one with Kirsch syrup and spread it with a ½-in layer of apricot jam. Top with the other layer and sprinkle with syrup. Refrigerate for 30 minutes.

Cover the entire surface of the sponge with ganache using a palette knife. Refrigerate for about 10 minutes, or until the ganache is firm and cool. Heat the remaining ganache in a saucepan. Place the Sachertorte on a wire rack and pour the warm ganache over until the entire cake is covered. Smooth the glaze immediately with a warm palette knife.

Decoration: Make a small paper pastry bag. Melt the milk chocolate, cool and pour it into the pastry bag; snip off the tip. Pipe the word "Sacher" on the surface of the cake.

Chocolate Truffle Cake

SERVES 8

DIFFICULTY ★ ★ ★

PREPARE: 2 hours

COOK: 25 minutes

REFRIGERATE: 25 minutes

Sponge

4 tsp unsalted butter

4 eggs

$^2/_3$ cup superfine sugar

$^3/_4$ cup flour, sifted

6 tbsp unsweetened cocoa
  powder, sifted

Cointreau Syrup

$^2/_3$ cup water

1 cup superfine sugar

$3^1/_2$ tbsp Cointreau

Ganache

9 oz bittersweet chocolate

1 cup heavy whipping
  cream

$3^1/_2$ tbsp Cointreau

Decoration

Unsweetened cocoa
  powder, sifted

◊ See p.12: Preparing a
basic ganache.

Preheat the oven to 350°F. Butter and flour an $8^1/_2$-in round cake pan.

Sponge: Melt the unsalted butter in a saucepan over low heat; set aside. Place the sugar and the eggs in a heatproof bowl; whisk to combine. Stand the bowl over a bain-marie and whisk continuously for 5–8 minutes, or until the mixture becomes light and doubles in volume. Do not allow it to become too hot. Remove the bowl from the bain-marie and continue whisking quickly by hand, or with an electric mixer on high speed, until cool and the batter falls in a ribbon from the whisk or mixer. Gently fold in the sifted flour and cocoa powder, adding it in 2 or 3 batches. Quickly add the melted butter and pour the batter into the prepared pan. Bake for about 25 minutes, or until the surface of the sponge is firm but springy to the touch. Cool for several minutes before turning out onto a wire rack.

Cointreau Syrup: Place the water and sugar in a saucepan over low heat, stirring until the sugar is completely dissolved, then bring to the boil; cool. Add the Cointreau to the cold syrup.

Ganache: Coarsely chop the chocolate and place in a bowl. Heat the cream until simmering and pour it over the chocolate. Stir until smooth and add the Cointreau. Set the ganache aside until it can be easily spread.

Using a long, serrated knife, cut the cooled sponge horizontally into 3 layers of equal thickness. Sprinkle or brush the first layer with Cointreau syrup and spread it with a $^3/_4$-in layer of ganache. Place the second layer on top and repeat with the syrup and ganache. Top with the remaining layer and brush with syrup. Refrigerate for 15 minutes, or until the ganache is firm.

Coat the entire surface of the cake with the remaining ganache. To obtain a spiked effect, tap the ganache lightly with a spatula and carefully pull away. Refrigerate for another 10 minutes, or until firm. Lightly dust with cocoa powder.

Tarts to die for

The best way to prepare pastry dough

Adapt this version of pastry using the ingredients indicated in the recipe of your choice (for example, p.110). You could also add sifted almond flour/meal or cocoa powder at the same time as the flour.

(1) Put ¹⁄₂ cup soft + 2¹⁄₂ tbsp unsalted butter, 2 cups flour (sifted), 1 pinch salt, ³⁄₄ cup confectioners' sugar and ¹⁄₄ tsp natural vanilla extract into a bowl. Rub the butter into the dry ingredients with your fingertips until the mixture resembles fine breadcrumbs.

(2) Using a wooden spoon, incorporate an egg; form the dough into a ball.

(3) Dust the work surface with flour and place the dough on it. Use the heel of your hand to push pieces of the dough away from you, smearing them across the work surface until smoothly blended. Work quickly; if you overwork the dough, it will be easily broken. Scrape into a ball, flatten slightly and wrap in plastic wrap; refrigerate for 30 minutes to rest before using.

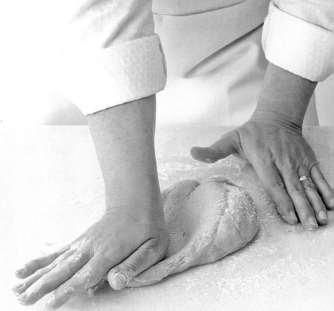

The best way to roll out pastry dough

Prepare the pastry for the tart or tartlet recipe of your choice.

① Dust a cool work surface with flour; flatten the chilled ball of dough between your hands.

② Using a rolling pin, place it on the center of the dough. Roll, in a backward and forward motion, to the edge of the dough. To form a round of even thickness, give the dough quarter-turns; work quickly so that it remains cool. If the dough starts to stick, add more flour to the work surface.

③ If the dough is too fragile to turn by hand, but not yet large enough to line the tart pan, carefully roll it around the rolling pin and lift to make the quarter-turns.

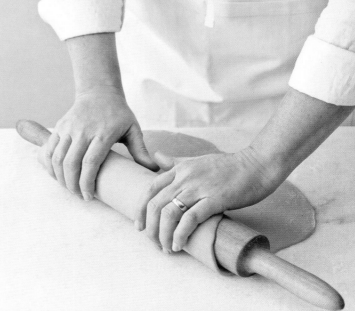

The best way to line a tart pan with pastry

Prepare the pastry for the tart of your choice. Roll the dough out to a thickness of 1/8 in and into a circle approximately 2 in larger than the diameter of the pan.

① Gently roll the dough around the rolling pin, place it over the pan and unroll loosely, allowing the excess to hang over the rim.

② Press the dough gently into the pan to cover the base, inside seam, and side.

③ Roll the rolling pin over the rim of the pan, pressing down firmly with your hand to remove excess dough. If indicated in the recipe, prick the base of the dough-lined pan with a fork and bake as described.

The best way to line a tartlet mold with pastry

Prepare the pastry dough for the tartlet recipe of your choice. Roll the dough out to a thickness of $^1/_8$ in.

(1) Use an upturned bowl or pastry cutter of the required size or shape to cut out the dough.

(2) Place the dough in each tartlet mold.

(3) Press the dough gently into each pan to cover the base, seam, and side. If indicated in the recipe, prick the base of the dough-lined tartlet mold with a fork and bake as described.

Milk Chocolate Mousse Boats

MAKES 12—14

DIFFICULTY ★ ★ ★

PREPARE: 45 minutes

COOK: 10—15 minutes

REFRIGERATE: 45 minutes

Sweet Pastry

$1/2$ cup + $1/2$ tbsp soft
   unsalted butter

$3/4$ cup confectioners'
   sugar

1 pinch salt

1 egg

$1^2/3$ cup flour, sifted

Milk Chocolate Mousse

$5^1/2$ oz milk chocolate

1 cup heavy whipping
   cream

Decoration

Unsweetened cocoa
   powder and/or
   confectioners' sugar

◊ See p.86: Preparing pastry
dough.

◊ See p.208: Forming
quenelles.

Sweet Pastry: Beat the unsalted butter with the confectioners' sugar and salt; combine well. Blend in the egg then the sifted flour; mix roughly to combine. Press the crumbs into a ball then, on a lightly floured work surface, use the heel of your hand to push bits of dough away from you, smearing them across the work surface to blend the butter and flour. Work quickly; repeat if necessary. Then form into a ball, flatten slightly, and wrap in plastic wrap. Refrigerate for 30 minutes.

Preheat the oven to 350°F. Butter 12—14 small ($3^1/4$ x $1^1/4$ in) fluted oval molds. Dust the work surface with flour. Roll out the dough to a thickness of $1/8$ in. Cut out 12—14 ovals about $5/8$ inch larger than the molds. Use the dough to line the molds and prick the bases using a fork. Refrigerate for 15 minutes.

Bake the dough-lined molds for 10—15 minutes, or until lightly golden. Set aside to cool on a wire rack.

Milk Chocolate Mousse: Coarsely chop the chocolate and place in a bowl; melt over a slowly simmering bain-marie until the temperature reaches approximately 113°F on a candy thermometer. Beat the cream until firm peaks cling to the whisk. Whisking quickly, add about $1/3$ of the whipped cream to the hot chocolate. Pour the mixture over the remaining cream and gently fold in with the whisk or a spatula to evenly blend the ingredients.

Shape the mousse into quenelles using 2 tablespoons and place one in each pastry boat. Using a fine-mesh strainer, dust the mousse boats with cocoa powder and/or confectioners' sugar.

Peruvian Style Chocolate Cheesecake

SERVES **6**

DIFFICULTY ★ ★ ★

DRAIN: Overnight

PREPARE: 45 minutes

COOK: 1¼ hours approx

REFRIGERATION: 4½ hours

Sweetened Potato Purée

7 oz russet potatoes

¾ cup milk

2 tbsp superfine sugar

Grated zest of ½ orange

Cocoa Paste

1½ tbsp unsweetened
  cocoa powder

2 tbsp water

Crunchy Chocolate Crust

2 tbsp unsalted butter

¾ cup graham cracker
  crumbs

3 tbsp grated bittersweet
  chocolate

2 tbsp chopped walnuts

Cheesecake Filling

4 oz full-fat fresh curd
  cheese or ricotta

½ cup heavy whipping
  cream

1 egg + 1 egg yolk

¼ cup superfine sugar

1 tbsp mild honey

Honey Glaze

½ sheet or ½ tsp gelatin

2 tbsp mild honey

2 tbsp water

This recipe must be started the day before.

Sweetened Potato Purée: Peel, wash, and dice the potatoes. Bring the milk, sugar, and orange zest to the boil. Add the potatoes and cook for about 30 minutes, or until they crush easily; drain. Purée the potatoes using a ricer or food mill set over a bowl; cool.

Cocoa Paste: Put the cocoa powder and water in a small saucepan, stir to combine and bring to the boil. Set aside.

Preheat the oven to 350°F. Cover a baking sheet with parchment. Butter the ring of a 7-in springform pan and place it on the baking sheet.

Crunchy Chocolate Crust: Melt the unsalted butter. Combine the graham cracker crumbs and the grated chocolate. Stir the butter and chopped walnuts into the crumbs; mix thoroughly. Pack the crust mixture firmly in an even layer at the base of the ring.

Cheesecake Filling: Place the cheese in a strainer to drain over night. Refrigerate. Combine the cheese with the potato purée. In a separate bowl, mix the whipping cream, egg and yolk, sugar, honey, and the cocoa paste until well combined; stir into the cheese-potato mixture. Pour the filling into the prepared ring and bake for 45 minutes. Cool the cheesecake without removing the ring then, refrigerate for 4 hours.

Honey Glaze: Soften the gelatin in a little cold water. Put the honey and water into a saucepan and stir over low heat until the honey melts completely; remove from the heat. (Squeeze the water out of the sheet gelatin.) Add the gelatin to the honey syrup, stir to dissolve; cool. Spread the honey glaze over the surface of the cold cheesecake and refrigerate for 15– 20 minutes. Slide the point of a knife around the ring to release the cheesecake; serve.

Chocolate Flan with a Crumble and Cream Topping

SERVES **6**

DIFFICULTY ★ ★ ★

PREPARE: 55 minutes

COOK: 1 hour 10 minutes

REST: 20 minutes

REFRIGERATE: 2 hours

Chocolate Flan

2³/₄ oz Cuzco or dark (70%)
  chocolate, chopped

³/₄ cup water

2¹/₂ cups milk

²/₃ cup heavy whipping
  cream

1 clove

1 stick cinnamon

5 eggs

²/₃ cup superfine sugar

Crumble

1 oz quinoa grains

¹/₄ cup (packed) brown sugar

3¹/₂ tbsp unsalted butter

6¹/₂ tbsp flour

Cinnamon powder

Chantilly Cream

²/₃ cup heavy whipping
  cream

Vanilla extract

2 tbsp confectioners' sugar

Chocolate Flan: Place the chocolate in a saucepan with the water; melt gently over very low heat. Bring to the boil, lower the heat, and cook for about 5 minutes. Add the milk, cream, clove, and cinnamon stick; heat until simmering. In a separate bowl, combine the eggs and sugar; beat until pale yellow and creamy. Stir in the cooked chocolate mixture and set aside to rest for 20 minutes.

Preheat the oven to 175°F. Strain the chocolate flan mixture and divide it evenly between six 3¹/₄-in ramekins (to come ³/₄ up the side); bake for 40 minutes, or until firm. Remove from the oven and cool; refrigerate for 2 hours.

Crumble: Wash and drain the quinoa. Fill a saucepan with water and add the quinoa. Bring to the boil, cover, and simmer for 20 minutes, or until the grains open; drain in a colander and set aside until dry. Increase the oven temperature to 350°F; cover a baking sheet with parchment paper. Put all the crumble ingredients into a bowl; mix until it resembles coarse breadcrumbs. Spread a ¹/₂-in layer of the crumble mixture on the baking sheet and bake for 10–15 minutes, or until golden. Break or crush the cooked crumble into small pieces; set aside to cool.

Chantilly Cream: Combine the cream and a few drops of vanilla extract, whisk until firm peaks form and cling to the whisk; add the confectioners' sugar.

Decorate each flan with a spoonful of the quinoa crumble and Chantilly cream.

Chocolate Crumble with Sweet Mango Slices

SERVES **6**

DIFFICULTY ★ ★ ★

PREPARE: 30 minutes

COOK: 20– 25 minutes

Chocolate Crumble

5 tbsp unsalted butter

6$^1/_2$ tbsp flour

5 tbsp unsweetened cocoa
  powder

$^1/_3$ cup (packed) brown
  sugar

$^1/_2$ cup hazelnut flour/
  meal

Mangoes

3 mangoes

4 tbsp unsalted butter

$^2/_3$ cup (packed) brown
  sugar

Preheat the oven to 350°F. Cover a baking sheet with parchment paper.

Chocolate Crumble: Put all the crumble ingredients into a bowl; mix until they resemble breadcrumbs. Spread a $^1/_2$-in layer of crumble mixture on the baking sheet and bake for 10– 15 minutes, or until firm. Break or crush the cooked crumble into small pieces; set aside to cool.

Mangoes: Peel and thinly slice the mangoes. Melt the butter in a frying pan, add the sliced mangoes, and sprinkle with brown sugar. Cook over low heat for 10 minutes, or until tender.

Prepare 6 plates and put several mango slices on each one. Divide the chocolate crumble equally between each plate and top with the remaining sliced mango; serve hot.

Crunchy Chocolate-Almond Tart

SERVES **10**

DIFFICULTY ★ ★ ★

PREPARE: 2 hours

COOK: 50 minutes to 1 hour

REFRIGERATE: 1 hour

Sweet Pastry

$1/2$ cup + $2^1/2$ tbsp soft
  unsalted butter

$3/4$ cup confectioners'
  sugar

1 pinch salt

1 egg

$1^2/3$ cups flour, sifted

Almond Cream

$6^1/2$ tbsp soft unsalted
  butter

$1/2$ cup superfine sugar

1 pinch vanilla powder

2 eggs

1 cup almond flour/meal

Ganache

$4^1/2$ oz bittersweet
  chocolate

$1/2$ cup heavy whipping
  cream

2 tbsp superfine sugar

5 tsp soft unsalted butter

Cocoa Syrup

3 tbsp water

3 tbsp superfine sugar

3 tbsp unsweetened cocoa
  powder

Crunchy Chocolate

1 oz milk chocolate

2 tbsp soft unsalted butter

$1/2$ cup praline paste (p.314)

$2^1/4$ cups Frosties®

Pastry: Beat the unsalted butter with the confectioners' sugar and salt; combine well. Blend in the egg then add the sifted flour; roughly mix to combine. Press the crumbs into a ball then, on a lightly floured work surface, use the heel of your hand to push bits of dough away from you, smearing them across the work surface to blend the butter and flour. Work quickly; repeat if necessary. Form into a ball, flatten slightly and wrap in plastic wrap. Refrigerate for 30 minutes.

Preheat the oven to 350°F. Butter a $9^1/2$-in round tart pan. Dust the work surface with flour. Roll out the dough to a thickness of $1/8$ in. Cut out a 12-in round of dough; line the pan with it. Refrigerate for 10 minutes. Cut out a 14-in round of parchment paper and place it in the dough-lined pan; fill with baking beans. Bake for about 10 minutes, or until lightly colored; remove the parchment and beans. Lower the oven temperature to 325°F and bake for another 8 minutes. Remove from the oven and set aside on a wire rack.

Almond Cream: Cream the unsalted butter and sugar; add the vanilla powder. Incorporate the eggs one at a time then fold in the almond flour. Pour the almond cream into the pastry shell and bake for about 30– 40 minutes, or until firm.

Ganache: Coarsely chop the chocolate and place in a bowl. Heat the cream and sugar until simmering, stir until the sugar dissolves. Pour the mixture over the chocolate, stirring until smooth; add the butter. Set the ganache aside at room temperature until it can be easily spread.

Cocoa Syrup: Put the water and sugar into a saucepan and stir over low heat until the sugar completely dissolves; boil for 2 minutes. Add the cocoa powder, whisking to combine and bring to the boil again. Set aside to cool.

Crunchy Chocolate: Finely chop the milk chocolate and melt over a bain-marie. Blend in the butter, praline paste, and 2 cups of lightly crushed Frosties®. Trace an 8-in circle on parchment paper and spread the chocolate mixture inside the circle to form a disc; refrigerate for 20 minutes. Unmold the tart, sprinkle the almond cream with cocoa syrup, and spread it with a thin layer of ganache. Place the crunchy chocolate disc on top and spread with the remaining ganache. Lightly crush the rest of the Frosties® and scatter over the surface of the tart.

Bitter Chocolate Tart

SERVES 6

DIFFICULTY ★ ★ ★

PREPARE: 35 minutes

COOK: 50 minutes approx

REFRIGERATE: 40 minutes

Pastry

1²/₃ cup flour, sifted

2¹/₂ tbsp superfine sugar

1 pinch salt

7 tbsp unsalted butter, cut
  in pieces

1 egg, beaten

1 tbsp water

Bitter Chocolate Cream

5¹/₂ oz dark (55– 70%)
  chocolate

¹/₂ cup + 2¹/₂ tbsp unsalted
  butter

3 eggs

1 cup superfine sugar

¹/₂ cup flour

¹/₄ cup heavy whipping
  cream

Crème Anglaise (Optional)

6 egg yolks

1 scant cup superfine
  sugar

1 vanilla pod, split

2 cups milk

Decoration

Confectioners' sugar,
  sifted

◊ See p.206: Making crème
anglaise.

Pastry: Combine the sifted flour, sugar, and salt in a bowl. Rub in the butter until the mixture resembles coarse breadcrumbs. Make a well in the center of the mixture and place the egg and water in it; roughly mix to combine. Press the crumbs into a ball then, on a lightly floured work surface, use the heel of your hand to push bits of dough away from you, smearing them across the work surface to blend the butter and flour. Work quickly; repeat if necessary. Form into a ball, flatten slightly, and wrap in plastic wrap. Refrigerate for 30 minutes.

Preheat the oven to 350°F. Butter a 10¹/₂-in round tart pan. Dust the work surface with flour. Roll out the dough to a thickness of ¹/₈ in. Cut out a 12¹/₂-in round of dough; line the pan with it. Refrigerate for 10 minutes.

Cut out a 14-in round of parchment paper and place it in the dough-lined pan; fill with baking beans. Bake for about 10 minutes or until colored then remove the parchment and beans. Lower the oven temperature to 325°F; bake for another 8 minutes. Remove from the oven and set aside on a wire rack. Lower the oven temperature to 250°F.

Bitter Chocolate Cream: Coarsely chop the chocolate and melt with the butter over a bain-marie. Remove from the heat and quickly blend in the eggs. Add the sugar, flour, and cream. Pour the chocolate cream into the pastry shell and bake for 30 minutes, or until firm.

Crème Anglaise (Optional): Put the egg yolks and sugar into a bowl and beat until pale yellow and creamy. Using the point of a knife, scrape the seeds from the vanilla pod into the milk, add the pod; bring slowly to the boil. Stir ¹/₃ of the hot milk quickly into the egg-sugar mixture and mix well to combine; pour the mixture into the remaining hot milk. Cook over low heat, stirring continuously with a wooden spoon, until thickened and the sauce coats the back of the spoon. (Do not allow to boil!) Remove from the heat immediately and strain into a bowl.

Dust the tart with sifted confectioners' sugar and serve warm. If desired, accompany with the crème anglaise.

CHEF'S TIP: If you want to create a lattice effect, cut strips of cardboard and lay them on the surface of the tart. Sift the confectioners' sugar over the top then carefully remove the strips.

Chocolate Tart with a Hint of Lime

SERVES 8-10

DIFFICULTY ★ ★ ★

PREPARE: 1¾ hours; lime slices need to be prepared 24 hrs ahead

COOK: 1½ hours approx

REFRIGERATE: 1 hour 10 minutes

Glazed Lime Slices
2 limes, finely sliced
$^1/_2$ cup superfine sugar
$^1/_2$ cup water

Sweet Pastry
$^1/_2$ cup + $^1/_2$ tbsp soft unsalted butter
$^3/_4$ cup confectioners' sugar
1 pinch salt
1 egg
1$^2/_3$ cup flour, sifted

Chocolate-Lime Ganache
2 limes
10$^1/_2$ oz bittersweet chocolate
1 cup heavy whipping cream
4$^1/_2$ oz unsalted butter

Decoration
Unsweetened cocoa powder, sifted

◊ See p.88: Lining a tart pan with dough.
◊ This recipe must be started a day ahead.

Glazed Lime Slices: Prepare at least 12 hours before cooking the tart. Place the sugar and water in a saucepan over low heat and stir until the sugar dissolves completely. Raise the heat and boil for 2 minutes; then remove pan from the heat. Place the lime slices in the syrup and macerate for 1 hour. Meanwhile, preheat the oven to 200°F and cover a baking sheet with parchment paper. Drain the slices and place on the baking sheet and transfer to the oven to dry for 1 hour, remove and set aside overnight.

Pastry: The next day, beat the butter with the confectioners' sugar and salt; combine well. Add the egg then the sifted flour; mix roughly to combine. Press the crumbs into a ball then, on a lightly floured work surface, use the heel of your hand to push bits of dough away from you, smearing them across the work surface to blend the butter and flour. Work quickly; repeat if necessary. Form into a ball, flatten slightly and wrap in plastic wrap. Refrigerate for 30 minutes.

Preheat the oven to 350°F. Butter an 8$^1/_2$-in round tart pan. Dust the work surface with flour. Roll out the dough to a thickness of $^1/_8$ in. Cut out a 10$^1/_2$-in round of dough; line the pan with it. Refrigerate for 10 minutes.

Cut out a 13-in round of parchment paper and place it in the dough-lined pan; fill with baking beans. Bake for about 10 minutes or until lightly colored then, remove the parchment and beans. Lower the oven temperature to 325°F; bake the pastry for another 10– 15 minutes, or until golden. Remove from the oven and set aside on a wire rack.

Chocolate-Lime Ganache: Zest the limes and cut the zests into long thin threads. Coarsely chop the chocolate and place in a bowl. Bring the cream and lime zest to the boil in a small saucepan then pour the mixture over the chocolate. Stir until well combined and add the butter. Pour the ganache into the cooked pastry shell, saving some for decoration; refrigerate for 30 minutes.

Before serving, sprinkle the tart with the cocoa powder. Fit a piping bag with a star nozzle, fill it with the reserved ganache and pipe rosettes on the top of the tart. Add the lime slices.

Chocolate-Fig Tart

SERVES 10

DIFFICULTY ★ ★ ★

PREPARE: 45 minutes

COOK: 1¼ hours approx

REFRIGERATE: 1 hour 10 minutes

Pastry

½ cup + 2½ tbsp soft unsalted butter

2 cups flour, sifted

3 tbsp unsweetened cocoa powder, sifted

1 pinch salt

¾ cup confectioners' sugar

1 egg

Fig Compote

2¾ cup dried figs

7 tbsp superfine sugar

¾ cup red wine

½ cup raspberry purée

Ganache

10½ oz bittersweet chocolate

1½ cups heavy whipping cream

7 tbsp soft unsalted butter

◇ See p.12: Making a basic ganache.

◇ See p.87: Making pastry.

Pastry: Rub the unsalted butter into the sifted flour and cocoa powder, salt and confectioners' sugar with the fingertips until the mixture resembles fine breadcrumbs. Add the egg and roughly mix to combine. Press the crumbs into a ball then, on a lightly floured work surface, use the heel of your hand to push bits of dough away from you, smearing them across the work surface to blend the butter and flour. Work quickly; repeat if necessary. Form into a ball, flatten slightly and wrap in plastic wrap. Refrigerate for 30 minutes.

Preheat the oven to 350°F. Butter a 9½-in round tart pan. Dust the work surface with flour. Roll the dough out to a thickness of ⅛ in. Cut out a 12-in round of dough; line the pan with it. Refrigerate for 10 minutes.

Cut out a 14-in round of parchment paper and place it in the dough-lined pan; fill with baking beans. Bake for about 10 minutes or until colored then, remove the parchment and beans. Lower the oven temperature to 325°F; bake the pastry for another 10–15 minutes, or until firm. Remove from the oven and set aside on a wire rack.

Fig Compote: Soften the figs in boiling water for 3 minutes; drain. Put the softened figs, sugar, wine, and raspberry purée into a saucepan and simmer very slowly for 40 minutes, or until the figs are tender and the mixture thickens; cool. Pour the fig compote into the cooked pastry shell to come ⅔ up the side; smooth the surface with a spatula.

Ganache: Coarsely chop the chocolate and place in a bowl. Heat the cream to simmering and pour it over the chocolate, stir until smooth; add the unsalted butter. Pour the ganache into the pastry shell over the fig compote; refrigerate for 30 minutes.

CHEF'S TIP: If you prefer smooth fig compote, work the cooked mixture in a food processor to the desired consistency before placing in the pastry shell.

"Grand Cru" Chocolate Tart

SERVES 10

DIFFICULTY ★ ★ ★

PREPARE: 45 minutes

COOK: 20– 25 minutes

REFRIGERATE: 40 minutes

Sweet Pastry

$1/2$ cup + $1/2$ tbsp soft
  unsalted butter

$3/4$ cup confectioners'
  sugar

1 pinch salt

1 egg

$1 2/3$ cup flour, sifted

'Grand Cru' Chocolate Cream

2 egg yolks

3 tbsp superfine sugar

$1/2$ cup milk

$1/2$ cup heavy whipping
  cream

$6 3/4$ oz 'grand cru' or dark
  (70%) chocolate, chopped

◇ See p.88: Lining a tart pan
with pastry.

Sweet Pastry: Beat the unsalted butter with the confectioners' sugar and salt; combine well. Add the egg then the sifted flour; mix roughly to combine. Press the crumbs into a ball then, on a lightly floured work surface, use the heel of your hand to push bits of dough away from you, smearing them across the work surface to blend the butter and flour. Work quickly; repeat if necessary. Form into a ball, flatten slightly and wrap in plastic wrap. Refrigerate for 30 minutes.

Preheat the oven to 350°F. Butter a $9 1/2$-in round tart pan. Dust the work surface with flour. Roll out the dough to a thickness of $1/8$ in. Cut out a 12-in round of dough; line the pan with it. Refrigerate for 10 minutes.

Cut out a 14-in round of parchment paper and place it in the dough-lined pan; fill with baking beans. Bake for about 10 minutes or until lightly colored then, remove the parchment and beans. Lower the oven temperature to 325°F; bake the pastry for another 10– 15 minutes, or until golden. Remove from the oven and set aside on a wire rack.

'Grand Cru' Chocolate Cream: Put the egg yolks and sugar into a bowl and beat until pale yellow and creamy. Heat the milk and cream until simmering. Stir a third of the hot milk-cream mixture quickly into the eggs and sugar and mix well to combine; return the mixture to the remaining hot milk. Cook over low heat, stirring continuously, until thickened and the mixture coats the back of a spoon. (Do not allow to boil!) Remove from the heat immediately and strain over the chopped chocolate, stirring carefully until smooth. Pour the chocolate cream into the pastry shell. Refrigerate the tart until serving.

CHEF'S TIP: The term "grand cru," used here designates a specific type of chocolate coming from Cuba, Sao Tomé, or Venezuela containing 66% cocoa solids. You can replace it by using a dark (70%) chocolate. If you want to give the tart a fruity taste, scatter fresh raspberries over the base of the cooked pastry shell before filling it with the chocolate cream.

Chocolate-Coconut Tart

SERVES **8–10**

DIFFICULTY ★ ★ ★

PREPARE: 1 hour

COOK: 40 minutes approx

REFRIGERATE: 40 minutes

Coconut Pastry

$1/2$ cup + $31/2$ tbsp soft
  unsalted butter

Scant $2/3$ cup
  confectioners' sugar

$1/3$ cup almond flour/meal

$1/3$ cup shredded coconut

1 pinch salt

1 egg

$11/2$ cups flour, sifted

Coconut Filling

$13/4$ cups shredded
  coconut

$3/4$ cup superfine sugar

3 tbsp apple sauce

3 egg whites

Crumble Topping

$31/2$ tbsp unsalted butter

$1/3$ cup flour

3 tbsp unsweetened cocoa
  powder

$1/4$ cup (packed) brown
  sugar

$1/2$ cup shredded coconut

$1/2$ tsp baking powder

◊ See p.88: Lining a tart pan
with pastry.

Coconut Pastry: Beat the unsalted butter with the confectioners' sugar, ground almonds, coconut, and salt; blend well. Add the egg then the sifted flour; mix roughly to combine. Press the crumbs into a ball then, on a lightly floured work surface, use the heel of your hand to push bits of dough away from you, smearing them across the work surface to blend the butter and flour. Work quickly; repeat if necessary. Form into a ball, flatten slightly and wrap in plastic wrap. Refrigerate for 30 minutes.

Preheat the oven to 350°F. Butter an $81/2$-in tart ring and place on a baking sheet. Dust the work surface with flour. Roll out the dough to a thickness of $1/8$ in. Cut out a $101/2$-in round of dough; line the ring it. Refrigerate for 10 minutes.

Cut out a $121/2$-in round of parchment paper and place it in the dough-lined ring; fill with baking beans. Bake for about 10 minutes, or until lightly colored, then remove the parchment and beans. Lower the oven temperature to 325°F; bake for another 8 minutes, or until set. Remove from the oven and set aside on a wire rack (leave the oven on).

Coconut Filling: Combine the coconut, sugar, and apple sauce. Beat the egg whites until stiff peaks form. Stir a third of the beaten egg whites into the coconut mixture; gently fold in the remainder of the egg whites. Pour the coconut filling into the pastry shell.

Crumble Topping: Put all the crumble ingredients into a bowl; mix with the fingertips to obtain a breadcrumb-like consistency. Scatter the crumble mixture over the coconut filling.

Bake the tart for 20 minutes, or until the pastry is golden. Cool and cut in 8–10 servings; serve warm or cold.

Chocolate-Orange Tart with a Hint of Coriander

SERVES 10

DIFFICULTY ★ ★ ★

PREPARE: 1¾ hours

COOK: 20– 25 minutes

REFRIGERATE: 40 minutes

Coriander-Orange Slices

²/₃ cup water

¾ cup superfine sugar

2 tbsp coriander seeds

1 orange, finely sliced

Pastry

½ cup + 2½ tbsp soft
  unsalted butter

2 cups flour, sifted

1 pinch salt

1 scant cup confectioners'
  sugar

¼ tsp natural vanilla
  extract

1 egg

Chocolate Cream

3 egg yolks

¼ cup superfine sugar

2 cups milk

1 vanilla pod, split

9¾ oz bittersweet
  chocolate, chopped

Decoration

Coriander sprig

◊ See p.87: Roll out pastry
dough.

Coriander-Orange Slices: Place the sugar and water in a saucepan over low heat, stir until the sugar is dissolved then raise the heat and boil for 2 minutes; remove the pan from the heat. Add the coriander seeds to the syrup and infuse for 5– 10 minutes. Strain the syrup into a bowl then add the orange slices; macerate for 1 hour.

Pastry: Rub the unsalted butter into the sifted flour, salt, confectioners' sugar and vanilla extract with your fingertips until the mixture resembles fine breadcrumbs. Blend in the egg and roughly mix to combine. Press the crumbs into a ball then, on a lightly floured work surface, use the heel of your hand to push bits of dough away from you, smearing them across the work surface to blend the butter and flour. Work quickly; repeat if necessary. Form into a ball, flatten slightly and wrap in plastic wrap. Refrigerate for 30 minutes.

Preheat the oven to 350°F. Butter a 9½-in tart pan. Dust the work surface with flour. Roll out the dough to a thickness of ⅛ in. Cut out a 12-in round of dough; line the pan with it. Refrigerate for 10 minutes.

Cut out a 14-in round of parchment paper and place it in the dough-lined pan; fill with baking beans. Bake for about 10 minutes, or until lightly colored, then remove the parchment and beans. Lower the oven temperature to 325°F; bake the pastry for another 10– 15 minutes, or until golden. Remove from the oven and set aside on a wire rack.

Chocolate Cream: Put the egg yolks and sugar into a bowl and beat until pale and creamy. Using the point of a knife, scrape the seeds from the vanilla pod into the milk, add the pod; bring slowly to the boil. Stir a third of the hot milk quickly into the egg and sugar and mix well to combine; pour the mixture into the remaining hot milk. Cook over low heat, stirring continuously with a wooden spoon, until thickened and the mixture coats the back of the spoon. (Do not allow to boil!) Remove from the heat and strain over the chopped chocolate, stirring carefully until smooth. Pour the chocolate cream into the pastry shell and refrigerate.

Just before serving, drain and dry the orange slices on kitchen paper; arrange on the surface of the tart with a sprig of coriander.

Chocolate and Caramelized Pear Tart

SERVES 8–10

DIFFICULTY ★ ★ ★

PREPARATION: 1 hour

COOK: 40 minutes

REFRIGERATE: 40 minutes

Chocolate Pastry

³/₄ cup soft unsalted butter

1 cup confectioners' sugar

1 egg

2 cups flour, sifted

¹/₄ cup unsweetened cocoa powder, sifted

Chocolate Filling

3¹/₂ oz bittersweet chocolate

³/₄ cup heavy whipping cream

2¹/₂ tbsp mild honey

5 egg yolks

Caramelized Pears

30 oz canned pear halves

2¹/₂ tbsp mild honey

4 tsp unsalted butter

◇ See p.88: Lining a tart pan with pastry.

Chocolate Pastry: Beat the unsalted butter with the confectioners' sugar; blend well. Add the egg then the sifted flour and cocoa powder; roughly mix to combine. Press the crumbs into a ball then, on a lightly floured work surface, use the heel of your hand to push bits of dough away from you, smearing them across the work surface to blend the butter and flour. Work quickly; repeat if necessary. Form into a ball, flatten slightly and wrap in plastic wrap. Refrigerate for 30 minutes.

Preheat the oven to 350°F. Butter an 8¹/₂-in round tart pan. Dust the work surface with flour. Roll out the dough to a thickness of ¹/₈ in. Cut out a 10³/₄-in round of dough; line the pan with it. Refrigerate for 10 minutes.

Cut out a 12-in round of parchment paper and place it in the dough-lined pan; fill with baking beans or rice. Bake for about 10 minutes, or until colored, and then remove the parchment and beans. Lower the oven temperature to 325°F; bake the pastry for another 8 minutes, or until set. Remove from the oven and set aside on a wire rack.

Lower the oven temperature to 275°F.

Chocolate Filling: Coarsely chop the chocolate and place in a bowl. Heat the cream and honey until simmering. Whisk the eggs and quickly stir in the hot honey cream. Strain the mixture over the chocolate and stir carefully until smooth; set aside.

Caramelized Pears: Strain the pear halves. Heat the honey and unsalted butter in a non-stick pan, add the pears and cook over high heat until pears turn golden. Transfer cut-side down to a cutting board, cool and slice crosswise into half-moons.

Pour the chocolate filling into the cooked pastry shell. Transfer the pear slices to the tart using a flat spatula. Bake for 20 minutes; serve.

Chocolate Praline Tart

SERVES 10–12

DIFFICULTY ★ ★ ★

PPEPARE: 1 hour

COOK: 20–25 minutes

REFRIGERATE: 1 hour

Almond Pastry

6¹/₂ tbsp soft unsalted butter

¹/₄ cup almond flour/meal

1¹/₂ cups flour, sifted

1 pinch salt

¹/₂ cup confectioners' sugar

¹/₄ tsp natural vanilla extract

1 egg

Chocolate Praline Cream

14 oz bittersweet chocolate

1²/₃ cups heavy whipping cream

¹/₄ cup praline paste (p.314)

1 or 2 drops vanilla extract

6 tbsp unsalted butter

Caramelized Nuts

¹/₄ cup water

¹/₂ cup superfine sugar

¹/₃ cup blanched almonds

¹/₃ oz blanched hazelnuts

2 tsp unsalted butter

Almond Pastry: Rub the unsalted butter into the almond flour/meal, sifted flour, salt, confectioners' sugar, and vanilla extract with the tips of your fingers until the mixture resembles breadcrumbs. Blend in the egg and roughly mix to combine. Press the crumbs into a ball then, on a lightly floured work surface, use the heel of your hand to push bits of dough away from you, smearing them across the work surface to blend the butter and flour. Work quickly; repeat if necessary. Form into a ball, flatten slightly and wrap in plastic wrap. Refrigerate for 30 minutes.

Preheat the oven to 350°F. Butter a rectangular tart pan (10 x 4 in). Dust the work surface with flour. Roll out the dough to a thickness of ¹/₈ in. Cut out a 12 x 6-in rectangle of dough; line the pan with it. Refrigerate for 10 minutes.

Cut out a 14 x 8-in rectangle of parchment paper and place it in the dough-lined pan; fill with baking beans. Bake for about 10 minutes, or until colored, and then remove the parchment and beans. Lower the oven temperature to 325°F; bake for another 10–15 minutes, or until golden. Remove from the oven and set aside on a wire rack.

Chocolate Praline Cream: Coarsely chop the chocolate and place in a bowl. Heat the cream until simmering, pour it over the chocolate; stir carefully until smooth. Blend in the praline paste, vanilla extract, and unsalted butter. Pour the chocolate praline cream into the pastry shell; refrigerate 20 minutes.

Caramelized Nuts: Put the sugar and water into a saucepan over low heat; stir until the sugar is completely dissolved. Increase the heat and boil the syrup without stirring for about 5 minutes. Remove from the heat; add the nuts and stir with a wooden spoon until the syrup crystalizes, covering them with a white powder. Cook the crystalized sugar and nuts over low heat until the nuts turn golden brown then incorporate the unsalted butter. Remove from the heat immediately and spread on parchment paper; stir until cool. When cold, rub between your hands to separate the nuts and arrange on the tart just before serving.

CHEF'S TIP: If a rectangular pan is not available, use a 10¹/₂-in round flan or tart pan. Simply roll the dough into a round and line the pan with it.

Chocolate Cream Tart with Caramelized Nuts

SERVES **8–10**

DIFFICULTY ★ ★ ★

PREPARE: 1 hour

COOK: 1 hour 10 minutes

REFRIGERATE: 40 minutes

Almond Pastry

$1/2$ cup + $1/2$ tbsp soft
   unsalted butter

$2/3$ cup confectioners'
   sugar

1 pinch salt

$1/4$ cup almond flour/meal

1 egg

$1 2/3$ cup flour, sifted

Chocolate Cream

$3/4$ cup milk

6 tbsp unsweetened cocoa
   powder

$3/4$ oz bittersweet
   chocolate

$3/4$ cup crème fraîche

4 egg yolks

$2/3$ cup superfine sugar

Chocolate Glaze

$1/4$ cup crème fraîche

1 tbsp superfine sugar

$1 1/2$ tsp mild honey

$2 1/4$ oz bittersweet
   grated chocolate

2 tsp unsalted butter

Caramelized Nuts

$1/2$ cup superfine sugar

$1/3$ cup each blanched
   almonds and hazelnuts

2 tsp unsalted butter

Almond Pastry: Beat the unsalted butter with the salt, almond flour/meal, and confectioners' sugar; combine well. Blend in the egg then the sifted flour; mix roughly to combine. Press the crumbs into a ball then, on a lightly floured work surface, use the heel of the hand to push bits of dough away from you, smearing them across the work surface to blend the butter and flour. Work quickly; repeat if necessary. Form into a ball, flatten slightly and wrap in plastic wrap. Refrigerate for 30 minutes.

Preheat the oven to 350°F. Butter an $8 1/2$-in tart pan and dust the work surface with flour. Roll the dough out to a thickness of $1/8$ in; cut out a $10 3/4$-in round. Line the pan with the dough. Refrigerate for 10 minutes.

Cut out a 12-in round of parchment paper and place it in the dough-lined pan; fill with baking beans. Bake for about 10 minutes, or until colored, and then remove the parchment and beans. Lower the oven temperature to 325°F; bake the pastry for another 8 minutes, or until set. Remove from the oven and set aside on a wire rack.

Chocolate Cream: Bring the milk, cocoa powder, and chocolate to the boil, add the cream and remove the saucepan from the heat. Place the egg yolks and sugar in a bowl, beat until pale yellow and creamy; stir in the milk-chocolate-cream mixture. Pour the chocolate cream into the pastry shell and bake for 45 minutes; set aside to cool.

Chocolate Glaze: Heat the crème fraîche, sugar, and honey; pour over the grated chocolate and stir until smooth. Blend in the butter.

Caramelized Nuts: Put the sugar and one-quarter cup water into a small saucepan over low heat and stir until the sugar is completely dissolved. Increase the heat and boil the syrup for about 2 minutes without stirring. Remove from the heat, add the nuts and stir with a wooden spoon until the syrup crystalizes, covering them with a white powder. Cook the crystalized sugar and nuts over low heat until the nuts turn golden brown then incorporate the unsalted butter. Remove from the heat immediately and spread on parchment paper, stir until cool. When cold, pour the chocolate glaze over the surface of the tart, scatter the caramelized nuts on top; serve.

Chocolate Tart topped with Caramelized Apple

SERVES **8**

DIFFICULTY ★ ★ ★

PREPARE: 1 hour

COOK: 40 minutes approx

REFRIGERATE: 1 hour
40 minutes

Chocolate Pastry

1 cup flour, sifted

2 tbsp unsweetened cocoa
  powder, sifted

Scant $\frac{1}{2}$ cup superfine
  sugar

1 pinch salt

5 tbsp unsalted butter, cut
  in pieces

1 egg yolk

3 tbsp water

3 tbsp chocolate sprinkles

Chocolate Nib Ganache

$3\frac{1}{2}$ oz dark chocolate
  with nibs

$6\frac{1}{2}$ tbsp heavy whipping
  cream

2 pinches ground nutmeg

1 tsp natural vanilla
  extract

Caramelized Apples

2 Granny Smith apples

2 tbsp unsalted butter

$2\frac{1}{2}$ tbsp superfine sugar

Decoration (Optional)

Chocolate nibs or chocolate
  sprinkles

Chocolate Pastry: Combine the sifted flour and cocoa powder, sugar, and salt in a bowl. Rub in the unsalted butter until the mixture resembles coarse breadcrumbs. Make a well in the center of the mixture, place the egg and water in it and roughly mix to combine; add the chocolate sprinkles. Press the crumbs into a ball then, on a lightly floured work surface, use the heel of your hand to push bits of dough away from you, smearing them across the work surface to blend the unsalted butter and flour. Work quickly; repeat if necessary. Form into a ball, flatten slightly and wrap in plastic wrap. Refrigerate for 30 minutes.

Preheat the oven to 350°F. Butter an 8-in round tart pan. Dust the work surface with flour. Roll out the dough to a thickness of $\frac{1}{8}$ in. Cut out a 10-in round of dough; line the pan with it. Refrigerate for 30 minutes.

Cut out a 12-in round of parchment paper and place it in the dough-lined pan; fill with baking beans. Bake for about 10 minutes then remove the parchment and beans. Lower the oven temperature to 325°F; bake the pastry for a further 10–15 minutes or until firm and golden. Remove from the oven and set aside on a wire rack.

Chocolate Nib Ganache: Coarsely chop the chocolate and place in a bowl. Bring the cream and nutmeg to the boil, pour over the chocolate and stir until smooth; incorporate the vanilla extract. Pour the ganache into the pastry shell; refrigerate for about 1 hour.

Caramelized Apples: Peel and cut the apples into quarters. Heat the unsalted butter and sugar in a non-stick pan. Add the apples and cook over low heat for about 10 minutes, or until tender, then increase the heat until the apples turn golden; cool.

Use a flat spatula to place the cooled apples on the tart; refrigerate. Remove from the refrigerator 30 minutes before serving; scatter the surface with chocolate nibs or sprinkles.

CHEF'S TIP: Chocolate or cocoa nibs are roasted cocoa beans separated from their husks and broken into small bits. If unavailable, they could be replaced with chocolate sprinkles.

Candy-topped Tart

SERVES 8

DIFFICULTY ★ ★ ★

PREPARE: 40 minutes

COOK: 20– 25 minutes

REFRIGERATE: 1 hour
10 minutes

Sweet Pastry

$^1/_2$ cup + $^1/_2$ tbsp soft
    unsalted butter
$^3/_4$ cup confectioners'
    sugar
1 pinch salt
1 egg
1 $^2/_3$ cup flour, sifted

Ganache

3 $^1/_2$ oz dark (55– 70%)
    chocolate
6 $^1/_2$ tbsp heavy whipping
    cream
$^1/_2$ cup M&M's®

◊ See p.12: Making
a basic ganache.

Sweet Pastry: Beat the unsalted butter with the confectioners' sugar and salt; blend well. Add the egg, then add the sifted flour; mix roughly to combine. Press the crumbs into a ball then, on a lightly floured work surface, use the heel of your hand to push bits of dough away from you, smearing them across the work surface to blend the unsalted butter and flour. Work quickly; repeat if necessary. Form into a ball, flatten slightly and wrap in plastic wrap. Refrigerate for 30 minutes.

Preheat the oven to 350°F. Butter an 8-in round tart pan. Dust the work surface with flour. Roll the dough out to a thickness of $^1/_8$ in. Cut out a 10-in round of dough; line the pan with it. Refrigerate for 10 minutes.

Cut out a 12-in round of parchment paper and place it in the dough-lined pan; fill with baking beans. Bake for about 10 minutes, or until lightly colored, then remove the parchment and beans. Lower the oven temperature to 325°F; bake the pastry for a further 10– 15 minutes, or until golden. Remove from the oven and set aside on a wire rack.

Ganache: Coarsely chop the chocolate and place in a bowl. Heat the cream until simmering and pour over the chocolate; stir until smooth. Pour the ganache evenly into the pastry shell, arrange the M&M's® on the surface; refrigerate for 30 minutes before serving.

Chocolate Walnut Tartlets

SERVES 8

DIFFICULTY ★ ★ ★

PREPARE: 1¼ hours

COOK: 25–30 minutes

REFRIGERATE: 1¾ hours

Chocolate Pastry

¾ cup soft unsalted
  butter

1 cup confectioners' sugar

1 pinch salt

1 egg

2 cups flour, sifted

¼ cup unsweetened
  cocoa powder, sifted

Walnut Caramel

1⅔ cup walnut halves

1 cup superfine sugar

2½ tbsp mild honey

2 tbsp unsalted butter

⅔ cup heavy whipping
  cream

Decoration

8 walnut halves

◇ See p.89: Lining tartlet
molds with pastry.

Chocolate Pastry: Beat the unsalted butter with the confectioners' sugar and salt; blend well. Add the egg then the sifted flour and cocoa powder; mix roughly to combine. Press the crumbs into a ball then, on a lightly floured work surface, use the heel of your hand to push bits of dough away from you, smearing them across the work surface to blend the unsalted butter and flour. Work quickly; repeat if necessary. Form into a ball, flatten slightly and wrap in plastic wrap. Refrigerate for 30 minutes.

Preheat the oven to 350°F. Butter eight 3¼-in fluted tartlet molds. Dust the work surface with flour. Roll out the dough to a thickness of ⅛ in. Use a 4-in pastry cutter to stamp out 8 rounds of dough, line the molds and prick the bases using a fork. Refrigerate for 10 minutes.

Bake the dough-lined molds for 20 minutes, or until firm. Set aside to cool on a wire rack.

Walnut Caramel: Maintain the oven at the 350°F. Coarsely chop the walnuts, place on a baking sheet and toast in the oven for 5–10 minutes, or until lightly colored. Place the sugar and honey in a saucepan over low heat and stir until the sugar dissolves completely. Increase the heat and boil (do not stir) for about 10 minutes until the syrup becomes a golden caramel color. Remove from the heat and add the unsalted butter. Return the saucepan to the heat and very slowly pour the cream into the caramel to stop the cooking. (Be careful as it will spit violently when the liquid is added.) Reduce the heat and stir with a wooden spoon until the mixture is smooth. Strain it into a bowl to cool then add the toasted walnuts; set aside.

Spoon the cooled walnut caramel into the tartlet shells, refrigerate for 1 hour before serving; decorate each tartlet with a walnut half.

CHEF'S TIP: If you want the tartlets to have a nuttier flavor, you could combine fresh pistachios with the walnuts.

Chocolate Nougatine Tartlets

SERVES 12–14

DIFFICULTY ★ ★ ★

PREPARE: 1½ hours

COOK: 20 minutes

REFRIGERATE: 1 hour

Almond Pastry

½ cup + ½ tbsp soft
  unsalted butter

⅔ cup confectioners'
  sugar

1 pinch salt

5 tbsp almond flour/meal

1 egg

1⅔ cups flour, sifted

Nougatine

½ cup sliced almonds

6 tbsp superfine sugar

4¼ tsp mild honey

Chocolate Cream

1¼ cups heavy whipping
  cream

3 eggs

⅓ cup superfine sugar

4½ oz dark (70%)
  chocolate, chopped

◇ See p.89: Lining tartlet
molds with pastry.

Almond Pastry: Beat the unsalted butter with the confectioners' sugar, salt, and almond flour/meal; blend well. Add the egg then the sifted flour; roughly mix to combine. Press the crumbs into a ball then, on a lightly floured work surface, use the heel of your hand to push bits of dough away from you, smearing them across the work surface to blend the butter and flour. Work quickly; repeat if necessary. Form into a ball, flatten slightly and wrap in plastic wrap. Refrigerate for 30 minutes.

Preheat the oven to 350°F. Butter 12–14 tartlet molds (3¼ in). Dust the work surface with flour. Roll out the dough to a thickness of ⅛ in. Using a 4-in pastry cutter, stamp out 12–14 rounds of dough. Line the molds with the dough and prick the pastry bases using a fork. Refrigerate for 10 minutes.

Bake the dough-lined molds for 20 minutes, or until firm. Set aside to cool on a wire rack. Lower the oven temperature to 300°F.

Nougatine: Cover a baking sheet with parchment paper and place the sliced almonds on it. Toast in the oven for 5 minutes, or until lightly colored. Place the sugar and honey in a saucepan and stir over low heat until the sugar dissolves completely. Increase the heat and boil (do not stir) for about 10 minutes, or until the syrup becomes amber colored. Remove from the heat and carefully stir in the toasted almonds. Pour the mixture onto the prepared baking sheet and place another sheet of parchment on top. Use a rolling pin to spread the nougatine into a layer 1/16 in thick. When cool, coarsely grind in a food processor.

Chocolate Cream: Heat the cream until simmering. Place the eggs and sugar in a bowl and beat until pale yellow and creamy. Stir a third of the cream quickly into the eggs and sugar and mix well to combine; return the mixture to the saucepan. Cook over low heat, stirring continuously with a wooden spoon, until thickened and the mixture coats the back of the spoon. (Do not allow to boil!) Remove from the heat immediately and strain over the chopped chocolate; stir carefully until smooth.

Spoon the nougatine into the tartlet shells to come ¾ up the side and fill with the chocolate cream. Refrigerate for 30 minutes, or until the cream is firm. Sprinkle with the remaining nougatine.

Chocolate Chestnut Tartlets

SERVES 8

DIFFICULTY ★ ★ ★

PREPARE: 1 hour approx.

COOK: 20 minutes

REFRIGERATE: 40 minutes

16 canned chestnuts in vanilla syrup or 16 glacé chestnuts (marrons glacés)

Pastry

$5^1/_2$ tbsp soft unsalted butter

1 scant cup flour, sifted

2 tbsp unsweetened cocoa powder, sifted

1 pinch salt

$^2/_3$ cup confectioners' sugar

1 egg

Chestnut Ganache

$4^1/_2$ oz dark chocolate

$^1/_4$ cup heavy whipping cream

6 tbsp sweet chestnut cream (crème de marrons)

Decoration (Optional)

$3^1/_2$ oz dark chocolate, tempered (p.315)

$^1/_4$ cup superfine sugar

◊ Start this recipe the day before.

The day before, drain the canned chestnuts. Then, cut in pieces and set aside overnight.

Pastry: The next day, rub the unsalted butter into the sifted flour, cocoa powder, salt, and confectioners' sugar with the tips of the fingers, until the mixture resembles breadcrumbs. Incorporate the egg and roughly mix to combine. Press the crumbs into a ball then, on a lightly floured work surface, use the heel of your hand to push bits of dough away from you, smearing them across the work surface to blend the unsalted butter and flour. Work quickly; repeat if necessary. Form into a ball, flatten slightly and wrap in plastic wrap. Refrigerate for 30 minutes.

Preheat the oven to 350°F. Butter 2 baking sheets.

Dust the work surface with flour. Roll out the dough to a thickness of $^1/_8$ in. Using a 4-in pastry cutter, stamp out 8 rounds of dough, prick with a fork and transfer to the baking sheets; refrigerate for 10 minutes.

Bake for 20 minutes, or until firm and golden. Set the pastry rounds aside to cool on a wire rack.

Chestnut Ganache: Coarsely chop the chocolate and place in a bowl. Heat the cream and sweet chestnut purée until simmering and pour it over the chocolate; stir until smooth. Set the ganache aside until firm and can be spread easily.

Spread each pastry round with the chestnut ganache and top with chestnut pieces. Cool before serving.

Decoration (Optional): If desired, decorate the tartlets with sugared chocolate medallions. Make a small paper pastry bag (p.319) and fill with the tempered chocolate (p.315). Put a layer of sugar on a large plate and pipe a chocolate design in the sugar, for each tartlet (see photo opposite). Let the medallions harden in the sugar then place one on each tartlet.

Chocolate Soufflé Tartlets

SERVES 12

DIFFICULTY ★ ★ ★

PREPARATION: 1¼ hours

COOK: 30 minutes

REFRIGERATE: 40 minutes

Sweet Pastry

½ cup + ½ tbsp soft
  unsalted butter

¾ cup confectioners' sugar

1 pinch salt

1 egg

1⅔ cups flour, sifted

Chocolate Pastry Cream

¼ cup unsweetened cocoa
  powder, sifted

¼ cup tbsp water

¾ cup milk

3 egg yolks

3 tbsp superfine sugar

2½ tbsp flour

3 egg whites

2 tbsp sugar

◇ See p.89: Lining tartlet
molds with pastry.

Pastry: Beat the unsalted butter with the confectioners' sugar and salt; combine well. Blend in the egg then add the sifted flour; roughly mix to combine. Press the crumbs into a ball then, on a lightly floured work surface, use the heel of your hand to push bits of dough away from you, smearing them across the work surface to blend the unsalted butter and flour. Work quickly; repeat if necessary. Form into a ball, flatten slightly and wrap in plastic wrap. Refrigerate for 30 minutes.

Preheat the oven to 350°F. Butter 12 tartlet molds (3¼ in). Dust the work surface with flour. Roll out the dough to a thickness of ⅛ in. Using a 4-in pastry cutter, stamp out 12 rounds of dough; line the molds with the dough and prick the bases using a fork. Refrigerate for 10 minutes.

Bake the dough-lined molds for 15 minutes, or until lightly golden. Turn out to cool on a wire rack.

Chocolate Pastry Cream: Put the cocoa powder and water into a saucepan; stir to combine. Add the milk and bring to the boil; remove from the heat. Put 2 egg yolks and the sugar into a bowl and beat until pale yellow and creamy; add the flour. Whisk half the hot chocolate milk quickly into the egg-and-sugar mixture. Add the remaining milk and return the mixture to the saucepan. Cook over low heat, whisking continuously until the cream thickens. Boil for 1 minute while continuing to whisk. Remove from the heat and when cooled, stir in the remaining egg yolk. Pour the chocolate pastry cream into a bowl, cover the surface with plastic wrap; cool.

Preheat the oven to 350°F. Beat the egg whites, gradually adding the sugar, until the whites are smooth, shiny, and stiff peaks form. Stir a third into the chocolate pastry cream and carefully fold in the remainder using a spatula. Divide the mixture evenly between the tartlet shells to come ⅔ up the side. Bake for 15 minutes, or until the chocolate soufflé rises in each tartlet.

CHEF'S TIP: These tartlets could be served with a pistachio cream, see page 64.

Chocolate-Hazelnut Soufflé Tartlets

SERVES 10

DIFFICULTY ★ ★ ★

PREPARATION: 1¼ hours

COOK: 30 minutes approx

REFRIGERATE: 40 minutes

Hazelnut Pastry

6½ tbsp soft unsalted
  butter

⅓ cup confectioners'
  sugar

1 pinch salt

⅓ cup hazelnut flour/
  meal, sifted

¼ tsp natural vanilla
  extract

1 egg

1⅔ cups flour, sifted

Chocolate Cream

⅓ cup unsweetened
  cocoa powder

⅓ cup water

¾ cup milk

3 egg yolks

4 tsp superfine sugar

3 tbsp flour

1 tbsp hazelnut liqueur
  (such as Frangelico®)

3 egg whites

¼ cup superfine sugar

Decoration

Confectioners' sugar,
  sifted

Hazelnut Pastry: Beat the unsalted butter with confectioners' sugar, salt, hazelnut flour/meal, and vanilla extract; combine well. Blend in the egg then the sifted flour and roughly mix to combine. Press the crumbs into a ball then, on a lightly floured work surface, use the heel of your hand to push bits of dough away from you, smearing them across the work surface to blend the unsalted butter and flour. Work quickly; repeat if necessary. Form into a ball, flatten slightly and wrap in plastic wrap. Refrigerate for 30 minutes.

Preheat the oven to 350°F. Butter ten tartlet molds (3¼ in). Dust the work surface with flour. Roll out the dough to a thickness of ⅛ in. Using a 4-in pastry cutter, stamp out 10 rounds of dough; line the molds with dough and prick the bases with a fork. Refrigerate 10 minutes.

Bake the dough-lined molds for 15 minutes, or until lightly golden. Cool before turning out onto a wire rack; set aside.

Chocolate Cream: Put the cocoa powder and water into a saucepan and stir to combine. Add the milk and bring to the boil; remove from the heat. Put the egg yolks and sugar into a bowl and beat until pale yellow and creamy; add the flour. Whisk half the hot chocolate milk quickly into the eggs-and-sugar mixture. Add the remaining milk and return the mixture to the saucepan. Cook over low heat, whisking continuously until the cream thickens. Boil for 1 minute while continuing to whisk. Pour the chocolate cream into a bowl; cover the surface with plastic wrap. When cool, add the hazelnut liqueur.

Preheat the oven to 350°F. Beat the egg whites until foamy. Gradually add the sugar, beating until the egg whites are smooth, shiny, and stiff peaks form. Stir a third into the chocolate cream; carefully fold in the remainder using a spatula. Divide the mixture evenly between the tartlet shells to come ⅔ up the side. Bake for 15 minutes, or until the chocolate soufflé rises in each tartlet. Dust with sifted confectioners' sugar and serve immediately.

Mouth-watering mousses & creams

The best way to prepare a chocolate meringue

You can adapt this version of chocolate meringue using the ingredients shown in the recipe of your choice (see p.168).

(1) Put the egg whites into a bowl and whisk until frothy. Add a third of the sugar a little at a time, whisking until the egg whites are smooth and shiny.

(2) Gradually add the remaining sugar, whisking until stiff peaks form on the whisk.

(3) Use a wooden spoon to fold the sifted confectioners' sugar and unsweetened cocoa powder into the whisked egg whites. Cut straight down to the bottom of the bowl with a wooden spoon, then lift up the contents, bringing the spoon up the side of the bowl while giving it a quarter turn. Continue until the mixture is smooth and shiny.

The best way to prepare soufflé dishes or ramekins

Prepare a soufflé using the recipe of your choice (see pp.192 and 200). The following technique is the same whatever the size of the ramekin or dish.

(1) Brush the ramekins with butter. Dust evenly with superfine sugar, tipping out the excess.

(2) Divide the soufflé mixture evenly between the ramekins and smooth with a spatula.

(3) Run your thumb around the inside rim of the ramekin to open a ¼-in channel, which will allow the soufflé mixture to rise cleanly and evenly during cooking. Cook according to the directions indicated in the recipe.

Chocolate Charlotte

SERVES **10–12**

DIFFICULTY ★ ★ ★

PREPARE: 1½ hours

COOK: 8 minutes

REFRIGERATE: 1 hour

Sponge Fingers
4 egg yolks
Scant $^2/_3$ cup superfine sugar
4 egg whites
1 cup flour, sifted
Confectioners' sugar

Chocolate Bavarian Cream
7 oz bittersweet chocolate, chopped
3 sheets or $2^1/_4$ tsp gelatin
$^3/_4$ cups milk
2 cups heavy whipping cream
$^1/_3$ cup superfine sugar
6 egg yolks

Decoration (Optional)
Chocolate shavings (p.209)

◊ See Making a pastry, batter, or meringue disc, p.13.

Preheat the oven to 350°F. Butter and dust an $8^1/_2$-in springform pan with sugar. Trace an $8^1/_2$-in circle on a sheet of parchment paper and turn the marked side over onto a baking sheet.

Sponge Fingers: Combine the egg yolks and half the sugar; beat until the mixture is pale yellow and creamy. In a separate bowl, whisk the egg whites, gradually adding the remaining sugar, until the egg whites are smooth, shiny, and stiff peaks form. Gently fold in the egg yolks and sugar mixture then the sifted flour. Fit a pastry bag with a plain round tip and fill it with the batter. Start piping in the center of the traced circle, working outward in a spiral and finishing a $^1/_2$ in from the inside edge. On the same or another baking sheet, pipe touching fingers of batter to form a band at least $8^1/_2$-in long; it should be the same width as the height of the springform pan. Dust the piped fingers with confectioners' sugar, wait 5 minutes then, dust generously a second time. Bake for 8 minutes, or until golden. Set the sponge disc and band of sponge fingers aside to cool.

Chocolate Bavarian Cream: Place the chopped chocolate in a large bowl. Soften the gelatin in cold water. Heat the milk, $^3/_4$ cup of the whipping cream and 2 tbsp of the sugar until simmering. Beat the egg yolks and remaining sugar, until pale yellow and creamy. Add a third of the hot milk mixture and mix well to combine. Pour it into the remaining hot milk mixture, stirring constantly with a wooden spoon; cook over low heat until the cream thickens and coats the back of the spoon. (Do not allow to boil!) Remove from the heat immediately, add the gelatin, and stir to dissolve. Strain the hot mixture over the chopped chocolate; stir until smooth. Stand the bowl in crushed ice to cool. Beat the remaining whipping cream until firm and clinging to the whisk; gently fold into the cooled chocolate cream.

Place the sponge disc in the bottom of the springform pan. Trim the band of sponge fingers to the height of the pan and place the sugared side against the inner wall, with the rounded ends pointing upward. Fill with the chocolate Bavarian cream and refrigerate 1 hour, or until firm. Remove the side of the pan and decorate with chocolate shavings.

Chocolate Crème Brûlée

SERVES 4
DIFFICULTY ★ ★ ★
PREPARE: 10 minutes
COOK: 25 minutes
REFRIGERATE: 1 hour

4 egg yolks
$^1/_4$ cup superfine sugar
$^1/_2$ cup milk
$^1/_2$ cup heavy whipping
  cream
$3^1/_2$ oz bittersweet
  chocolate, chopped

Decoration
• Superfine sugar

Preheat the oven to 200°F. Prepare 4 small baking dishes or low-sided ramekins.

Combine the egg yolks and 3 tbsp of the sugar in a large bowl; beat until the mixture is pale and creamy.

Heat the milk, whipping cream, and remaining sugar until simmering. Add the chopped chocolate and stir until well combined and smooth. Slowly stir the chocolate mixture into the egg yolks-sugar mixture. Pour the chocolate mixture into the dishes, to come $^3/_4$ up the side.

Bake for 25 minutes, or until firm; cool. Refrigerate for 1 hour.

Preheat the broiler to its maximum temperature. Sprinkle the creams evenly with superfine sugar and place under the broiler until the sugar becomes a dark brown topping. Let cool and serve once the topping has hardened.

CHEF'S TIP: To correctly brown, or caramelize creams, put the broiler rack as close to the heat source as possible.

White Chocolate Crème Brûlée

SERVES 6

DIFFICULTY ★ ★ ★

PREPARE: 30 minutes + 5 min

INFUSE: 1 hour

REFRIGERATE: Overnight

1³/₄ cups crème fraîche

1 vanilla pod, split

5 oz white chocolate

6 egg yolks

¹/₃ cup (packed) soft
  brown sugar

◊ The white chocolate
crème brûlée should be
prepared the day before
serving.

Place the crème fraîche in a saucepan. Using the point of a knife, scrape the seeds from the vanilla pod into the cream; add the pod, and heat until simmering. Remove from the heat and set aside to infuse for 1 hour.

Chop the white chocolate and melt over a bain-marie; remove from the heat, stirring until smooth. Add the egg yolks and mix well to combine; stir in the vanilla-flavored cream. Pour the mixture into a clean saucepan. Stirring constantly with a wooden spoon, cook over low heat until the cream thickens and coats the back of the spoon. (Do not allow to boil!) Strain and divide the mixture equally between six ramekins (3¹/₄ in diameter) and refrigerate overnight.

When ready to serve, preheat the broiler to its maximum temperature. Sprinkle the creams evenly with the brown sugar and place under the broiler until the sugar melts and turns golden. Serve immediately.

Chocolate Cream topped with Peppered Chantilly Cream and Caramel "Leaves"

SERVES 12–14
DIFFICULTY: ★ ★ ★
PREPARE: 1 hour
REFRIGERATE: 30 minutes

Chocolate Cream
8 oz bittersweet chocolate
2 sheets or 1 1/2 tsp gelatin
1 cup milk
1 cup heavy whipping cream
1 vanilla pod, split
5 egg yolks
1/3 cup superfine sugar

Caramel Leaves
1 1/4 cups superfine sugar
Scant 1/2 cup mild honey

Peppered Chantilly Cream
3/4 cup heavy whipping cream
1 pinch freshly ground pepper
3 tbsp confectioners' sugar

Chocolate Cream: Chop the chocolate and set aside in a large bowl. Soften the gelatin in cold water. Pour the milk and whipping cream into a saucepan. Using the point of a knife, scrape the seeds from the vanilla pod into the milk-and-cream mixture, add the pod and heat to simmering. Beat the egg yolks and sugar until pale yellow and creamy. Slowly whisk in a third of the hot cream mixture and mix well to combine; pour the egg yolks-and-sugar mixture into the remaining hot cream. Stirring constantly with a wooden spoon, cook over low heat until the cream thickens and coats the back of the spoon. (Do not allow to boil!) Remove from the heat immediately and discard the vanilla pod. (Squeeze the excess water from the sheet gelatin.) Stir the gelatin into the cream to dissolve. Pour over the chopped chocolate and stir until smooth. Divide the chocolate cream equally between 12–14 glasses and refrigerate for 30 minutes.

Caramel Leaves: Lightly brush a baking sheet with oil. Heat the sugar and honey over low heat, stirring until the sugar dissolves completely. Increase the heat and boil without stirring for about 10 minutes, or until the syrup turns a dark gold. Pour a thin layer of this caramel onto the baking sheet. When hard, break in large pieces.

Peppered Chantilly Cream: Combine the cream and ground pepper; whisk until the cream begins to firm. Add the confectioners' sugar and continue whisking until stiff peaks cling to the whisk. Fit a pastry bag with a plain tip and fill with the peppered Chantilly cream. Decorate each glass of chocolate cream with Chantilly and a caramel "leaf."

CHEF'S TIP: There are several types of pepper such as Sarawak, Sichuan, or Cubeb that will give your Chantilly a hot spicy flavor; they also marry well with chocolate. Grind your pepper just before using to give it a stronger taste.

Irish Coffee Cream

SERVES **4**

DIFFICULTY: ★ ★ ★

PREPARE: 25 minutes

REFRIGERATE: 30 minutes

Ganache

7 oz dark (55–70%)
  chocolate

1 scant cup crème fraîche

2 tbsp superfine sugar

2 tbsp whisky

Coffee Cream

3/4 cup heavy whipping
  cream

1/4 cup confectioners'
  sugar, sifted

1 tbsp coffee extract

Decoration

Unsweetened cocoa
  powder, sifted

Ganache: Coarsely chop the chocolate and place in a bowl. Heat the cream and sugar until simmering and pour over the chocolate. Stir until smooth and then add the whisky. Divide the mixture evenly between four glasses; refrigerate until required.

Coffee Cream: Whisk the cream until it begins to firm. Add the confectioners' sugar and continue whisking until stiff peaks cling to the whisk; fold in the coffee extract. Fit a pastry bag with a plain round tip and fill with the coffee cream.

Just before serving, remove the glasses from the refrigerator and pipe the coffee cream on top. Dust with sifted cocoa powder and serve.

CHEF'S TIP: If you don't have coffee extract, make your own by dissolving 1 tbsp of instant coffee in 1 tsp of hot water.

Old Fashioned Cream Soufflé

SERVES 4

DIFFICULTY ★ ★ ★

PREPARE: 15– 20 minutes

COOK: 7 or 8 minutes

3¹/₂ oz dark (55– 70%)
  chocolate
4 tbsp unsalted butter
¹/₃ cup unsweetened cocoa
  powder, sifted
2 egg yolks
3 egg whites
¹/₄ cup superfine sugar
Confectioners' sugar, sifted

Preheat the oven to 400°F. Butter four, shallow, 6 fl oz gratin or baking dishes with unsalted butter. Dust evenly with superfine sugar, tipping out the excess.

Chop the chocolate, place in a large bowl and melt over a bain-marie. Add the unsalted butter, stirring until smooth then blend in the cocoa powder. Remove from the bain-marie and cool. Slowly stir the egg yolks into the cooled chocolate and butter mixture.

Put the egg whites into a bowl and whisk until frothy. Add 1 tbsp of the sugar a little at a time, whisking until the egg whites are smooth and shiny. Gradually add the remaining sugar, whisking until stiff peaks form.

Whisk a third of the egg whites into the chocolate mixture to lighten it. Using a spatula, carefully fold in the remainder, in two separate batches. Divide the soufflé mixture equally between the prepared dishes and bake for 7– 8 minutes, or until risen. As soon as they come out of the oven, dust with sifted confectioners' sugar; serve immediately.

CHEF'S TIP: Room temperature egg whites whisk more successfully than refrigerated ones.

Two-Mousse Terrine

SERVES 10–12

DIFFICULTY ★ ★ ★

PREPARE: 1½ hours

COOK: 8 minutes

REFRIGERATE: 2 hours or freeze 1 hour

Chocolate Sponge

4 tsp unsalted butter

⅔ cup superfine sugar

4 eggs

¾ cup flour, sifted

6 tbsp unsweetened cocoa powder, sifted

Milk Chocolate Mousse

3½ oz milk chocolate

¾ cup heavy whipping cream

2 egg yolks

2 tbsp water

2 tbsp superfine sugar

Bittersweet Chocolate Mousse

5½ oz bittersweet chocolate

1¼ cups heavy whipping cream

2 egg yolks

3 tbsp water

2½ tbsp superfine sugar

Preheat the oven to 400°F. Line a jelly roll pan with baking parchment. Set a 10 x 4-in terrine aside.

Chocolate Sponge: Melt the unsalted butter in a saucepan over low heat; set aside. Place the sugar and eggs in a heatproof bowl; whisk to combine. Stand the bowl over a bain-marie and whisk continuously for 5–8 minutes, or until the batter becomes light and thick and falls in an unbroken ribbon from the whisk or beater. Do not allow it to become too hot. Remove the bowl from the bain-marie and continue whisking quickly by hand, or with an electric mixer on high speed, until cool. Gently fold in the flour and cocoa powder, adding them in 2 or 3 batches. Quickly add the melted butter. Pour the batter into the jelly roll pan and smooth with a palette knife. Bake approximately 8 minutes, or until the surface of the sponge is firm but springy to the touch and it starts to pull away from the parchment. Slide the cooked sponge, with the parchment attached, onto a wire rack. Place a sheet of parchment paper and a rack on the sponge and turn everything over, remove the rack; cool. Peel off the cooking parchment. Cut the sponge in strips and use to line the terrine, placing the crusty side against the walls and base. Reserve a piece of sponge, the same dimensions as the terrine, for the final assembly.

Milk Chocolate Mousse: Chop the chocolate and melt in a bain-marie. Whisk the cream until stiff peaks cling to the whisk; refrigerate. Whisk the egg yolks in a large bowl until pale yellow. Put the water and sugar into a saucepan and stir over low heat until the sugar dissolves; bring to the boil and cook for 2 minutes. Pour the syrup slowly down the side of the bowl into the egg yolks, whisking continuously until the mixture thickens and cools. Using a spatula, gradually blend in the melted chocolate then fold in the whipped cream.

Bittersweet Chocolate Mousse: Repeat the previous step using bittersweet chocolate instead of milk chocolate.

Pour the milk-chocolate mousse into the sponge-lined terrine then add the bittersweet chocolate mousse. Cover with the reserved piece of sponge. Refrigerate for 2 hours or freeze for 1 hour. Serve cold.

Chocolate-Coffee Dessert

SERVES **6–8**

DIFFICULTY ★ ★ ★

PREPARE: 1 hour

COOK: 15 minutes

REFRIGERATE: 2 hours

Chocolate Cake

1 3/4 oz dark (70%) chocolate

3 1/2 tbsp soft unsalted butter

2 egg yolks

2 egg whites

2 tbsp superfine sugar

3 1/2 tbsp flour, sifted

Coffee Syrup

3 tbsp water

3 tbsp superfine sugar

1 tsp instant coffee

Coffee Mousse

3 oz dark (55%) chocolate

3/4 cup heavy whipping cream

3 egg yolks

3 tbsp superfine sugar

4 tsp coffee extract

Chocolate Glaze

1 3/4 oz bittersweet chocolate

1/3 cup heavy whipping cream

1 tbsp mild honey

Decoration (Optional)

Coffee beans

Preheat the oven to 350°F. Line a baking sheet with parchment paper. Butter a 7-in square dessert frame; place it on the baking sheet.

Chocolate Cake: Finely chop the chocolate and melt over a bain-marie. Remove from the heat, add the unsalted butter, stir until smooth; add the egg yolks. In a separate bowl, whisk the egg whites gradually adding the sugar until the egg whites are smooth, shiny, and stiff peaks form. Whisk a third of the egg whites into the chocolate mixture to lighten it. Using a flexible spatula, carefully fold in the remainder then add the flour. Pour the batter into the dessert frame and bake for 15 minutes, or until a knife inserted in the center comes out clean. Cool in the frame.

Coffee Syrup: Put the water and sugar into a saucepan and stir over low heat until the sugar dissolves completely, increase the heat and boil for 2 minutes, add the coffee; cool.

Coffee Mousse: Finely chop the chocolate and melt over a bain-marie; cool. Beat the cream until firm peaks cling to the whisk; refrigerate. Whisk the egg yolks and sugar in a bowl until pale yellow and creamy; add the coffee extract. Use a spatula and gradually blend in the chocolate then, fold in the whipped cream.

Sprinkle or brush the chocolate cake with the coffee syrup and pour the coffee mousse over the top filling the dessert frame. Smooth the surface with a palette knife; refrigerate 1 hour.

Chocolate Glaze: Finely chop the chocolate and place in a bowl. Heat the cream and honey until simmering, pour over the chocolate and stir until smooth.

Remove the cake from the refrigerator, spread the glaze evenly over the surface; refrigerate for 1 hour. Remove the frame when the glaze is firm. Decorate with coffee beans, if desired.

White Chocolate and Blood Orange Mousse Dessert

SERVES **6–8**

DIFFICULTY ★ ★ ★

PREPARE: 1½ hours

COOK: 15 minutes

REFRIGERATE: 4 hours

Flourless Chocolate Cake
2 egg whites

6½ tbsp superfine sugar

2 egg yolks

5 tbsp unsweetened cocoa
   powder, sifted

Orange Syrup
⅓ cup water

6 tbsp superfine sugar

⅔ cup blood-orange juice

Blood Orange Mousse
2 sheets or 1½ tsp gelatin

1¼ cup heavy whipping
   cream

⅔ cup blood orange juice
   (with pulp)

4 tsp superfine sugar

White Chocolate Mousse
3½ oz white chocolate

¾ cup heavy whipping
   cream

Glaze (Optional)
1 sheet or ¾ tsp gelatin

3 tbsp mild honey

¼ cup water

3 blood orange segments

Flourless Chocolate Cake: Preheat the oven to 350°F. Line a jelly roll pan with parchment paper. Put the egg whites into a bowl and whisk until frothy. Add 2 tbsp of the sugar a little at a time, whisking until the egg whites are smooth and shiny. Gradually add the remaining sugar, whisking until stiff peaks form. Carefully fold in the egg yolks then the cocoa powder. Spread the batter onto the pan and bake for 15 minutes, or until firm; cool. Use a 7-in springform pan as a template and cut out 2 cake discs. Cover the leftover cake so it does not dry out and reserve.

Orange Syrup: Put the water and sugar into a saucepan, stir over low heat until the sugar dissolves, increase the heat and boil; cool. Add the blood orange juice to the cooled syrup.

Blood Orange Mousse: Soften the gelatin in cold water. Beat the cream until firm and clinging to the whisk. Heat half the blood orange juice; remove the saucepan from the heat. (Squeeze the excess water from the sheet gelatin.) Add the gelatin and the sugar to the hot juice; stir to dissolve. Pour the mixture into a bowl, add the remaining juice and stir in a third of the whipped cream; gently fold in the remainder.

White Chocolate Mousse: Chop the chocolate and melt over a slowly simmering bain-marie until the temperatures reaches approximately 115°F on a candy thermometer. Beat the cream until stiff peaks cling to the whisk. Quickly whisk about a third of the whipped cream into the hot chocolate. Pour the mixture over the remaining cream and fold in gently with the whisk or a spatula to evenly blend the ingredients.

Line a baking sheet with parchment paper and place the ring of the springform pan on it. Put one cake disc into the ring, sprinkle or brush with orange syrup and spread it with a 1¼-in layer of blood orange mousse. Place the other disc on top, sprinkle or brush with the orange syrup and spread with the white chocolate mousse. Smooth the surface with a palette knife; refrigerate for 4 hours. If desired, prepare the optional glaze using the listed ingredients and following the directions on p.92; carefully brush the glaze over the dessert's surface. Remove the ring. Crush the leftover cake into large crumbs and press around the bottom of the dessert. Decorate with blood orange segments.

Chocolate-Raspberry Mogador

SERVES 10

DIFFICULTY ★ ★ ★

PREPARE: 1 hour

COOK: 35 minutes

Raspberry Chocolate Cake

$3^1/_2$ oz bittersweet
  chocolate

7 tbsp unsalted butter

4 egg yolks

4 egg whites

3 tbsp superfine sugar

$6^1/_2$ tbsp flour, sifted

$3^1/_2$ oz frozen raspberries

Raspberry Syrup

$^1/_4$ cup water

$^1/_4$ cup superfine sugar

2 tbsp raspberry eau-de-vie

Chocolate Mousse

$2^3/_4$ oz dark (55%) chocolate

$^3/_4$ cup heavy whipping
  cream

3 egg yolks

2 tbsp water

$^1/_4$ cup superfine sugar

Decoration

$^1/_4$ cup raspberry jam

$4^1/_2$ oz raspberries

$3^1/_2$ oz chocolate shavings
  (p.209)

Preheat the oven to 325°F. Line a baking sheet with parchment paper. Butter an $8^1/_2$-in tart ring and place it on the baking sheet.

Raspberry Chocolate Cake: Finely chop the chocolate and melt over a bain-marie. Remove from the heat, add the unsalted butter, stir until smooth; add the egg yolks. In a separate bowl, whisk the egg whites, gradually adding the sugar until smooth, shiny, and stiff peaks form. Whisk a third of the egg whites into the chocolate mixture to lighten it. Using a flexible spatula, carefully fold in the remainder in two batches then add the sifted flour. Pour the batter into the tart ring, arrange the raspberries on the surface and bake for 35 minutes, or until firm and springy to the touch. Cool in the tart ring.

Raspberry Syrup: Put the water and sugar into a saucepan, stir over low heat until the sugar dissolves, increase the heat and boil for 2 minutes; cool. Add the raspberry eau-de-vie to the cold syrup.

Chocolate Mousse: Chop the chocolate and melt in a bain-marie. Beat the cream until stiff peaks cling to the whisk; refrigerate. Whisk the egg yolks in a large bowl until light and creamy. Put the water and sugar into a saucepan and stir over low heat until the sugar dissolves; bring to the boil and cook for 2 minutes. Carefully pour the syrup down the side of the bowl into the egg yolks, whisking continuously until the mixture thickens and cools. Using a spatula, gradually mix in the melted chocolate then fold in the whipped cream. Fit a pastry bag with a plain tip and fill with the mousse; set aside.

Put the cake onto a plate and remove the tart ring. Sprinkle or brush with the raspberry syrup; spread with the raspberry jam. Pipe touching balls of chocolate mousse in decreasing layers to form a pyramid. Decorate with raspberries and chocolate shavings.

Chocolate-Mascarpone Dessert

SERVES 8–10

DIFFICULTY ★ ★ ★

PREPARE: 30 minutes

INFUSE: 30 minutes

COOK: 20 minutes

REFRIGERATE: Overnight

2$^1/_2$ cups milk

1 vanilla pod, split

$^1/_3$ cup semolina

$^1/_4$ cup superfine sugar

8 oz bittersweet chocolate, chopped

$^1/_4$ cup rum

8 oz mascarpone

Decoration

Strawberries

Mascarpone

◇ This recipe must be prepared the day before serving.

Pour the milk into a saucepan. Using the point of a knife, scrape the seeds from the vanilla pod into the milk, add the pod and bring to the boil. Remove from the heat, cover and infuse for 30 minutes.

Discard the vanilla pod and bring the milk to the boil again. Remove the saucepan from the heat and stirring continuously, add the semolina in a thin, steady stream. Continue stirring, add the sugar and return the pan to the heat and bring to the boil. Reduce the heat to low and cook for about 20 minutes, stirring often to stop the semolina sticking. Remove from the heat, add the chopped chocolate and stir until melted. Blend in the rum and mascarpone.

Rinse a 10 x 3$^1/_4$-in loaf pan with cold water (do not dry) then fill with the mascarpone-chocolate mixture. Cover with plastic wrap; refrigerate overnight.

Just before serving, turn the dessert out; decorate with fresh strawberries and mascarpone.

CHEF'S TIP: When cooking the semolina, add some raisins, if desired.

Creole Chocolate Flan with Guava Caramel

SERVES 8
DIFFICULTY: ★ ★ ★
PREPARE: 30 minutes
COOK: 30 minutes
REFRIGERATE: 2 hours

Guava Caramel
7 tbsp water
1 cup superfine sugar
Scant $3/4$ cup guava pulp

Creole Chocolate Flan
$4^1/2$ oz bittersweet
  chocolate
5 eggs
$1^1/2$ cups milk
$2/3$ cup dulce de leche
7 tbsp sweetened
  condensed milk
1 tsp natural vanilla extract
1 pinch ground cinnamon

Preheat the oven to 300°F.

Guava Caramel: Heat the water and sugar in a saucepan; stir until the sugar dissolves. Increase the heat and boil (without stirring) for about 10 minutes, or until the syrup becomes a golden caramel color. Remove from the heat and add the guava pulp; take care as the caramel will spit violently when the liquid is added. Return to boil, cook 3 minutes. Pour an equal amount of the guava caramel into eight small bowls or ramekins.

Creole Chocolate Flan: Finely chop the chocolate and place in a large bowl. Whisk the eggs in a separate bowl. Combine the milk, dulce de leche and sweetened condensed milk in a saucepan; heat until simmering. Pour the milk mixture over the chocolate and stir until smooth. Stir the chocolate mixture into the whisked eggs then add the vanilla extract and ground cinnamon. Strain the flan mixture through a sieve over a bowl and distribute between the bowls of guava caramel.

Stand the bowls in a large roasting pan and half-fill the pan with boiling water. Transfer to the oven and cook for 30 minutes, or until the flans are firm. Remove the bowls from the roasting pan, cool and refrigerate for 2 hours before serving.

Chocolate Fondant with Praline Cream

SERVES **10**

DIFFICULTY ★ ★ ★

PREPARE: 1 hour

REFRIGERATE: 4 – 5 hours

Chocolate Fondant

9¹/₂ oz bittersweet
  chocolate

¹/₂ cup + 3¹/₂ tbsp soft
  unsalted butter

4 egg yolks

4 egg whites

¹/₃ cup superfine sugar

Praline Cream

6¹/₂ tbsp praline paste
  (p.314)

1 cup milk

3 egg yolks

6 tbsp superfine sugar

◊See p.206: Making a crème anglaise.

Line a 10 x 4-in loaf pan with parchment paper.

Chocolate Fondant: Chop the chocolate and melt over a bain-marie. Remove from the heat and add the unsalted butter, stir until smooth; blend in the egg yolks. Put the egg whites into a bowl and whisk until frothy. Add 2 tbsp of the sugar a little at a time, whisking until the egg whites are smooth and shiny. Gradually add the remaining sugar, whisking until stiff peaks form. Whisk a third of the egg whites into the chocolate mixture to lighten it. Using a spatula, carefully fold in the remainder in two batches. Pour the mixture into the prepared loaf pan and refrigerate for 4–5 hours, or until firm.

Praline Cream: Bring the milk to the boil. Beat the egg yolks and sugar until pale yellow and creamy. Whisk in a third of the hot milk and mix well to combine; pour the mixture into the remaining hot milk. Stirring constantly with a wooden spoon, cook over low heat until the cream thickens and coats the back of the spoon. (Do not allow to boil!) Remove from the heat immediately, strain into a bowl and blend in the praline paste. Cool the cream; refrigerate until required.

Dip the bottom of the loaf pan momentarily into very hot water to loosen. Place a serving platter on top and turn everything upside down to unmold the fondant onto the platter. Serve the praline cream separately.

CHEF'S TIP: You can also prepare individual fondants by using small ramekins or molds instead of the loaf pan.

Chocolate Fondue

SERVES 4

DIFFICULTY ★ ★ ★

PREPARE: 20 minutes

18 oz bittersweet chocolate

1 1/3 cups heavy whipping cream

1/4 cup milk

1 vanilla pod, split

1 banana

3 kiwis

3–4 slices pineapple, fresh or tinned

9 oz strawberries

Chop the chocolate and set aside. Put the heavy whipping cream and milk into a saucepan. Using the point of a knife, scrape the seeds from the vanilla pod into the saucepan, add the pod and heat slowly until simmering. Remove from the heat and discard the vanilla pod. Add the chopped chocolate to the cream and milk mixture and stir until completely melted. Place over a bain-marie to keep warm.

Slice or cut the fruit in pieces but leave the strawberries whole.

Thread the fruit on four metal skewers and serve with individual bowls of melted chocolate. Or, place a larger bowl of the chocolate, along with the fruit and skewers in the center of the table and let the guests help themselves.

CHEF'S TIP: Vary your choice of fruit, according to the season.

Chocolate Hedgehog

SERVES 8

DIFFICULTY ★ ★ ★

PREPARE: 1 hour

COOK: 20 minutes

Chocolate Sponge

3 egg yolks

6 tbsp superfine sugar

3 egg whites

Scant $^2/_3$ cup flour, sifted

3 tbsp unsweetened cocoa
  powder, sifted

Syrup

$^1/_4$ cup water

$^1/_4$ cup superfine sugar

Chocolate Whipped Cream

$4^1/_2$ oz bittersweet
  chocolate

$1^1/_3$ cups heavy whipping
  cream

Decoration

$^1/_2$ cup sliced almonds

Unsweetened cocoa
  powder, sifted

◇ See Making pastry, batter,
and meringue discs, page
13.

Preheat the oven to 325°F. Prepare two baking sheets and two pieces of parchment paper. Trace three circles – $6^1/_4$ in, $5^1/_2$ in and $4^1/_2$ in – on the paper; turn the marked sides over onto the baking sheets.

Chocolate Sponge: Whisk the egg yolks and 3 tbsp of the sugar until pale yellow and creamy. Whisk the egg whites in a separate bowl, gradually adding the remaining sugar until the egg whites are smooth, shiny, and stiff peaks form. Gently fold in the egg yolk and sugar mixture then the sifted flour and cocoa powder. Fit a pastry bag with a plain tip, and fill with the batter. Start piping in the center of each traced circle, working outward in a spiral until filled. Bake the layers for 15 minutes, or until firm, then set aside. (Do not turn off the oven; maintain it at the same temperature.)

Syrup: Heat the water and sugar in a saucepan over low heat until the sugar dissolves then increase the heat and boil for 2 minutes; cool.

Chocolate Whipped Cream: Chop the chocolate and melt over a bain-marie. Beat the whipping cream until stiff peaks cling to the whisk. Quickly whisk in the warm melted chocolate. Fit a pastry bag with a plain tip and fill with the chocolate whipped cream; set aside.

Line a baking sheet with parchment and sprinkle the sliced almonds over it. Toast the almonds in the oven for about 5 minutes, or until lightly golden.

Place the $6^1/_4$-in sponge layer on a plate and sprinkle or brush with syrup. Pipe touching balls of chocolate whipped cream over the surface. Put the $5^1/_2$-in layer on top, repeat the syrup and the cream; repeat the operation for the $4^1/_2$-in layer. Pipe additional chocolate whipped cream balls over the surface of the cake to form a pyramid. Dust with sifted cocoa powder and insert the sliced almonds to resemble "spikes."

Chocolate Marquise

SERVES **12**

DIFFICULTY ★ ★ ★

PREPARE: 1 hour

FREEZE: 30 minutes

REFRIGERATE: 1 hour 20 minutes

Chocolate Discs

5$\frac{1}{2}$ oz bittersweet chocolate

$\frac{3}{4}$ cup praline paste (314)

4 oz Frosties®, lightly crushed

Chocolate Mousse

9$\frac{3}{4}$ oz bittersweet chocolate

2$\frac{1}{4}$ cups heavy whipping cream

Bittersweet Chocolate Glaze

5$\frac{1}{2}$ oz bittersweet chocolate

$\frac{2}{3}$ cup heavy whipping cream

3 tbsp mild honey

4 tsp unsalted butter

Decoration, optional

Chocolate wafers

◇ See p.15: Glazing a cake or tart.

Chocolate Discs: Trace two 8-in circles on parchment paper. Finely chop the chocolate and melt over a bain-marie. Add the praline paste (see p. 314), stir until smooth then add the crushed Frosties®. Spread a layer of the mixture, $\frac{1}{4}$ in thick, in each of the traced circles; freeze the discs for 30 minutes.

Chocolate Mousse: Place the chocolate in a bowl and melt over a slowly simmering bain-marie until the temperature reaches approximately 115°F on a candy thermometer. Beat the cream until firm peaks cling to the whisk. Whisking quickly, add about a third of the whipped cream to the hot chocolate. Pour the mixture over the remaining cream and fold in gently with the whisk or a spatula to evenly blend the ingredients; set aside.

Place an 8$\frac{1}{2}$ x 1$\frac{1}{4}$-in dessert ring on a plate; put a chocolate disc into it. Fit a pastry bag with a plain tip, and fill with the mousse. Pipe a $\frac{1}{2}$-in layer of chocolate mousse over the disc. Place the other disc on top, press down lightly and pipe on enough chocolate mousse to fill the dessert ring; smooth with a spatula. Refrigerate the cake for 1 hour, or until firm.

Bittersweet Chocolate Glaze: Finely chop the chocolate and place in a large bowl. Heat the cream and honey in a saucepan until simmering and pour over the chocolate; stir until smooth. Add the unsalted butter and set aside at room temperature.

Remove the cake from the refrigerator. Warm the ring by running a hot, damp dish towel around it and slide it off the cake. Put the cake back into the refrigerator for 10 minutes. Put a wire rack over a bowl, place the cake on it and pour the glaze over the entire surface; smooth with a palette knife. When the glaze stops trickling into the bowl, transfer the marquise to a serving platter; if desired, cut chocolate wafers in half and press into the side as decoration. Refrigerate for about 10 minutes until firm. Cut into individual portions; serve.

CHEF'S TIP: The praline paste can be replaced with a chocolate-hazelnut spread.

Chocolate Meringue Nests

SERVES 10

DIFFICULTY ★ ★ ★

PREPARE: 30 minutes

COOK: 1 hour

COOL: 1 hour

Chocolate Meringue Nests

4 egg whites

Scant ⅔ cup superfine sugar

¾ cup confectioners' sugar, sifted

¼ cup unsweetened cocoa powder, sifted

Chocolate Chantilly Cream

3½ oz dark (66%) chocolate, chopped

¾ cup heavy whipping cream

3 tbsp confectioners' sugar

Decoration

7 oz raspberries

Confectioners' sugar

◇ See Making meringue, batter. and pastry discs, p.13.

Preheat the oven to 215°F. Trace ten 3¼-in circles on parchment paper and turn the marked sides over onto the baking sheet(s).

Chocolate Meringues: Put the egg whites into a bowl and whisk until frothy. Add 3 tbsp of the superfine sugar a little at a time, whisking until the egg whites are smooth and shiny. Gradually add the remaining sugar, whisking until stiff peaks form. Carefully fold in the sifted confectioners' sugar and cocoa powder. Fit a pastry bag with a star tip and fill with the chocolate meringue. Start piping in the center of the traced circles, working outward in a spiral until filled. Pipe a raised border on each edge to form a "nest." Bake the meringues for 1 hour, or until crisp. Remove from the baking sheet(s); cool on a rack at room temperature for 1 hour.

Chocolate Chantilly Cream: Melt the chocolate over a bain-marie. Whisk the cream until it begins to firm, add the confectioners' sugar and continue whisking until stiff peaks cling to the whisk. Quickly whisk in the warm melted chocolate.

Divide the chocolate Chantilly cream evenly between the meringue nests. Decorate with raspberries and dust with sifted confectioners' sugar.

CHEF'S TIP: You can make the meringues several weeks in advance if you store them in a dry place.

Chocolate Mousse

SERVES 8

DIFFICULTY ★ ★ ★

PREPARE: 30 minutes

REFRIGERATE: 3 hours min.

4$^1/_2$ oz dark (55%) chocolate
3$^1/_2$ tbsp unsalted butter
$^2/_3$ cup heavy whipping
  cream
2 egg yolks
3 egg whites
$^1/_4$ cup superfine sugar

Chop the chocolate and melt over a bain-marie, add the unsalted butter; stir until smooth. Set aside to cool.

Whisk the cream in a large bowl until stiff peaks cling to the whisk. Beat the egg yolks and blend into the cream. Refrigerate.

Put the egg whites into a bowl and whisk until frothy. Add 1 tbsp of the sugar a little at a time, whisking until the egg whites are smooth and shiny. Gradually add the remaining sugar, whisking until stiff peaks form.

Whisk a third of the egg whites into the cream-egg yolk mixture to lighten it. Using a spatula, carefully fold in the remainder in two separate batches. Quickly whisk in the melted chocolate mixture, making sure it is thoroughly incorporated. Refrigerate the chocolate mousse for at least 3 hours, or until firm before serving.

CHEF'S TIP: To obtain a lighter mousse, remove the eggs from the refrigerator well before starting the recipe.

White Chocolate Mousse

SERVES 10

DIFFICULTY ★ ★ ★

PREPARE: 20 minutes

REFRIGERATE: 3 hours min.

White Chocolate Mousse

2¹/₃ cups heavy whipping
  cream

10¹/₂ oz white chocolate

Decoration

5¹/₄ oz bittersweet
  chocolate shavings (p.209)

Beat the cream until firm peaks cling to the whisk. Set aside ¹/₂ cup in a bowl and refrigerate the rest. Finely chop the chocolate and melt over a slowly simmering bain-marie until the temperature reaches approximately 115°F on a candy thermometer. Whisking quickly, pour the melted chocolate over the whisked cream. Then, using a whisk or spatula, fold in the refrigerated whipped cream gently until the ingredients are evenly blended.

Divide the mousse equally between 10 dessert glasses and refrigerate for at least 3 hours, or until firm.

About 30 minutes before serving, remove the mousse-filled glasses from the refrigerator, to take the chill off them; decorate with bittersweet chocolate shavings.

CHEF'S TIP: To whisk cream more easily, refrigerate it for 15 minutes in the bowl you are going to use.

Darjeeling Infused Chocolate Mousse with Columbian Coffee Cream

DIFFICULTY ★ ★ ★

PREPARE: 50 minutes

REFRIGERATE: 3 hours min.

Darjeeling Infused Chocolate Mousse

$1/4$ cup water

1 Darjeeling tea bag

7 oz bittersweet chocolate

2 tbsp unsalted butter

6 tbsp superfine sugar

$1/3$ cup toasted hazelnuts, crushed (optional)

3 egg yolks

3 egg whites

Columbian Coffee Cream

1 cup milk

3 egg yolks

$1/3$ cup superfine sugar

1 tsp instant Columbian coffee

Chantilly Cream

$3/4$ cup heavy whipping cream

1 or 2 drops natural vanilla extract

3 tbsp confectioners' sugar

Decoration

Mint leaves

Darjeeling Infused Chocolate Mousse: Boil the water then add the tea bag; infuse for 10 minutes then discard the bag. Chop the chocolate and place in a bowl with the unsalted butter and 3 tbsp of the sugar; melt over a bain-marie without stirring. Add the hazelnuts (if desired) and pour in the tea. Remove the mixture from the bain-marie and add the egg yolks; set aside to cool. In a separate bowl, whisk the egg whites, gradually adding the remaining sugar until the whites are smooth, shiny, and stiff peaks form. Whisk a third of the egg whites into the chocolate mixture to lighten it, gently fold in the remainder in two separate batches. Divide the mousse evenly between four dessert bowls; refrigerate for at least 3 hours, or until firm.

Columbian Coffee Cream: Bring the milk and coffee slowly to the boil. Beat the egg yolks and sugar until pale yellow and creamy. Stir in a third of the hot milk and mix well to combine; pour the mixture into the remaining hot milk. Stir constantly with a wooden spoon over low heat until the cream thickens and coats the back of the spoon. (Do not allow to boil!) Remove from the heat immediately, strain into a bowl and cool; refrigerate.

Chantilly Cream: Combine the cream and vanilla extract; whisk until the cream begins to firm. Add the confectioners' sugar and continue whisking until firm peaks cling to the whisk. Fit a pastry bag with a plain round tip and fill with the Chantilly.

Decorate the surfaces of the mousses with Chantilly and mint leaves. Serve the Columbian coffee cream separately.

Hazelnut and Whisky Chocolate Mousse

SERVES **8–10**

DIFFICULTY ★ ★ ★

PREPARE: 30 minutes

COOK: 10 minutes

REFRIGERATE: 3 hours min.

1 $1/_3$ cups blanched
  hazelnuts, crushed

16 oz dark (55%) chocolate

2 tbsp unsalted butter

1 cup superfine sugar

6 egg yolks

$1/_3$ cup whisky

6 egg whites

Decoration

Chocolate shavings (p.209)

Preheat the oven to 350°F.

Cover a baking sheet with parchment paper. Spread the crushed hazelnuts on it, toast in the oven for about 5 minutes or until fragrant and golden.

Chop the chocolate and place in a bowl with the unsalted butter and $1/_2$ cup of the sugar; melt over a bain-marie without stirring. Remove from the heat and stir in the egg yolks then add about $1/_2$ cup of the toasted hazelnuts and the whisky.

Put the egg whites into a separate bowl and whisk until frothy. Add 2 tbsp of the remaining sugar a little at a time whisking until the egg whites are smooth and shiny. Gradually blend in the remaining sugar, whisking until stiff peaks form. Whisk a third of the egg whites into the chocolate mixture to lighten it, gently fold in the remainder in two separate batches.

Divide the mousse evenly between 8–10 dessert bowls; refrigerate for at least 3 hours, or until firm. Just before serving, decorate with the remaining hazelnuts and chocolate shavings.

Chocolate Praline Mousse

SERVES **10**

DIFFICULTY ★ ★ ★

PREPARE: 1 hour

REFRIGERATE: 3 hours min.

**Almond-Hazelnut
Praline Paste**

2 tbsp water

$3/4$ cup superfine sugar

$1/2$ cup blanched almonds

$1/2$ cup blanched hazelnuts

Dark Chocolate Mousse

$10^1/_2$ oz dark (55%)
  chocolate

$1^1/_2$ cups heavy whipping
  cream

6 egg yolks

6 egg whites

6 tbsp superfine sugar

◊ See p.314: Making praline
paste.

Almond-Hazelnut Praline Paste: Put the water and sugar in a medium saucepan over low heat and stir until the sugar dissolves completely. Increase the heat and bring to the boil. Stir in the blanched almonds and hazelnuts using a wooden spoon. Remove from the heat and continue stirring until the sugar crystalizes covering the nuts with a white powder. Return the saucepan to the heat until the sugar melts and the nuts turn golden brown. Spread the mixture on an oiled baking sheet; cool. When cold, break the praline in pieces, place in a food processor and grind, first to a powder then, to a creamy paste. To do so, it will be necessary to stop the food processor often, and stir the powder with a spatula. (To avoid overworking the food processor, grind the praline in several batches.) Set the praline paste aside in a bowl.

Dark Chocolate Mousse: Chop the chocolate and melt over a bain-marie; cool. Whisk the cream until stiff peaks cling to the whisk, blend in the egg yolks; refrigerate. Put the egg whites into a bowl and whisk until frothy. Add 2 tbsp of the sugar a little at a time, whisking until the egg whites are smooth and shiny. Gradually add the remaining sugar, whisking until stiff peaks form. Whisk one-third of the egg whites into the whipped cream and egg mixture to lighten it. Using a flexible spatula, carefully fold in the remainder in two separate batches. Quickly whisk in the melted chocolate.

Blend the praline paste into the dark chocolate mousse using a spatula. Refrigerate for at least 3 hours before serving.

Chocolate-Orange Mousse

MAKES 6

DIFFICULTY ★ ★ ★

PREPARE: 45 minutes

COOK: 15 minutes

REFRIGERATE: 3 hours min.

Glazed Orange Zests

2 oranges

¹/₄ cup water

¹/₂ cup superfine sugar

Chocolate Mousse

5¹/₂ oz bittersweet
   chocolate

³/₄ cup heavy whipping
   cream

3 egg yolks

3 egg whites

¹/₄ cup superfine sugar

Glazed Orange Zests: Zest the oranges using a vegetable peeler to remove strips of rind (without the pith). Cut the zest into long thin shreds. Bring a small saucepan of water to the boil. Add the zests, blanch for 1 minute, drain and rinse under cold water. Heat the water and sugar over low heat, and stir until the sugar dissolves; increase the heat and boil for 2 minutes. Lower the heat, add the orange zests and simmer for 15 minutes until tender; drain and set aside.

Chocolate Mousse: Chop the chocolate and melt over a bain-marie; cool. Whisk the cream until stiff peaks cling to the whisk, blend in the egg yolks; refrigerate. Put the egg whites into a bowl and whisk until frothy. Add 2 tbsp of the sugar a little at a time, whisking until the egg whites are smooth and shiny. Gradually blend in the remaining sugar, whisking until stiff peaks form. Whisk one-third of the egg whites into the whipped cream-egg yolk mixture to lighten it; carefully fold in the remainder in two separate batches. Quickly whisk in the melted chocolate, making certain it is thoroughly incorporated.

Set a few glazed orange zests aside for decoration. Add the remainder to the chocolate mousse; refrigerate for at least 3 hours until firm. Before serving, decorate with the reserved glazed orange zests.

Chocolate "Eggs"

MAKES 12

DIFFICULTY ★ ★ ★

PREPARE: Overnight + 1 hour

COOK: 10 minutes

REFRIGERATE: 30 minutes

12 eggs

Chocolate Fondant
4 oz bittersweet chocolate
6 1/2 tbsp unsalted butter
1/2 cup superfine sugar
2 tbsp Kirsch

Milk Cream
2 sheets or 1 1/2 tsp gelatin
1/3 cup milk
3/4 cup heavy whipping
  cream
2 tbsp superfine sugar
1/2 vanilla pod, split

◇ This recipe must be started the day ahead. You will need a cardboard egg carton.

The day before: Using a knife, spoon, or egg scissors, cut the tops off the eggs and empty the shells. Save 2 whole eggs and 1 egg yolk for the recipe. Use the remainder in another recipe. Rinse and carefully dry the eggshells; set aside overnight.

The next day, preheat the oven to 325°F.

Chocolate Fondant: Chop the chocolate and melt with the unsalted butter over a bain-marie. Put the 2 reserved whole eggs and single egg yolk, sugar, and Kirsch into a bowl and whisk to combine; blend in the melted chocolate. Soak the carton in water to prevent it burning when it is in the oven. Place the eggshells upright in the egg carton. Fill the shells with the chocolate fondant to come 3/4 up the side. Transfer to the oven and cook in the carton for 10 minutes.

Milk Cream: Soften the gelatin in cold water. Put the milk, cream, and sugar into a saucepan. Using the point of a knife, scrape the seeds from the vanilla pod into the milk mixture, add the pod; heat slowly until simmering. Remove from the heat and allow to infuse for 10 minutes; strain the mixture into a bowl. (Squeeze the excess water from the sheet gelatin.) Stir the gelatin into the cream to dissolve. Refrigerate for 30 minutes.

Place each chocolate egg in an egg cup; top with cold milk cream and serve.

CHEF'S TIP: Make sure you clean the eggshells well; use cold running water.

Nutty Chocolate Spread

SERVES 8

DIFFICULTY ★ ★ ★

PREPARE: 40 minutes

3 oz bittersweet chocolate
1 tbsp mild honey
$^2/_3$ cup heavy whipping
  cream

**Hazelnut-Almond
Praline Paste**
$^1/_4$ cup water
1 cup superfine sugar
1 cup blanched hazelnuts
$^1/_3$ cup blanched almonds
2 tbsp hazelnut oil

◇ See p.314: Making praline paste.

Finely chop the chocolate and place in a bowl with the honey. Heat the whipping cream until simmering, pour over the chocolate and honey; stir to combine. Set aside.

Hazelnut-Almond Praline Paste: Put the water and sugar into a saucepan over low heat and stir until the sugar is completely melted. Increase the heat and bring to the boil without stirring. Using a wooden spoon, stir in the hazelnuts and almonds. Remove from the heat and continue stirring until the sugar crystalizes covering the nuts with a white powder. Return the saucepan to the heat until the sugar melts and the nuts turn golden brown. Spread the mixture on an oiled baking sheet; cool. When cold, break the praline into pieces, place in a food processor and grind – first to a powder then to a creamy paste. To do so, it will be necessary to stop the food processor often, and stir the powder with a flexible spatula. (To avoid overworking the food processor, grind the praline in several batches.) Set the praline paste aside in a bowl.

Add a little praline paste to the chocolate mixture using a spatula then add the remainder; add the hazelnut oil. Cut down to the bottom of the mixture with the spatula, lift up the contents, and bring the spatula up the side of the bowl; continue until the mixture is shiny. Transfer to the bowl of a food processor and pulse or process until smooth. Store the spread in a glass container at room temperature for 2– 3 weeks.

CHEF'S TIP: The bittersweet chocolate in this recipe can be replaced with milk chocolate. Also, the hazelnut oil could be substituted with walnut oil.

Little Chocolate Pots

MAKES 6

DIFFICULTY ★ ★ ★

PREPARE: 15 minutes

COOK: 25-30 minutes

5^1/$_2$ oz dark (66%) chocolate

^{3}/$_4$ cup milk

1^1/$_4$ cups heavy whipping
cream

4 egg yolks

^{1}/$_3$ cup superfine sugar

Preheat the oven to 350°F.

Chop the chocolate and place in a saucepan; add the milk and cream. Heat slowly until the chocolate melts and the mixture barely simmers. Remove from the heat. Beat the egg yolks and sugar until pale yellow and creamy. Stir in the chocolate mixture using a wooden spoon; strain into a bowl. Skim the froth from the surface of the chocolate cream with a spoon.

Divide the chocolate cream equally between six 3^1/$_2$-in ramekins (^{1}/$_2$ cup capacity). Stand the ramekins in a large roasting pan half filled with boiling water. Transfer to the oven and cook for 25–30 minutes or until the chocolate creams puff very slightly and still tremble in the middle. Remove from the roasting pan and cool. Serve the chocolate pots cold.

CHEF'S TIP: The little chocolate pots can be kept refrigerated for 2–3 days. If desired, decorate with Chantilly cream and grated chocolate.

Coffee, Chocolate, and Vanilla Cream Pots

MAKES 12

DIFFICULTY ★ ★ ★

PREPARE: 10 minutes

COOK: 20–25 minutes

1 tsp instant coffee

2 tbsp unsweetened cocoa
  powder

3 cups milk

$^3/_4$ cup superfine sugar

1 vanilla pod, split

3 eggs

2 egg yolks

Preheat the oven to 350°F.

Prepare three large bowls: Place the instant coffee in one, the cocoa powder in another, and leave the third bowl empty.

Place the milk and 6 tbsp of the sugar in a saucepan. Using the point of a knife, scrape the seeds from the vanilla pod into the milk and sugar mixture, add the pod and bring to the boil. Remove from the heat.

Beat the whole eggs, egg yolks and remaining sugar until pale yellow and creamy; whisk into the hot milk. Strain and divide the mixture equally between the three large bowls. Whisk the coffee and cocoa mixtures to blend the flavors.

Set aside twelve $3^1/_2$-in ramekins ($^1/_2$ cup capacity).

Fill four ramekins with the coffee cream, another four with the chocolate cream and the remaining four with the vanilla cream. If necessary, skim the froth from the surface of the creams with a spoon. Stand the ramekins in a large roasting pan half filled with boiling water. Transfer to the oven and cook for 20 – 25 minutes, or until the point of a knife, inserted into center of the cream(s) comes out clean. Remove from the roasting pan, cool then refrigerate. Serve the little pots of cream cold – one of each of the flavors per person.

CHEF'S TIP: If you line the bottom of the roasting pan with absorbent paper, it will stop bubbles from forming in the creams giving them a smooth rather than a grainy texture.

Empress Pudding with Passion Fruit Granita

SERVES **10**

DIFFICULTY ★ ★ ★

PREPARE: 1½ hours

COOK: 30 minutes

REFRIGERATE: 3½ hours approx.

Creamed Rice

1 cup milk

3 tbsp heavy whipping cream

4 cups water

6 tbsp short grain rice

²/₃ cup passion fruit juice

1 tbsp superfine sugar

Chocolate Cream

5¹/₂ oz bittersweet chocolate

2 sheets or 1¹/₂ tbsp gelatin

2 egg yolks

¹/₄ cup superfine sugar

¹/₂ cup milk

1²/₃ cups heavy whipping cream

1 vanilla pod, split

Passion Fruit Granita

²/₃ cup water

3 tbsp superfine sugar

²/₃ cup passion fruit juice

Creamy Raspberries

2 sheets or 1¹/₂ tsp gelatin

²/₃ cup raspberry coulis

Decoration

Fresh raspberries

Creamed Rice: Heat the milk and cream until simmering. Bring the water to the boil in a separate saucepan, add the rice and cook for 2 minutes. Strain and pour into the simmering milk and cream. Add the passion fruit juice and cook over low heat for 20 minutes. Stir in the sugar and cook for a further 5 minutes; set aside to cool.

Chocolate Cream: Chop the chocolate and place in a large bowl. Soften the gelatin in a little cold water. Beat the egg yolks and 2 tbsp of the sugar until pale yellow and creamy. Put the milk, 2 tbsp of the whipping cream and the remaining sugar into a saucepan. Using the point of a knife, scrape the seeds from the vanilla pod into the milk mixture; add the pod and heat slowly until simmering. Quickly stir a third of the hot milk into the eggs and sugar and mix well to combine. Pour the mixture into the remaining hot milk and cook over low heat, stirring constantly with a wooden spoon, until the cream thickens and coats the back of the spoon. (Do not allow to boil!) Remove from the heat immediately. (Squeeze the excess water from the sheet gelatin.) Stir the gelatin into the cream to dissolve. Strain the hot mixture over the chopped chocolate, stirring until smooth. Stand the bowl in crushed ice to cool; stir from time to time. Whisk the remaining whipping cream until firm and clinging to the whisk. Combine the cooled, creamed rice with the dark chocolate cream; carefully fold in the whisked cream. Pour the mixture into an 8-in Charlotte mold; refrigerate for 3 hours.

Passion Fruit Granita: Combine the water and sugar in a saucepan, stir over low heat to dissolve the sugar. Cool the syrup to room temperature, and add the passion fruit juice. Pour a shallow layer into a large container and freeze. Stir with a fork from time to time, scraping the bottom and sides of the pan so the mixture will freeze evenly (about 2 hours).

Creamy Raspberries: Soften the gelatin in cold water. Heat 3 tbsp of the raspberry coulis, remove from the heat, add the softened gelatin; stir until smooth. Pour into the remaining coulis and refrigerate 20 minutes. Turn the empress pudding out onto a serving platter. Whisk the raspberry mixture, mound it on top, and decorate with fresh raspberries. Serve with glasses of passion fruit granita.

Chocolate Soufflé

SERVES 8

DIFFICULTY ★ ★ ★

PREPARE: 30 minutes

COOK: 45 minutes

Chocolate Pastry Cream

4 oz bittersweet chocolate
2 cups milk
1 vanilla pod, split
4 egg yolks
6 tbsp superfine sugar
$^1/_2$ cup flour

6 egg whites
3 tbsp superfine sugar

Decoration

Unsweetened cocoa
  powder, sifted

◊ See p.135: Preparing
soufflé dishes.

Chocolate Pastry Cream: Finely chop the chocolate, place in a bowl and melt over a bain-marie. Pour the milk into a saucepan. Using the point of a knife, scrape the seeds from the vanilla pod into the milk, add the pod and bring to the boil; remove from the heat. Put the eggs and sugar into a bowl and beat until pale yellow, thick, and creamy; blend in the flour. Remove the vanilla pod and stir half the hot milk quickly into the eggs-sugar-flour mixture, mix well to combine; add the remaining milk. Cook over low heat, stirring continuously with a wooden spoon until the cream thickens. Boil for 1 minute while continuing to stir. Remove from the heat and pour the pastry cream into the melted chocolate; stir until smooth. Cover the surface of the chocolate pastry cream with plastic wrap; cool.

Preheat the oven to 350°F. Brush a 9-in soufflé dish with butter and dust evenly with superfine sugar, tipping out the excess.

Put the egg whites into a bowl and whisk until frothy. Add half the sugar a little at a time, whisking until the egg whites are smooth and shiny. Gradually add the remaining sugar, whisking until stiff peaks form.

Whisk one-third of the egg whites into the pastry cream to lighten it. Using a spatula, carefully fold in the remainder in two separate batches. Pour the mixture into the prepared soufflé dish, filling it completely; smooth the surface with the spatula. Run your thumb around the top of the dish to open a narrow $^1/_4$-in channel between the mixture and the rim. (This will allow the soufflé to rise cleanly and evenly.) Cook the soufflé for 45 minutes, or until risen. As soon as it comes out of the oven, dust with sifted cocoa powder; serve immediately.

Bitter Chocolate Soufflés

SERVES 6

DIFFICULTY ★ ★ ★

PREPARE: 30 minutes

COOK: 15 minutes

1¼ oz dark (55–70%)
  chocolate
⅓ cup unsweetened cocoa
  powder
½ cup water
1 egg yolk
2 tbsp cornstarch
6 egg whites
7 tbsp superfine sugar

Decoration

Confectioners' sugar, sifted

◇ See p.135: Preparing
soufflé dishes.

Preheat the oven to 350°F. Brush six 3¼-in ramekins with butter and dust evenly with superfine sugar, tipping out the excess.

Finely chop the chocolate and place in a bowl. Put the cocoa powder and water into a saucepan, stir to combine and bring to the boil. Pour the hot mixture over the chocolate, stirring until smooth; set aside until cool. Blend in the egg yolk then the corn starch.

Put the egg whites into a bowl and whisk until frothy. Add 3 tbsp of the sugar a little at a time, whisking until the egg whites are smooth and shiny. Gradually add the remaining sugar, whisking until stiff peaks form.

Whisk a third of the egg whites into the chocolate mixture to lighten it. Use a spatula and carefully fold in the remainder in two separate batches. Divide the mixture evenly between the ramekins; smooth the surface with the spatula. Run your thumb around the tops of the ramekins to open a narrow (¼ in) channel between the mixture and the rim. (This will allow the soufflés to rise cleanly and evenly.) Cook the soufflés for 15 minutes, or until risen. As soon as they come out of the oven, dust with sifted confectioners' sugar; serve immediately.

Chocolate-Coffee Soufflés

SERVES **6**

DIFFICULTY ★ ★ ★

PREPARE: 1 hour

FREEZE: 2 hours

COOK: 15 minutes

Coffee Ganache Discs

2³/₄ oz bittersweet
   chocolate

¹/₃ cup heavy whipping
   cream

¹/₂ tsp instant coffee

Chocolate Soufflé

2¹/₄ oz bittersweet
   chocolate

³/₄ cup unsweetened cocoa
   powder

1 cup water

2 egg yolks

4 egg whites

¹/₄ cup superfine sugar

◇ See p.135: Preparing
soufflé dishes.

Coffee Ganache Discs: Cover a baking sheet with parchment paper. Coarsely chop the chocolate and place in a bowl. Heat the whipping cream and instant coffee until simmering, pour over the chocolate; stir until smooth. Use a teaspoon to form 24 small discs on the baking sheet; freeze for 2 hours.

Preheat the oven to 350° F. Brush six 3¹/₄-in ramekins with butter and dust evenly with superfine sugar, tipping out the excess.

Chocolate Soufflé: Finely chop the chocolate and place in a bowl. Put the cocoa powder and water into a saucepan, stir to combine and bring to the boil. Pour the hot mixture over the chocolate, stirring until smooth; set aside until cold then, blend in the egg yolks.

Put the egg whites into a bowl and whisk until frothy. Add 1 tbsp of the sugar a little at a time, whisking until the egg whites are smooth and shiny. Gradually add the remaining sugar, whisking until stiff peaks form.

Whisk a third of the egg whites into the chocolate mixture to lighten it. Use a spatula and carefully fold in the remainder in two separate batches. Pour the mixture into the ramekins, filling them to the half-way mark. Place four ganache discs in each ramekin then fill with the remaining soufflé mixture; smooth the surface with the spatula. Run your thumb around the tops of the ramekins to open a narrow (¹/₄ in) channel between the mixture and the rim. (This will allow the soufflés to rise cleanly and evenly.) Cook the soufflés for 15 minutes, or until risen. As soon as they come out of the oven, dust with confectioners' sugar; serve immediately.

White Chocolate Soufflés

SERVES 6

DIFFICULTY ★ ★ ★

PREPARE: 30 minutes

COOK: 20 minutes

**White Chocolate
Pastry Cream**

$4^1/_2$ oz white chocolate

$1^1/_3$ cups milk

4 egg yolks

$6^1/_2$ tbsp superfine sugar

3 tbsp flour

10 egg whites

$6^1/_2$ tbsp superfine sugar

Decoration

Confectioners' sugar, sifted

◊ See p.135: Preparing
soufflé dishes.

Preheat the oven to 350°F. Brush six $3^1/_4$-in ramekins with butter and dust evenly with superfine sugar, tipping out the excess.

White Chocolate Pastry Cream: Finely chop the chocolate and place in a bowl. Pour the milk into a saucepan and bring to the boil; remove from the heat. Put the eggs and sugar into a bowl and beat until pale yellow and creamy; add the flour. Whisk half of the hot milk quickly into the eggs-sugar-flour mixture; add the remaining milk. Return to the heat and cook over low heat, whisking continuously until the cream thickens. Boil for 1 minute while continuing to whisk. Remove from the heat and pour the mixture over the chopped chocolate; stir until smooth. Cover the surface of the chocolate pastry cream with plastic wrap; cool.

Put the egg whites into a bowl and whisk until frothy. Add 2 tbsp of the sugar a little at a time, whisking until the egg whites are smooth and shiny. Gradually add the remaining sugar, whisking until stiff peaks form.

Whisk a third of the egg whites into the chocolate mixture to lighten it. Using a spatula, carefully fold in the remainder in two separate batches. Divide the mixture evenly between the ramekins, filling them completely; smooth the surface with the spatula. Run your thumb around the tops of the ramekins to open a narrow ($^1/_4$ in) channel between the mixture and the rim. (This will allow the soufflés to rise cleanly and evenly.) Cook the soufflés for 15 minutes, or until risen. As soon as the soufflés come out of the oven, dust with confectioners' sugar; serve immediately.

Chocolate Duo

SERVES 6

DIFFICULTY ★ ★ ★

PREPARE: 45 minutes

COOK: 15 minutes

FREEZE: 1½ hours approx.

Chocolate Sorbet

7 oz bittersweet chocolate

1 cup water

1 cup milk

1 scant cup superfine sugar

$^1/_3$ cup unsweetened cocoa
  powder

Moist Chocolate Soufflés

$3^1/_2$ oz bittersweet
  chocolate

$^1/_4$ cup unsalted butter

4 egg yolks

4 egg whites

$^1/_4$ cup superfine sugar

Decoration

Confectioners' sugar, sifted

Chocolate Sorbet: Finely chop the chocolate and place in a bowl. Put the water, milk, sugar, and cocoa powder in a saucepan, stir until the sugar dissolves and bring to the boil. Pour over the chopped chocolate, stirring until smooth and strain. Stand the bowl in crushed ice until the mixture is cold. Pour the mixture into an ice-cream maker (pre-frozen, if necessary) and freeze-churn according to the manufacturer's instructions (about 30 minutes). Remove the sorbet from the machine and transfer it to the freezer to harden for a minimum of 1 hour before using.

Preheat the oven to 350°F. Brush six $3^1/_4$-in ramekins with butter and dust evenly with superfine sugar, tipping out the excess.

Moist Chocolate Soufflés: Finely chop the chocolate and melt with the unsalted butter over a bain-marie. Remove from the heat and when cool, add the eggs; set aside until cold. Put the egg whites into a bowl and whisk until frothy. Add 2 tbsp of the sugar a little at a time, whisking until the egg whites are smooth and shiny. Gradually add the remaining sugar, whisking until stiff peaks form. Whisk a third of the egg whites into the chocolate mixture to lighten it. Use a spatula and carefully fold in the remainder, in two separate batches. Divide the mixture evenly between the ramekins; smooth the surface with the spatula. Run your thumb around the tops of the ramekins to open a narrow ($^1/_4$ in) channel between the mixture and the rim. (This will allow the soufflés to rise cleanly and evenly.) Cook the soufflés for about 15 minutes, or until risen. As soon as the soufflés come out of the oven, dust with confectioners' sugar; serve immediately with the chocolate sorbet in separate bowls.

Chocolate Fondant with Apricot Coulis and Pistachios

SERVES **10**

DIFFICULTY ★ ★ ★

PREPARE: 1 hour

COOK: 15 minutes

REFRIGERATE: Overnight + 30 minutes

Chocolate Fondant

$^1/_2$ cup + $2^1/_2$ tbsp soft unsalted butter

$2^3/_4$ oz dark (66%) chocolate

1 cup unsweetened cocoa powder, sifted

4 egg yolks

$^2/_3$ cup superfine sugar

1 tbsp coffee extract

$1^1/_4$ cups heavy whipping cream

Apricot Coulis

1lb 2 oz apricots

7 tbsp superfine sugar

Juice of $^1/_2$ lemon, strained

$1^2/_3$ cup water

Decoration

Crushed pistachios

◇ The dessert should start to be prepared the day before serving.

Chocolate Fondant: The day before serving, place the unsalted butter in a bowl and beat until creamy. Chop the chocolate and melt over a bain-marie. Remove from the heat, add the unsalted butter and the sifted cocoa powder; whisk until smooth. Put the eggs and sugar into a bowl and beat until pale yellow and creamy; add the coffee extract. Using a flexible spatula, blend in the chocolate mixture carefully. Place the heavy whipping cream in a separate bowl and whisk until stiff peaks cling to the whisk. Quickly whisk a third of the chocolate mixture into the whipped cream then fold in the remainder. Pour the mixture into a 10 x 4-in porcelain terrine, cover the surface with plastic wrap; refrigerate overnight.

Apricot Coulis: The day of serving, wash and dry the apricots, remove the pits and coarsely chop the fruit. Place the chopped apricots in a saucepan with the sugar, lemon juice, and water; bring to the boil. Lower the heat, cook for 15 minutes, or until apricots are tender, then purée in a food processor or blender. If the coulis is not sweet enough, add a little more sugar; refrigerate for 30 minutes.

Stand the terrine briefly in hot water before turning the fondant out; slice using a knife dipped in hot water. Place one or two slices of the chocolate fondant on each plate, spoon a little apricot coulis beside it and scatter with crushed pistachios.

CHEF'S TIP: You can, if you like, use Caribbean chocolate, which is a "grand cru" dark couverture chocolate made from cocoa beans grown on the Caribbean Islands.

Iced desserts
& sweet drinks

The best way to prepare crème anglaise

Adapt this version of crème anglaise using the ingredients listed in the recipe of your choice (see pp. 168 or 230).

(1) Beat 5 egg yolks and ²/₃ cup sugar until pale yellow and creamy.

(2) Using the point of a knife, scrape the seeds from a vanilla pod into 2 cups milk; add the pod and bring the milk slowly to the boil. Beating quickly, pour a third of the hot milk onto the egg yolk-and-sugar mixture.

(3) Pour the mixture into the remaining hot milk. Stirring constantly with a wooden spoon, cook over low heat until the cream thickens and coats the back of the spoon. (Do not allow to boil!) Remove from the heat immediately and strain into a bowl. Set in a container of crushed ice to cool; stir from time to time.

The best way to prepare choux pastry dough

Adapt this version of choux pastry dough using the ingredients shown in the recipe of your choice (see p. 262).

① Put 2¹/₂ tbsp unsalted butter, ¹/₂ cup water, ¹/₂ tsp salt, and ¹/₂ tsp sugar into a saucepan over low heat. When the butter melts, bring the mixture to the boil; remove from the heat immediately. Tip ²/₃ cup of flour into the hot liquid. Stir with a wooden spoon until a firm, smooth dough forms. Return the saucepan to low heat to dry out the dough; continue beating until it forms a ball and pulls away cleanly from the sides of the saucepan.

② Transfer the dough to a bowl; cool for 5–10 minutes. One by one, add 3 eggs to the paste, beating vigorously after each addition to incorporate as much air as possible. The dough should be smooth and shiny.

③ The dough is ready to be used, when it falls from the spoon in a point. If it doesn't, add half of another beaten egg. Depending on the egg size and/or flour quality it may be necessary to use all of the egg.

The best way to shape quenelles

Follow the recipe of your choice to create the mixture (see pp. 218, 220, or 234); then shape the quenelles as set out below.

(1) Place 2 tablespoons (or teaspoons) in a glass of hot water. Set out the mixture, serving dishes and/or pastry shells.

(2) Using one spoon, scoop out a mound of the mixture. Invert the second spoon over the top and shape it into an oval (a quenelle). Slide the top spoon under the quenelle and repeat the operation until the quenelle is smooth and oval.

(3) Slide the quenelle off the spoon, into the serving dish or pastry shell.

The best way to make chocolate shavings

Chocolate shavings are ideal to decorate your desserts (see p.212). You will need 7 oz chocolate. There are two different methods you can use. The first one produces shorter shavings.

① First method: Stand a block of chocolate, smooth side out, on a piece of parchment paper and use a hair dryer to soften the surface. Wait 2 minutes for the chocolate to return to room temperature. Hold the chocolate block at a slight angle and scrape off shavings using a fixed-blade vegetable peeler. Refrigerate until required.

② Second method (professional): Temper the chocolate (see p.315). Use a palette knife and spread it out thinly on marble work surface or a sheet of acetate or thick plastic; cool.

③ Holding a long-bladed knife at an angle, scrape up the chocolate, keeping the pressure steady along the blade to form curls. Refrigerate until required.

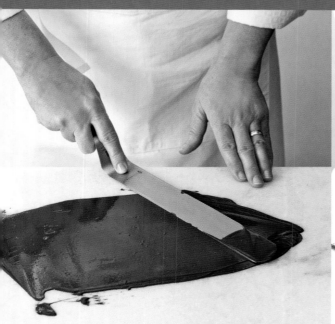

Iced Chocolate Log

SERVES 12

DIFFICULTY ★ ★ ★

PREPARE: 1¼ hours

COOK: 12 minutes

FREEZE: 3 hours

Chocolate Sponge

3½ oz dark (70%) chocolate

6½ tbsp soft unsalted
   butter

4 egg yolks

4 egg whites

3 tbsp superfine sugar

6½ tbsp flour, sifted

Chocolate Syrup

¼ cup water

6 tbsp superfine sugar

2 tbsp unsweetened cocoa
   powder

Chocolate Parfait

3½ oz bittersweet
   chocolate

1⅓ cups heavy whipping
   cream

5 egg yolks

2½ tbsp water

¼ cup superfine sugar

Chocolate Chantilly Cream

3½ oz bittersweet
   chocolate

¾ cup heavy whipping
   cream

3 tbsp confectioners' sugar

Chocolate Shards

9 oz bittersweet chocolate

◇ You will need a 14 x 2½-in
log mold.

Chocolate Sponge: Preheat the oven to 350°F. Line a 15 x 12-in jelly roll pan with parchment paper. Chop the chocolate and melt over a bain-marie. Remove from the heat; add the unsalted butter then the egg yolks. In a separate bowl, whisk the egg whites, gradually adding the sugar until the whites are smooth, shiny, and stiff peaks form; gently fold into the chocolate mixture. Blend in the sifted flour, stirring to combine. Pour a ½-in layer of the batter into the jelly roll pan, smooth with a palette knife. Bake for 12 minutes, or until firm but springy to the touch. Cool on a rack.

Chocolate Syrup: Combine all ingredients in a saucepan and stir over low heat until the sugar dissolves, bring to the boil; cool.

Chocolate Parfait: Chop the chocolate and melt in a bain-marie. Beat the cream until firm and clinging to the whisk; refrigerate. Whisk the egg yolks in a large bowl until pale yellow. Put the water and sugar into a saucepan and stir over low heat until the sugar dissolves; increase the heat and boil for 2 minutes. Pour the syrup slowly down the side of the bowl into the egg yolks, whisking continuously until the mixture thickens and cools. Using a spatula, gradually blend in the melted chocolate then fold in the whipped cream.

Pour the parfait into the log mold, filling it to the ⅓ mark. Cut the chocolate sponge into two rectangles, one measuring 14 x 1¼ in and the other, 14 x 2 in. Place the smaller rectangle on the parfait and brush it with chocolate syrup; cover with the remaining parfait. Brush the larger rectangle with chocolate syrup and place it, syrup side down, on the parfait. Freeze for 3 hours.

Chocolate Chantilly Cream: Melt the chopped chocolate over a bain-marie. Whisk the cream until it begins to firm, add the confectioners' sugar and continue whisking until stiff peaks cling to the whisk. Quickly whisk in the warm melted chocolate. Fit a pastry bag with a star tip and fill with the chocolate Chantilly cream; set aside.

Chocolate Shards: Temper the chocolate (p.315) and spread it on a baking sheet covered with parchment paper; refrigerate. When hard, remove from the refrigerator, bring to room temperature and break in large pieces.

Pipe chocolate Chantilly rosettes on top of log and decorate with chocolate shards.

Chocolate Ice Cream Sundae

SERVES 8

DIFFICULTY ★ ★ ★

PREPARE: 45 minutes

FREEZE: 30 minutes

Chocolate Ice Cream

4 1/2 oz dark (55-70%)
  chocolate

1 1/4 oz unsweetened
  cooking chocolate

2 cups milk

6 egg yolks

1/2 cup superfine sugar

Chocolate Sauce

9 oz bittersweet chocolate

2/3 cup milk

1/2 cup heavy whipping
  cream

Chantilly Cream

1 1/2 cups heavy whipping
  cream

1/3 cup confectioners' sugar

Decoration

Chocolate shavings
  (see p.209)

Chocolate Ice Cream: Finely chop the chocolates; place in a large bowl. Bring the milk slowly to the boil. In a separate bowl, beat the egg yolks and sugar until pale yellow and creamy. Whisk in a third of the hot milk and mix well to combine; pour the mixture into the remaining hot milk. Stirring constantly with a wooden spoon, cook over low heat until the mixture thickens and coats the back of the spoon. (Do not allow to boil!) Remove from the heat immediately. Pour over the chopped chocolate and stir until smooth; strain into a bowl. Stand the bowl in crushed ice until the mixture is cold. Pour the mixture into an ice-cream maker (pre-frozen, if necessary) and freeze-churn according to the manufacturer's instructions (about 30 minutes). Remove the ice cream from the machine and transfer it to the freezer before serving.

Chocolate Sauce: Chop the chocolate and place in a bowl. Heat the milk and heavy whipping cream until simmering and pour over the chopped chocolate; stir until smooth.

Chantilly Cream: Whisk the cream until it begins to stiffen, add the confectioners' sugar and continue whisking until firm peaks cling to the whisk. Fit a pastry bag with a star tip and fill with the Chantilly cream.

Place three scoops of chocolate ice cream in each glass and pour in a ribbon of chocolate sauce. Pipe a large rosette of Chantilly cream on top, and decorate with chocolate shavings.

CHEF'S TIP: If you can't find unsweetened cooking chocolate, use chocolate with a high percentage of cocoa, 72% for example.

Chocolate Ice Cream topped with Hot Chocolate Sauce

SERVES **8**

DIFFICULTY ★ ★ ★

PREPARE: 30 minutes

FREEZE: 30 minutes

Chocolate Ice Cream

4$^1/_2$ oz dark (55-70%)
  chocolate

1$^1/_4$ oz unsweetened
  cooking chocolate

2 cups milk

6 egg yolks

$^1/_2$ cup superfine sugar

Chocolate Sauce

9 oz bittersweet chocolate

$^2/_3$ cup milk

$^1/_2$ cup heavy whipping
  cream

Chocolate Ice cream: Finely chop the chocolates and place in a large bowl. Bring the milk slowly to the boil. In a separate bowl, beat the egg yolks and sugar until pale yellow and creamy. Whisk in a third of the hot milk and mix well to combine; pour the mixture into the remaining hot milk. Stirring constantly with a wooden spoon, cook over low heat until the mixture thickens and the mixture coats the back of the spoon. (Do not allow to boil!) Remove from the heat immediately. Pour over the chopped chocolate and stir until smooth; strain into a bowl. Stand the bowl in crushed ice until the mixture is cold. Pour the mixture into an ice-cream maker (pre-frozen, if necessary) and freeze-churn according to the manufacturer's instructions (about 30 minutes). Remove the ice cream from the machine and transfer it to the freezer before serving.

Chocolate Sauce: Chop the chocolate and place in a bowl. Heat the milk and heavy whipping cream until simmering and pour over the chopped chocolate; stir until smooth.

Place three or four scoops of chocolate ice cream in each bowl and pour over the hot chocolate sauce.

Chocolate Ice Cream Dessert with Hot Coffee Sabayon

SERVES **4**

DIFFICULTY ★ ★ ★

PREPARE: 1½ hours

COOK: 8 minutes

FREEZE: 30 minutes

Chocolate Ice Cream
4½ oz dark (55-70%) chocolate

1¼ oz unsweetened cooking chocolate

2 cups milk

6 egg yolks

½ cup superfine sugar

Sponge
3 egg yolks

3 egg whites

6 tbsp superfine sugar

⅔ cup flour, sifted

Coffee Syrup
¼ cup water

¼ cup superfine sugar

2 tbsp rum

1 tsp coffee liqueur

Coffee Sabayon
1½ tsp instant coffee

⅓ cup water

4 egg yolks

½ cup superfine sugar

1 tsp coffee liqueur

Decoration
½ cup Chantilly cream (p.212)

Unsweetened cocoa powder

Chocolate Ice cream: Prepare as in the recipe on page 214. Pour the mixture into an ice-cream maker (pre-frozen, if necessary) and freeze-churn according to the manufacturer's instructions (about 30 minutes). Remove the ice cream from the machine and transfer it to the freezer before serving.

Preheat the oven to 350°F. Prepare 1 or 2 baking sheets, depending on the oven size. Trace four 3¼-in circles on parchment paper and turn the marked side over onto the baking sheet(s).

Sponge: Beat the egg yolks until pale yellow. In a separate bowl, whisk the egg whites until frothy. Add 2 tbsp of the sugar a little at a time, whisking until the egg whites are smooth and shiny. Gradually add the remaining sugar, whisking until stiff peaks form. Gently fold in the egg yolks, then the sifted flour. Fit a pastry bag with a plain round tip and fill it with the batter. Start piping in the center of each traced circle, working outward in a spiral until filled. Bake for approximately 8 minutes, or until firm but springy to the touch; set aside until required.

Coffee Syrup: Put the water and sugar into a saucepan and stir over low heat until the sugar dissolves, increase the heat and boil; cool. When cold, add the rum and coffee liqueur.

Coffee Sabayon: Dissolve the instant coffee in the water; set aside. Place the egg yolks and sugar in a heatproof bowl over a bain-marie; whisk until pale and creamy. Pour in the coffee and continue whisking until thick and light and the sabayon falls in a ribbon trail from the whisk; add the coffee liqueur.

Place a 4-in dessert ring (depth 1¾ in) on each plate. Put one sponge disc into each ring and sprinkle or brush with coffee syrup. Fill with chocolate ice cream and briefly return to the freezer until firm. To serve, remove the rings, decorate with Chantilly cream, pour the hot coffee sabayon over; dust with sifted cocoa powder.

Vanilla Ice in Hot Chocolate Sauce with Crunchy Spice Biscuits

SERVES 8

DIFFICULTY ★ ★ ★

PREPARE: 1½ hours

REFRIGERATE: Overnight

FREEZE: 30 minutes

COOK: 20 minutes

Crunchy Spice Biscuits

½ cup superfine sugar

2 tbsp soft brown sugar

1⅔ cups flour, sifted

7 tbsp unsalted butter

1 pinch salt

½ tsp baking powder

2 pinches ground nutmeg

½ tsp ground cinnamon

4 tsp milk

1 egg

Vanilla Ice

5 egg yolks

⅔ cup sugar

2 cups milk

1 vanilla pod, split

3 tbsp heavy whipping cream

Hot Chocolate Sauce

9 oz bittersweet chocolate

3½ tbsp praline paste (p.314)

2 cups milk

¾ cup heavy whipping cream

◇ This recipe must be started a day before serving.

Crunchy Spice Biscuits: The day before serving, put the sugars, sifted flour and unsalted butter into a bowl. Rub the butter into the dry ingredients with your fingertips until the mixture resembles fine breadcrumbs. Blend in the salt, baking powder, nutmeg, and cinnamon. Add the milk and egg and mix gently until the dough forms a ball, being careful not to overwork it. Wrap in plastic wrap and refrigerate overnight.

Vanilla Ice: The following day, beat the egg yolks with ⅓ cup of the sugar until pale yellow and creamy. Place the milk and remaining sugar in a saucepan. Using the point of a knife, scrape the seeds from the vanilla pod into the milk and sugar mixture, add the pod, and bring slowly to the boil. Whisk a third of the hot milk into the eggs-and-sugar mixture, mixing well to combine; pour the mixture into the remaining hot milk. Stirring constantly with a wooden spoon, cook over low heat until the mixture thickens and coats the back of the spoon. (Do not allow to boil!) Stir in the heavy whipping cream and remove from the heat immediately; strain into a bowl. Stand the bowl in crushed ice until the mixture is cold. Pour the mixture into an ice-cream maker (pre-frozen, if necessary) and freeze-churn according to the manufacturer's instructions (about 30 minutes). Remove the ice cream from the machine and transfer it to the freezer before serving.

Preheat the oven to 350°F. Line a baking sheet with parchment paper. Roll out the biscuit dough and cut it into 4 x 1-in rectangles. Transfer to the baking sheet and bake for 20 minutes, or until firm and golden; cool on a rack.

Hot Chocolate Sauce: Coarsely chop the chocolate and place in a bowl with the praline paste. Heat the milk and heavy whipping cream slowly until simmering. Pour the hot mixture over the chocolate and praline paste, whisking quickly to combine. Use a fine-mesh strainer and strain the sauce into a bowl.

Divide the hot chocolate sauce between 8 rimmed soup dishes. Form the ice cream into quenelles using 2 large spoons (p.208). Place two quenelles in each dish; serve the crunchy spice biscuits on the rim.

White Chocolate Islands in Strawberry Soup

SERVES 8

DIFFICULTY ★ ★ ★

PREPARE: 30 minutes

INFUSE: 30 minutes

REFRIGERATE: 6 hours

White Chocolate Islands
5 1/2 oz white chocolate
1 vanilla pod, split
2/3 cup passion fruit juice
1 cup coconut milk

Strawberry Soup
1 3/4 lbs strawberries
2 lemongrass stalks

Decoration
Reserved vanilla pods

◊ See p.208: Shaping quenelles.

White Chocolate Islands: Chop the white chocolate and place in a bowl. Combine the passion fruit juice and coconut milk in a saucepan. Using the point of a knife, scrape the seeds from a vanilla pod into the saucepan, add the pod and heat slowly until simmering. Remove the saucepan from the heat; allow to infuse for 30 minutes. Remove and rinse the vanilla pod; set aside for decoration. Pour the passion fruit mixture over the chopped chocolate, stir until smooth; let cool. Then place in the refrigerator for 6 hours.

Strawberry Soup: Wash the strawberries. Coarsely chop the lemongrass stalks and 12 ounces of the strawberries. Place in the bowl of a food processor and process; strain the juice into a bowl using a fine-mesh strainer. Hull and cut the remaining strawberries into quarters and add to the strawberry juice. Refrigerate for at least 30 minutes, or until cold.

Divide the strawberry soup between 8 small dishes. Use 2 spoons to form the white chocolate into quenelles; place 4 in each dish. Use the reserved vanilla pod, along with any extra vanilla pods, to decorate.

White Chocolate-Aniseed Ice Cream topped with Pecans

SERVES **8**

DIFFICULTY ★ ★ ★

PREPARE: 35 minutes

FREEZE: 1½ hours

White Chocolate-Aniseed Ice Cream

5½ oz white chocolate

6 egg yolks

½ cup superfine sugar

2 cups milk

½ tsp pastis (or ouzo)

Decoration

Chopped pecans

◊ See p.208: Shaping quenelles.

White Chocolate-Aniseed Ice cream: Finely chop the chocolate and place in a large bowl. In a separate bowl, beat the egg yolks and sugar until pale yellow and creamy. Bring the milk slowly to the boil. Whisk a third of the hot milk into the egg yolks-sugar mixture, mixing well to combine; pour the mixture into the remaining hot milk. Stirring constantly with a wooden spoon, cook over low heat until the mixture thickens and coats the back of the spoon. (Do not allow to boil!) Remove from the heat immediately. Pour over the chopped chocolate and stir until smooth; strain into a bowl. Stand the bowl in crushed ice until the ice cream mixture is cold. Add the pastis. Pour the mixture into an ice-cream maker (pre-frozen, if necessary) and freeze-churn according to the manufacturer's instructions (about 30 minutes). Remove the ice cream from the machine and transfer it to the freezer before serving.

Prepare 8 rimmed soup dishes. Use 2 spoons to form the white chocolate-aniseed ice cream into quenelles; place 3 in each dish. Sprinkle with chopped pecans.

CHEF'S TIP: This ice cream is delicious with caramelized pecans incorporated into it. Heat ¼ cup sugar in a saucepan. When it starts to melt and turns a golden color, add 5½ oz pecans and cook for 1–2 minutes, stirring with a wooden spoon. Add 1 tbsp unsalted butter; pour onto parchment paper until cool. When you take the ice cream out of the maker and before you freeze it, add half of the nuts. Use the other half as decoration.

Chocolate Granita

SERVES 4
DIFFICULTY ★ ★ ★
PREPARE: 10 minutes
FREEZE: 2 hours

1 3/4 oz bittersweet chocolate
3/4 cup water
3 tbsp superfine sugar

Chop the chocolate and place in a bowl. Combine the water and sugar in a saucepan and stir over low heat until the sugar dissolves completely then bring to the boil. Pour over the chopped chocolate; stir until smooth.

Pour a shallow (1/2 in) layer of the chocolate mixture into a large container and freeze. Stir with a fork from time to time, crushing the crystals and scraping the bottom and sides of the container so the mixture will freeze evenly (about 2 hours).

Divide the chocolate granita evenly between mugs or glasses; serve immediately.

Iced Chocolate Nougat Mousse

SERVES 6

DIFFICULTY ★ ★ ★

PREPARE: 45 minutes

COOK: 5 minutes

FREEZE: 1 hour

Nougatine

³/₄ cup sliced almonds

¹/₂ cup superfine sugar

Chocolate Mousse

2 egg whites

²/₃ cups superfine sugar

3 oz dark (66%) chocolate

1 cup heavy whipping
   cream

²/₃ cup mixed candied fruit,
   chopped

1 tbsp Kirsch

Chantilly Cream

³/₄ cup heavy whipping
   cream

3 tbsp confectioners' sugar

Decoration

6 Amarena (or Maraschino)
   cherries

Preheat the oven to 300°F. Line a baking sheet with parchment paper. Prepare an 8¹/₂ x 2-in terrine.

Nougatine: Place the sliced almonds on the baking sheet. Toast in the oven for 5 minutes until lightly colored, remove from the lined baking sheet; set aside. Place the sugar in a saucepan and cook over medium heat (do not stir) for about 10 minutes until it melts and becomes a golden caramel color. Remove from the heat immediately and carefully stir in the toasted almonds. Pour onto the lined baking sheet and cover with another piece of parchment. Use a rolling pin to spread the nougatine into a layer ¹/₁₆ in thick. When cool, break in large pieces, wrap in a tea towel and coarsely crush using the rolling pin.

Chocolate Mousse: Whisk the egg whites until frothy. Add 3 tbsp of the sugar a little at a time, whisking until the egg whites are smooth and shiny. Gradually add the remaining egg yolk-and-sugar mixture sugar, whisking until stiff peaks form; refrigerate until required.

Chop the chocolate and melt over a bain-marie. Beat the cream until firm and clinging to the whisk; carefully blend in the melted chocolate. Quickly whisk a third of the chocolate cream into the whisked egg whites. Using a spatula, carefully fold in the remainder, in two separate batches. Add the crushed nougatine, chopped candied fruit and the Kirsch. Pour the mixture into the terrine; freeze for 1 hour.

Chantilly cream: Whisk the cream until it begins to stiffen, add the confectioners' sugar and continue whisking until firm peaks cling to the whisk. Fit a pastry bag with a star tip and fill with the cream.

Remove the terrine from the freezer and place it briefly in hot water then invert the chilled chocolate nougatine mousse onto a platter. Cut into 6 slices. Top each slice with a piped rosette of Chantilly cream and an Amarena cherry; serve immediately.

CHEF'S TIP: If you do not have Amarena cherries, use other cherries in syrup for the decoration. The nougat mousse could also be served with a cherry coulis.

Iced Chocolate Parfait with Orange-Basil Cream

SERVES 6

DIFFICULTY ★ ★ ★

PREPARE: 1 ¼ hours

FREEZE: 2 hours

Chocolate Parfait

3 ½ oz bittersweet chocolate

1 ⅓ cup heavy whipping cream

5 egg yolks

3 tbsp water

3 tbsp superfine sugar

Orange-Basil Cream

1 bunch basil

4 egg yolks

7 tbsp superfine sugar

1 ⅓ cups orange juice

Citrus Fruit Segments

2 oranges

1 pink grapefruit

Decoration

Small basil leaves

Chocolate Parfait: Chop the chocolate and melt in a bain-marie. Beat the cream until firm and clinging to the whisk; refrigerate. Whisk the egg yolks in a large bowl until pale yellow. Put the water and sugar into a saucepan and stir over low heat until the sugar dissolves completely; increase the heat and boil for 2 minutes. Pour the syrup slowly down the side of the bowl into the egg yolks, whisking continuously until the mixture thickens and cools. Using a spatula, gradually blend in the melted chocolate then fold in the whipped cream. Pour the mixture into an 7 x 2¾-in porcelain terrine; freeze for 2 hours.

Orange-Basil Cream: Wash and dry the basil. In a separate bowl, beat the egg yolks and sugar until pale yellow and creamy. Place the basil and orange juice in a saucepan and bring slowly to the boil. Whisk a third of the hot juice into the egg yolks-sugar mixture, mixing well to combine; pour the mixture into the remaining juice. Stirring constantly with a wooden spoon, cook over low heat until the mixture thickens and coats the back of the spoon. (Do not allow to boil!) Remove from the heat immediately. Strain the orange-basil cream into a bowl; cool and then refrigerate.

Citrus Fruit Segments: Using a very sharp knife, cut a small slice off both ends of the fruit. Stand the fruit on a board and cut off the peel and all the pith in wide strips, working from top to bottom. Hold the peeled fruit, and insert the knife between the membrane and the flesh cutting towards the center without cutting the membrane. Then, cut on the other side of the segment in the same way and ease it out. Continue until all the segments have been removed; set aside.

Remove the terrine from the freezer, wrap it in a hot, damp dish towel then turn the parfait out. Spoon the orange basil cream into six dessert bowls and place a slice of parfait in each bowl. Top with citrus segments and decorate with basil leaves.

Pears Belle-Hélène

SERVES 6

DIFFICULTY ★ ★ ★

PREPARE: 1 hour

REFRIGERATE: 2 hours

FREEZE: 30 minutes

Poached Pears

6 small pears

$^1/_2$ lemon

$2^3/_4$ cups water

$2^1/_4$ cups superfine sugar

$^1/_2$ vanilla pod, split

Vanilla Ice Cream

5 egg yolks

$^2/_3$ cup sugar

2 cups milk

1 vanilla pod, split

$^1/_4$ cup heavy whipping
  cream

Chocolate Sauce

$4^3/_4$ oz bittersweet
  chocolate

1 tbsp unsalted butter

$^2/_3$ cup crème fraîche

Poached Pears: Peel and cut the pears in half; remove the cores. Rub the pears with the lemon to prevent darkening. Combine the water and sugar in a saucepan. Using the point of a knife, scrape the seeds from the vanilla pod into the sugared water; add the pod. Stir over low heat until the sugar dissolves then bring to the boil. Lower the heat, add the pears and poach for 20 minutes, or until tender when pierced with the point of a knife. Transfer the poached pears and syrup to a bowl to cool then refrigerate for 2 hours.

Vanilla Ice Cream: Beat the egg yolks and $^1/_3$ cup of the sugar until pale yellow and creamy. Pour the milk into a saucepan; add the remaining sugar. Using the point of a knife, scrape the seeds from the vanilla pod into the milk, add the pod and bring the sugared milk slowly to the boil. Whisk a third of the hot mixture into the eggs-sugar mixture, stirring well to combine; pour the mixture into the remaining hot milk. Stirring constantly with a wooden spoon, cook over low heat until the mixture thickens and coats the back of the spoon. (Do not allow to boil!) Stir in the whipping cream and remove from the heat immediately; strain into a bowl. Stand the bowl in crushed ice until the mixture is cold. Pour the mixture into an ice-cream maker (pre-frozen, if necessary) and freeze-churn according to the manufacturer's instructions (about 30 minutes). Remove the ice cream from the machine and transfer it to the freezer before serving.

Warm Chocolate Sauce: Finely chop the chocolate and melt over a bain-marie with the unsalted butter and crème fraîche. Stir well until smooth; keep warm.

Place 1 scoop of vanilla ice cream and 2 pear halves in each footed ice cream dish; pour the warm chocolate sauce over the top. Serve immediately.

Iced Profiteroles with Hot Chocolate Sauce

SERVES **6**

DIFFICULTY ★ ★ ★

PREPARE: 45 minutes

COOK: 25 minutes

FREEZE: 1½ hours

Vanilla Ice Cream

5 egg yolks

²/₃ cup sugar

2 cups milk

1 vanilla pod, split

¼ cup heavy whipping
  cream

Choux Pastry Dough

3½ tbsp unsalted butter

½ cup water

½ tsp salt

½ tsp superfine sugar

Scant ²/₃ cup flour, sifted

2 eggs

1 beaten egg, for glazing

Hot Chocolate Sauce

3½ oz bittersweet
  chocolate

¼ cup milk

3½ tbsp unsalted butter

◊ See p.207: Making choux pastry dough.

Vanilla Ice Cream: Use the ingredients listed and prepare following the method on p.230. Freeze for a minimum of 1 hour.

Choux Pastry Dough: Preheat the oven to 350°F. Put the unsalted butter, water, salt, and sugar in a saucepan over low heat. When the butter melts, bring the mixture to the boil; remove from the heat immediately. Tip the sifted flour into the hot liquid. Stir with a wooden spoon until a firm smooth dough forms. Return the saucepan to low heat to dry out the dough; continue beating until it forms a ball and pulls away cleanly from the sides of the saucepan. Transfer the dough to a bowl; cool for 5– 10 minutes. Add the eggs, one by one to the choux pastry dough, beating vigorously after each addition to incorporate as much air as possible. When the dough is ready to be used, it will fall from the spoon in a point. If it doesn't, add half of the beaten egg; continue beating until the dough is smooth and shiny.

Fit a pastry bag with a plain tip, and spoon in the choux pastry dough. Butter a baking sheet with unsalted butter; pipe small 1¼-in diameter mounds of dough onto it. Brush the tops with the egg glaze and flatten slightly with the back of a fork. Transfer to the oven and bake for 15 minutes without opening the door. Then, lower the oven temperature to 325° F and continue baking for another 10 minutes, or until the choux are golden and sound hollow when tapped. Cool on a wire rack.

Hot Chocolate Sauce: Finely chop the chocolate. Bring the milk to the boil, remove from the heat and add the chocolate; stir until smooth. Add the unsalted butter and keep the sauce hot.

Cut the top third off the choux puffs. Place a scoop of vanilla ice cream in each base; replace the tops and pour the hot chocolate sauce over. Serve immediately.

CHEF'S TIP: If you want to save time, you could use 1 pint of ready-made vanilla ice cream.

Chocolate Sorbet on a Raspberry Coulis

SERVES 8

DIFFICULTY ★ ★ ★

PREPARE: 30 minutes

REFRIGERATE: 10 minutes

FREEZE: 30 minutes

Chocolate Sorbet

7 oz bittersweet chocolate

1 cup unsweetened cocoa powder

2 cups water

$^2/_3$ cup superfine sugar

Raspberry Coulis

1$^2/_3$ cups raspberries, fresh or frozen

2 or 3 drops lemon juice

$^1/_4$ cup confectioners' sugar

Decoration (Optional)

Fresh raspberries

◇ See p.208: Shaping quenelles.

Chocolate Sorbet: Finely chop the chocolate and place in a bowl. Put the cocoa powder into a saucepan, add $^1/_2$ cup of the water and stir over low heat until blended. Add the remaining water and the sugar; stir to dissolve then, bring to the boil.

Pour the syrup over the chopped chocolate, stir until smooth and strain the mixture into a bowl; cool. Pour the mixture into an ice-cream maker (pre-frozen, if necessary) and freeze-churn according to the manufacturer's instructions (about 30 minutes). Remove the sorbet from the machine and transfer it to the freezer before serving.

Raspberry Coulis: Puree the raspberries with the lemon juice in a food processor. Add the confectioners' sugar, to taste. Strain the coulis into a bowl through a fine-mesh strainer; refrigerate for 10 minutes.

Spoon the raspberry coulis into 8 small bowls. Use 2 spoons to form the chocolate sorbet into quenelles and place one in each bowl. If desired, decorate with fresh raspberries.

CHEF'S TIP: If you like, you can make the coulis with other berries.

Iced Chocolate Soufflés

SERVES **4**

DIFFICULTY ★ ★ ★

PREPARE: 30 minutes

FREEZE: 6 hours

REFRIGERATE: 15 minutes

Chocolate Cream

10$^1/_2$ oz bittersweet
  chocolate

7 egg yolks

1 cup superfine sugar

1 cup milk

1$^1/_2$ cups heavy whipping
  cream

French Meringue

4 egg whites

6$^1/_2$ tbsp superfine sugar

Decoration

Confectioners' sugar, sifted

Prepare four 3$^1/_4$ in soufflé dishes or ramekins. Create collars from doubled over, parchment paper rectangles to extend 1$^1/_4$ in above the rims of the dishes. Secure with adhesive tape.

Chocolate Cream: Finely chop the chocolate and melt over a bain-marie. Beat the egg yolks and sugar until pale yellow and creamy. Bring the milk to the boil and whisk a third into the eggs and sugar, mixing well to combine; pour the mixture into the remaining hot milk. Stirring constantly with a wooden spoon, cook over low heat until the mixture thickens and coats the back of the spoon. (Do not allow to boil!) Remove from the heat immediately, strain into a bowl, and blend in the melted chocolate; cool. Beat the cream until firm and clinging to the whisk then, carefully fold into the chocolate mixture.

Divide the chocolate cream among the prepared soufflé dishes. Fill to within $^1/_4$ in of the top of the collar, leaving sufficient space for the French meringue; freeze for 6 hours.

French Meringue: Whisk the egg whites until frothy. Add a third of the sugar a little at a time, whisking until the egg whites are smooth and shiny. Gradually add the remaining sugar, whisking until stiff peaks form.

Remove the soufflés from the freezer and spread with a $^1/_4$-in layer of French meringue. Dip a serrated knife (or a fork) in hot water and make wavy lines in the meringue to decorate the tops of the soufflés; refrigerate for 15 minutes until firm.

Preheat the broiler to its maximum temperature.

Place the soufflés briefly under the broiler (and at least 1 inch from the top so the collars don't burn) until the meringue is lightly colored. Discard the paper collars. Sprinkle with confectioners' sugar; serve immediately.

Triple Chocolate Iced Terrine

SERVES 8

DIFFICULTY ★ ★ ★

PREPARE: 45 minutes

FREEZE: 3 hours

White Chocolate Mousse

1 ³/₄ oz white chocolate

1 sheet or ³/₄ tsp gelatin

²/₃ cup heavy whipping
   cream

2 tbsp sugar

4 tsp water

Milk Chocolate Mousse

1 ³/₄ oz milk chocolate

1 sheet or ³/₄ tsp gelatin

²/₃ cup heavy whipping
   cream

2 tbsp sugar

4 tsp water

Bittersweet Chocolate Mousse

²/₃ cup heavy whipping
   cream

2 ¹/₄ oz bittersweet
   chocolate

White Chocolate Mousse: Chop the white chocolate and melt over a bain-marie. Soften the gelatin in cold water. Whisk the whipping cream until firm and clinging to the whisk; refrigerate. Place the sugar and water in a saucepan and swirl over low heat until the sugar dissolves then bring to the boil; add the gelatin. Pour into the melted chocolate whisking quickly; carefully fold in the whipped cream. Pour the white chocolate mousse into a 10 x 4-in terrine, smooth the surface with a rubber spatula, and transfer to the freezer.

Milk Chocolate Mousse: Repeat the preceding step replacing the white chocolate with the milk chocolate. Remove the terrine from the freezer and pour the milk chocolate mousse on top of the white chocolate mousse; smooth the surface with a spatula and return the terrine to the freezer.

Bittersweet Chocolate Mousse: Whisk the whipping cream until firm and clinging to the whisk; refrigerate. Chop the bittersweet chocolate and melt over a bain-marie; carefully fold in the whipped cream. Remove the terrine from the freezer, fill with the bittersweet chocolate mousse and smooth the surface with a rubber spatula; freeze for 3 hours.

When ready to serve, remove the terrine from the freezer and cut slices. Or, place the terrine briefly in very hot water and turn the dessert out onto a serving platter.

Chocolate-Coated Ice Cream Balls

MAKES **12**

DIFFICULTY ★ ★ ★

PREPARE: 30 minutes

FREEZE: 3 hours

Chocolate Ice cream

2^1/$_4$ oz dark (55-70%) chocolate

^{1}/$_2$ oz unsweetened cooking chocolate

1 cup milk

3 egg yolks

^{1}/$_4$ cup superfine sugar

Ganache Coating

9 oz bittersweet chocolate

1 cup heavy whipping cream

^{1}/$_4$ cup superfine sugar

Unsweetened cocoa powder, sifted

Line a baking sheet with parchment paper; transfer to the freezer to chill.

Chocolate Ice Cream: Finely chop the chocolates and place in a large bowl. Bring the milk slowly to the boil. In a separate bowl, beat the egg yolks and sugar until pale yellow and creamy. Whisk in a third of the hot milk, mixing well to combine; pour the mixture into the remaining hot milk. Stirring constantly with a wooden spoon, cook over low heat until the mixture thickens and coats the back of the spoon. (Do not allow to boil!) Remove from the heat immediately. Pour over the chopped chocolate and stir until smooth; strain into a bowl. Stand the bowl in crushed ice until the mixture is cold. Pour the mixture into an ice-cream maker (pre-frozen, if necessary) and freeze-churn according to the manufacturer's instructions (about 30 minutes). Remove the ice cream from the machine and transfer it to the freezer to harden for a minimum of 1 hour before serving.

Use a spoon to form 12 balls of chocolate ice cream. Transfer to the chilled baking sheet; freeze for 1 hour.

Ganache Coating: Chop the chocolate and place in a large bowl. Heat the cream and sugar until simmering, stir until the sugar dissolves completely. Pour the mixture over the chopped chocolate; stir until smooth. Then stir every 10 minutes until the ganache cools.

Spread the sifted cocoa powder on a large plate. When the ice cream balls are hard, immerse each one individually in the ganache coating then roll in the cocoa powder. Transfer to the freezer for at least 30 minutes before serving.

CHEF'S TIP: You can keep the chocolate coated ice cream balls frozen in an air-tight container for 15 days; just before serving, roll them in cocoa powder. Take care when coating the ice cream balls; if the ganache is warm, the ice cream will melt but if it is too cold, the coating will become very thick.

Iced Chocolate Creams with Apricot Compote and Almond Crumble

SERVES **10**

DIFFICULTY ★ ★ ★

PREPARE: 45 minutes

FREEZE: 30 minutes

COOK: 20 minutes

Chocolate Cream

3 oz bittersweet chocolate

$^3/_4$ cup heavy whipping cream

3 egg yolks

2 tbsp superfine sugar

Almond Crumble

$3^1/_2$ tbsp salted butter

$^1/_4$ cup superfine sugar

$6^1/_2$ tbsp flour

1 pinch baking powder

$^1/_2$ cup almond flour/meal

Apricot Compote

4 tsp unsalted butter

3 tbsp superfine sugar

12 canned apricot halves in syrup

1 or 2 drops vanilla extract

Decoration

Confectioners' sugar, sifted

Chocolate Cream: Chop the chocolate and place in a bowl. Heat the cream until simmering. In a separate bowl, beat the egg yolks and sugar until thick and creamy. Whisk a third of the hot cream into the eggs and sugar, mixing well to combine; pour the mixture into the remaining hot cream. Stirring constantly with a wooden spoon, cook over low heat until the mixture thickens and coats the back of the spoon. (Do not allow to boil!) Remove from the heat immediately, strain over the chopped chocolate; stir until smooth.

Pour a $^3/_4$-in layer of the chocolate cream into each of 10 dessert glasses; transfer to the freezer for 30 minutes.

Preheat the oven to 325°F. Line a baking sheet with parchment paper.

Almond Crumble: Put all the crumble ingredients into a bowl; rub the salted butter into the dry ingredients until the mixture resembles breadcrumbs. Spread the mixture on the baking sheet and bake for 20 minutes or until golden; cool. Break or crush the cooked crumble in small pieces; set aside.

Apricot Compote: Place the unsalted butter and sugar in a saucepan and heat over low heat. Add the apricots, $^1/_3$ cup of the syrup and the vanilla extract. Cook until the compote is smooth and thick; set aside until cold.

Remove the dessert glasses from the freezer and spoon a $^3/_4$-in layer of cold apricot compote into each. Divide the crumble between the glasses and sprinkle with confectioners' sugar; serve immediately.

CHEF'S TIP: If you don't have salted butter, use a pinch of sea salt flakes or fleur de sel in the crumble.

Creamy Hot Chocolate

SERVES 6

DIFFICULTY ★ ★ ★

PREPARE: 15 minutes

4¹/₂ oz bittersweet
  chocolate
4 cups milk
1 cup crème fraîche
1 tsp ground cinnamon
1 black peppercorn
2 tbsp superfine sugar

Decoration (Optional)
6 marshmallows

Chop the chocolate. Heat the milk and cream in a saucepan until simmering.

Add the chopped chocolate, ground cinnamon, peppercorn, and sugar to the hot milk and cream mixture. Place the saucepan over low heat for about 10 minutes; stir from time to time using a wooden spoon.

Strain the hot chocolate mixture then divide it between six mugs. Decorate each with a marshmallow, if desired; serve immediately.

CHEF'S TIP: The taste of the hot chocolate will be richer if it is refrigerated for several hours, or even up to three days and reheated before serving.

Iced Chocolate Milk with Chantilly Cream

SERVES 6

DIFFICULTY ★ ★ ★

PREPARE: 20 minutes

FREEZE: 30 minutes

Iced Chocolate Milk
2 cups milk

3 oz bittersweet chocolate

Chantilly Cream
$^1/_2$ cup heavy whipping cream

2 tbsp confectioners' sugar

Prepare 6 martini glasses.

Iced Chocolate Milk: Chop the chocolate and place in a bowl. Bring the milk to the boil and pour over the chopped chocolate; stir until smooth. Divide the mixture between six martini glasses. Transfer to the freezer for 30 minutes.

Chantilly Cream: Whisk the cream until it begins to stiffen, add the sugar and continue whisking until firm peaks cling to the whisk. Fit a pastry bag with a star tip and fill with the Chantilly cream. Remove the glasses of iced chocolate milk from the freezer and pipe rosettes of Chantilly on each one. Serve immediately.

CHEF'S TIP: If you have a Chantilly siphon in your kitchen, you could make Chantilly foam. Pour the cream and the confectioners' sugar into the siphon and insert the gas cartridge. Shake it vigorously to combine the ingredients and to make the mixture light and airy.

Chocolate Milkshake

SERVES 6–8

DIFFICULTY ★ ★ ★

PREPARE: 20 minutes

REFRIGERATE: 1 hour

3/4 cup milk

3 tsp unsweetened cocoa powder

2 tsp superfine sugar

6 scoops vanilla ice cream (p. 230)

6 scoops chocolate ice cream (p.214)

6 ice cubes

Pour half the milk into a saucepan, add the cocoa powder and sugar and bring to the boil. Add the remaining milk, stir well to combine; remove from the heat. When cold, refrigerate the chocolate milk for 1 hour.

Place the vanilla and chocolate ice creams, ice cubes, and cold chocolate milk in a food processor or blender and process on maximum speed for 1–2 minutes.

Divide the chocolate milkshake between 6–8 tall glasses; serve immediately.

CHEF'S TIP: If you like, you can use ready-prepared ice creams.

Chocolate Soup with Crunchy Pineapple Slices and Pineapple Kebabs

SERVES **6**

DIFFICULTY ★ ★ ★

PREPARE: 30 minutes

REFRIGERATE: Overnight

COOK: 4 – 5 hours

INFUSE: 30 minutes

Pineapple Kebabs

$^1/_2$ pineapple

2 cups water

$^3/_4$ cup superfine sugar

4 star anise

Crunchy Pineapple

$^1/_2$ pineapple

Confectioners' sugar

Chocolate Soup

$^2/_3$ cup milk

1 tsp mild honey

$^1/_2$ vanilla pod, split

$3^1/_2$ oz bittersweet
  chocolate, chopped

◇ This recipe must be started the day before.

Pineapple Kebabs: The day before, peel the pineapple and cut it in half lengthwise. Set one half aside for the crunchy pineapple. Cut the remaining half in $^1/_2$-in slices; cut the slices in small chunks. Combine the water, sugar, and star anise in a saucepan and stir over low heat until the sugar dissolves, bring to the boil; cool. Pour the syrup over the pineapple pieces; macerate overnight in the refrigerator.

Preheat the oven to 175°F. Line a baking sheet with parchment paper.

Crunchy Pineapple: Finely slice the reserved half pineapple, place on the baking sheet and sprinkle with confectioners' sugar. Transfer to the oven and dry the slices overnight or for at least 4– 5 hours until crunchy.

Chocolate Soup: The day of serving, place the milk and honey in a saucepan. Using the point of a knife, scrape the seeds from the vanilla pod into the milk-honey mixture, add the pod, and bring slowly to the boil. Remove from the heat and infuse for 30 minutes. Discard the vanilla pod and pour the mixture over the chopped chocolate; stir until smooth. Set aside to cool.

Thread the pineapple chunks onto 6 skewers. Divide the chocolate soup between 6 ramekins; top with the pineapple kebabs and crunchy pineapple slices.

Teatime treats
to share

The best way to fill éclairs

Make the éclairs and cream filling using the recipe of your choice, for example, on pp.274 or 296.

① Set aside a plain round tip with a small (⅛-in) opening. Fit a pastry bag with a larger plain round tip and fill with the cream to be used. Place the éclairs side by side on a work surface, flat side up.

② Holding an éclair in the palm of your hand, pierce two or three small holes in the flat side, using the small tip.

③ Continue holding the éclair and place the tip of the filled pastry bag over each hole and squeeze it, filling the éclair with the cream.

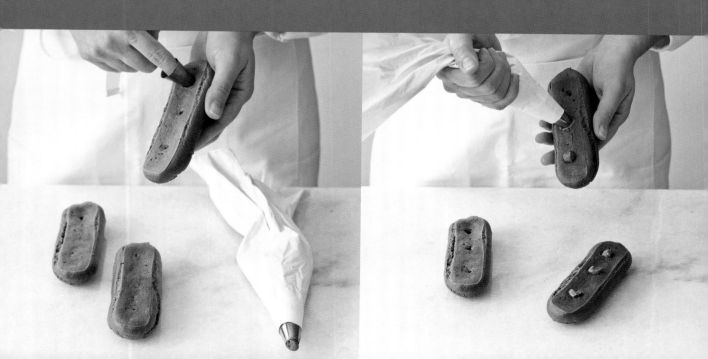

The best way to prepare chocolate containers

You can adapt this technique when using the chocolate design of your choice (cones, bowls, cases...) depending on the recipe chosen, see p.270.

(1) Prepare a pastry brush, a small knife, a bowl of tempered chocolate (p.315) and some cone-shaped paper cups.

(2) Brush a thin coat of tempered chocolate on the inside of the cone then invert it, placing the opening on your work surface, so the excess chocolate will run out. Set the cones aside at room temperature for 30 minutes, until firm. Then, apply a second coat of chocolate in the same manner. A third coat may be necessary.

(3) When the chocolate is hard, carefully peel off the paper. If necessary, use the knife. Store the chocolate containers in a cool location until required.

Field Marshall's Batons

MAKES 75

DIFFICULTY ★ ★ ★

PREPARE: 1 hour

COOK: 10–12 minutes

5 egg whites

2 tbsp superfine sugar

1 1/3 cups almond flour/meal, sifted

1 cup confectioners' sugar, sifted

1/4 cup flour, sifted

3/4 cup chopped almonds

Decoration

9 oz bittersweet chocolate

◇ See p.315: Tempering chocolate.

Preheat the oven to 325°F. Line a baking sheet with parchment paper.

Whisk the egg whites until frothy. Add a third of the sugar a little at a time, whisking until the egg whites are smooth and shiny. Gradually add the remaining sugar, whisking until stiff peaks form. Carefully blend in the sifted almond flour, confectioners' sugar, and flour. Fit a pastry bag with a medium round tip and fill with the mixture. Pipe small batons— 2 1/2-in long — on the baking sheet continuing until all the mixture is used; sprinkle with the chopped almonds. Bake the batons for 10–12 minutes, or until lightly golden. Remove from the oven and cool. When cold, peel off the parchment paper and store the batons at room temperature.

Decoration: Temper the chocolate: Coarsely chop the chocolate. Place 2/3 of the chopped chocolate in a bowl and melt over a bain-marie until the temperature reaches 115°F on a candy thermometer. Remove the bowl from the heat and add the remaining chocolate stirring until the temperature drops to 75°F. Return the bowl to the bain-marie, stir and reheat the chocolate to 90°F. Slide a regular or chocolate fork (ringed or pronged) under each baton and dip carefully into the tempered chocolate so it comes half way up the sides. Then lift the baton up, letting the excess chocolate drip into the bowl. Gently shake the fork.

Place on a wire rack, chocolate-coated side up; cool at room temperature until firm.

CHEF'S TIP: The Field Marshall's Batons can be kept several days in an airtight container.

Chocolate Fritters

MAKES **25–30** FRITTERS

DIFFICULTY ★ ★ ★

PREPARE: 40 minutes + 30 minutes

REFRIGERATE: 1 hour

FREEZE: overnight

COOK: 45 minutes

Chocolate Cream

7 oz dark (55–70%) chocolate

$^2/_3$ cup heavy whipping cream

Unsweetened cocoa powder

Batter

1 cup flour, sifted

1 tbsp cornstarch, sifted

1 tbsp vegetable oil

2 pinches salt

1 egg

$^1/_2$ cup beer

1 egg white

2 tbsp superfine sugar

Vegetable oil for frying

Flour

Unsweetened cocoa powder, sifted (optional)

◊ This recipe needs to be started one day ahead.

Chocolate Cream: The day before, chop the chocolate and melt over a bain-marie. Heat the cream in a saucepan until simmering, pour over the chocolate, and stir until smooth. Cover and refrigerate until the chocolate cream is firm enough to pipe. Fit a pastry bag with a round tip and fill with the cream. Line a baking sheet with parchment; pipe 25–30 neat mounds of chocolate cream on it. Refrigerate for 1 hour, or until firm. Wearing rubber gloves, roll the mounds by hand to form balls, and dust with cocoa powder; freeze overnight.

Batter: The next day, place the sifted flour and cornstarch in a large bowl; make a well in the center. Put the oil, salt, and egg into the well and gradually blend in the sifted ingredients; stir until the mixture is smooth then add the beer a little at a time.

Whisk the egg white, gradually adding the sugar until it is shiny and stiff peaks form. Gently fold it into the batter.

Pour the frying oil into a deep fat fryer (or heavy bottomed-saucepan) to a depth of about 3 in; heat to 400°F.

Remove 2 or 3 balls of chocolate from the freezer and roll them lightly in flour. Immerse in the batter then, using tongs, in the hot oil; deep fry for 3–5 minutes, or until lightly golden. Drain the fritters on kitchen paper and dust with cocoa powder, if desired. Repeat for the remaining chocolate balls; serve.

Brownies

SERVES 10

DIFFICULTY ★ ★ ★

PREPARE: 30 minutes

COOK: 30 minutes

$4\frac{1}{2}$ oz dark (55-70%)
  chocolate
1 cup unsalted butter
4 eggs
Scant $\frac{2}{3}$ cup soft brown
  sugar
$\frac{2}{3}$ cup superfine sugar
$6\frac{1}{2}$ tbsp flour, sifted
4 tbsp unsweetened cocoa
  powder, sifted
1 cup pecans, crushed

Preheat the oven to 325°F. Line an 8-in square cake pan with parchment paper.

Chop the chocolate and melt over a bain-marie with the unsalted butter; stir with a spatula until smooth.

In a separate bowl, combine the eggs and soft brown and superfine sugars and beat until thick and creamy; add to the chocolate-butter mixture. Then, using a spatula, fold in the sifted flour and cocoa powder followed by the crushed pecans; mix well.

Pour the mixture into the prepared cake pan and bake for 30 minutes, or until the point of a knife inserted into the center comes out clean. Cool on a wire rack and cut the brownies into squares to serve.

Chocolate and Raspberry Cream Puffs

MAKES **8–10** PUFFS

DIFFICULTY ★ ★ ★

PREPARE: 35 minutes

COOK: 30 minutes

Choux Pastry Dough
6¹/₂ tbsp unsalted butter

1 cup water

1 tsp salt

1 tsp superfine sugar

1¹/₄ cups cup flour, sifted

4 eggs

1 beaten egg for glazing

Chocolate Chantilly Cream
4¹/₂ oz bittersweet
   chocolate

1¹/₃ cups heavy whipping
   cream

¹/₄ cup confectioners' sugar,
   sifted

Decoration
2¹/₂ cups raspberries

Confectioners' sugar, sifted

◇ See p.207: Making choux pastry dough.

Preheat the oven to 350°F. Butter a baking sheet.

Choux Pastry Dough: Put the unsalted butter, water, salt, and sugar into a saucepan over low heat. When the butter melts, bring the mixture to the boil; remove from the heat immediately. Tip the sifted flour into the hot liquid. Stir with a wooden spoon until a firm, smooth dough forms. Return the saucepan to low heat to dry out the dough; continue beating until it forms a ball and pulls away cleanly from the sides of the saucepan. Transfer the dough to a bowl; cool for 5–10 minutes.

Place 1 egg in a small bowl; beat and set aside. Add the other 3 eggs, one at a time to the choux pastry dough, beating vigorously after each addition to incorporate as much air as possible. When the dough is ready to be used, it will fall from the spoon in a point. If not, add ¹/₂ of the remaining egg in the same manner, beating until the dough is smooth and shiny. Beat in the remainder of the egg only if necessary.

Fit a pastry bag with a plain round tip, and spoon in the choux pastry dough; pipe mounds (2-in diameter) onto the baking sheet. Brush the tops with the egg glaze and flatten slightly with the back of a fork. Transfer to the oven and bake for 15 minutes without opening the door. Lower the oven temperature to 325°F and continue baking for another 15 minutes, or until the puffs are golden and sound hollow when tapped. Cool on a wire rack.

Chocolate Chantilly Cream: Chop the chocolate and melt over a bain-marie. Whisk the cream until it begins to stiffen, add the confectioners' sugar, and continue whisking until the cream is firm and clinging to the whisk. Quickly whisk in the melted chocolate. Fit a pastry bag with a star tip and fill with the chocolate Chantilly cream; set aside.

Cut the top ¹/₃ off each puff. Pipe the chocolate Chantilly cream into the bases, decorate with fresh raspberries, and replace the tops; dust with sifted confectioners' sugar.

Chocolate Cigarettes

MAKES **45** CIGARETTES

DIFFICULTY ★ ★ ★

PREPARE: 30 minutes

REFRIGERATE: 20 minutes

COOK: 6–8 minutes

$^1/_3$ cup soft unsalted butter
1 cup confectioners' sugar
4 egg whites (4$^1/_2$ oz)
$^3/_4$ cup flour, sifted
$^1/_4$ cup unsweetened cocoa
  powder, sifted

Beat the unsalted butter and confectioners' sugar until creamy. Add the egg whites, a little at a time, mixing well after each addition. Blend in the sifted flour and cocoa powder; refrigerate the batter for 20 minutes.

Preheat the oven to 400°F. Line a baking sheet with parchment paper.

On a piece of cardboard trace a 3$^1/_4$-in circle. Cut out and discard the circle leaving a round hole in the cardboard. This is your template. Place it on the baking sheet, put a spoonful of the chocolate batter into the center of the hole, and spread the mixture out to form a 3$^1/_4$-in disc. Pick up the template and continue making batter discs, leaving about $^1/_4$ in between each one, until the baking sheet is covered. Bake for 6–8 minutes.

Set out a wooden spoon (or spatula) with a round handle to use for rolling the cigarettes. As soon as discs come out of the oven, roll each one around the handle of the spoon, waiting for a couple of seconds until it hardens. Slide each one off onto a wire rack. Store the chocolate cigarettes in a cool dry place.

Chocolate Chip Cinnamon Cookies

MAKES **40** COOKIES

DIFFICULTY ★ ★ ★

PREPARE: 15 minutes

REFRIGERATE: 1 hour

COOK: 10 minutes

2 egg yolks
1 tsp vanilla extract
2 tbsp water
$^1/_2$ cup + 2$^1/_2$ tbsp soft
  unsalted butter
1 scant cup confectioners'
  sugar
2$^1/_2$ cups flour, sifted
$^1/_2$ tsp baking powder, sifted
1 large pinch salt
1$^1/_2$ tsp ground cinnamon
$^2/_3$ cup chocolate chips
Confectioners' sugar, sifted

Combine the egg yolks, vanilla extract, and water. In a separate bowl, beat the soft, unsalted butter and confectioners' sugar until creamy. Add the egg yolk mixture a little at a time, beating after each addition. Blend in the sifted flour and baking powder, salt, and cinnamon. Fold in the chocolate chips being careful not to over-mix the dough.

Divide the dough in two even portions. Roll each one into a 1$^1/_4$-in diameter cylinder. Roll the cylinders in confectioners' sugar and wrap in plastic wrap. Roll again before chilling to ensure they are evenly shaped; refrigerate for at least 1 hour.

Preheat the oven to 325°F. Butter a baking sheet.

Remove and discard the plastic wrap from the dough cylinders. Cut the dough into $^1/_2$-in thick slices and place on the baking sheet. Bake for about 10 minutes, or until the cookies are golden; cool on a wire rack.

CHEF'S TIP: For a variation, you could also roll the dough cylinders in unsweetened cocoa powder.

Chocolate-Orange Cookies

MAKES 20 COOKIES

DIFFICULTY ★ ★ ★

PREPARE: 15 minutes

REFRIGERATE: 15 minutes

COOK: 7–8 minutes

6$\frac{1}{2}$ tbsp soft unsalted butter

3 tbsp superfine sugar

Zest of $\frac{1}{2}$ orange, finely grated

1 cup flour, sifted

$\frac{1}{2}$ tsp baking powder, sifted

3$\frac{1}{2}$ oz bittersweet chocolate

Preheat the oven to 375°F. Butter a baking sheet.

Place the soft unsalted butter in a bowl and beat until creamy. Add the sugar and grated orange zest, a little at a time, beating until the mixture is light. Blend in the sifted flour and baking powder. Using two teaspoons form the dough into balls about the size of a walnut and place on the baking sheet. Dip a fork in cold water and use the back of it to flatten the dough.

Put the baking sheet into the oven and bake for 7–8 minutes, or until the cookies are golden. Remove from the oven and cool on a wire rack.

Chop the chocolate and melt slowly over a bain-marie; remove from the heat. Put a sheet of parchment paper on the work surface. Using your fingers or plastic-coated tongs, dip each biscuit halfway into the melted chocolate and place it on the parchment; repeat until all the cookies have been dipped. Refrigerate for 15 minutes, or until the chocolate hardens.

Chocolate Cases, Bowls, and Cones

MAKES **10** CONTAINERS

DIFFICULTY ★ ★ ★

PREPARE: 45 minutes

18 oz bittersweet chocolate

◇ See p.315: Tempering chocolate.
◇ See p.255: Preparing chocolate containers.

Temper the chocolate: Coarsely chop the chocolate. Place two-thirds (12 oz) in a bowl; melt over a simmering bain-marie until the temperature reaches 115°F on a cooking thermometer. Remove the bowl from the heat and add the remaining chocolate, stirring until the temperature drops to 75°F. Return the bowl to the bain-marie, stir gently and reheat the chocolate to 90°F.

Chocolate Cases: Use either large (cupcake) or small (petits fours) individual paper baking cases. If the paper is flimsy, put one case inside another. Using a pastry brush, apply a thin coat of tempered chocolate to the inside of the case. Set aside at room temperature for 30 minutes, or until firm. Then apply a second coat of chocolate in the same manner. If necessary, apply a third coat. When the chocolate is hard, carefully remove the paper cases. Store the small chocolate cases in a cool, dry place until required.

Chocolate Bowls: Inflate and tie-off 10 small balloons. Dip the bottom half of each balloon into the tempered chocolate and place on a baking sheet covered with parchment paper. Refrigerate for 15 minutes, or until the chocolate firms. When the chocolate is hard, pierce the balloons with a needle and carefully peel them away. Store the chocolate bowls in a cool, dry place until required.

Chocolate Cones: Use small paper cups. Apply a thin coat of tempered chocolate on the inside of the cone then invert and place the opening on the work surface, so the excess chocolate will run out. Set the cones aside at room temperature for 30 minutes, or until firm. Then apply a second coat of chocolate in the same manner. It may be necessary to apply a third coat. When the chocolate is hard, carefully peel off the paper; use a knife if necessary. Store the chocolate cones in a cool dry place until required.

CHEF'S TIP: Use the differently shaped containers to serve your desserts. Fill with ice cream, mousse, or fruits.

Chocolate Crêpes

MAKES **15 CRÊPES**
DIFFICULTY ★ ★ ★
PREPARE: 10 minutes
REFRIGERATE: 2 hours
COOK: 45 minutes

Crêpe Batter
1 1/4 cups flour, sifted
1/3 cup unsweetened cocoa
  powder, sifted
2 eggs
1 3/4 cups milk
1 tbsp superfine sugar

Clarified Butter
1/2 cup + 1 tbsp unsalted
  butter

Garnish
Chantilly cream (p.174)
  and superfine sugar, or
  chocolate-hazelnut spread

Crêpe Batter: Tip the sifted flour and cocoa powder into a large bowl; make a well in the center. Put the eggs and 1/2 cup of the milk into the well and gradually blend in the sifted ingredients, stirring until the mixture is smooth. Continue stirring, gradually adding the remaining milk. Cover the batter and refrigerate for 2 hours.

Clarified Butter: Place the unsalted butter in a saucepan and melt completely over low heat. Remove from the heat and let stand for several minutes, allowing the milk solids to settle on the bottom. Skim the froth from the top of the melted butter and pour only the clear yellow liquid butter into a bowl; discard the milk solids left in the saucepan.

Put a little clarified butter into a crêpe or small frying pan and pour out or wipe away the excess with a paper towel. Heat the pan over medium heat until a drop of water sizzles in it. Using a small ladle, pour in about 2 tbsp of batter. Tilt and swivel the pan to thinly coat the bottom. Cook 1–2 minutes then flip or turn using a spatula and cook the other side for the same amount of time. Turn the crêpe out onto a warmed plate; cover with an upturned plate to keep warm. Continue cooking until all the batter is used; re-butter the pan only if the crêpes start to stick.

Serve the crêpes sprinkled with sugar and garnished with Chantilly cream or even covered with chocolate-hazelnut spread and folded.

CHEF'S TIP: Your crêpes can be prepared several hours in advance and reheated quickly in a lightly buttered or oiled pan. The clarified butter, which has its milk solids removed, can be heated more easily without burning and refrigerated for longer without becoming rancid, than non-clarified butter.

All Chocolate Éclairs

MAKES 12 ÉCLAIRS

DIFFICULTY ★ ★ ★

PREPARE: 1 hour

COOK: 25 minutes

REFRIGERATE: 25 minutes

Chocolate Choux Pastry Dough

1 cup water

6¹/₂ tbsp unsalted butter

1 tsp salt

1 tsp superfine sugar

1 cup flour, sifted

¹/₃ cup unsweetened cocoa powder, sifted

4 eggs

1 beaten egg for glazing

Chocolate Pastry Cream

5¹/₂ oz bittersweet chocolate

2 cups milk

1 vanilla pod, split

4 egg yolks

²/₃ cup superfine sugar

¹/₄ cup cornstarch

Chocolate Glaze

3¹/₂ oz bittersweet chocolate

1 scant cup confectioners' sugar

4 tsp water

◇See p.254: The best way to fill éclairs.

Preheat the oven to 350°F. Butter a baking sheet.

Chocolate Choux Pastry Dough: Using the ingredients listed, prepare as indicated on p.262, adding the sifted cocoa powder at the same time as the flour. When the dough is ready to be used, fit a pastry bag with a plain round tip, and spoon in the dough. Pipe 1¹/₄ x 4-in fingers of dough on the baking sheet. Brush the tops with the egg glaze. Transfer to the oven and bake for 15 minutes without opening the door. Then, lower the oven temperature to 325°F and continue baking for another 10 minutes, or until the choux pastry fingers are firm and sound hollow when tapped. Cool on a wire rack.

Chocolate Pastry Cream: Finely chop the chocolate and place in a bowl. Pour the milk into a saucepan. Using the point of a knife, scrape the seeds from the vanilla pod into the milk, add the pod and bring to the boil; remove from the heat. Put the eggs and sugar into a bowl and beat until pale yellow, thick, and creamy; add the cornstarch. Discard the vanilla pod. Whisking continuously, add half of the hot milk to the eggs-sugar-cornstarch mixture; whisk in the remaining milk. Return the mixture to the saucepan and cook over low heat, whisking continuously until the cream thickens. Boil for 1 minute while continuing to stir. Remove from the heat and pour the pastry cream over the chopped chocolate; stir until smooth. Cover the surface of the cream with plastic wrap; refrigerate for 25 minutes.

Chocolate Glaze: Melt the chocolate over a bain-marie. Combine the confectioners' sugar and water and blend into the melted chocolate. Heat the mixture until it registers 100°F on a candy thermometer.

Fit a pastry bag with a plain round tip and fill it with pastry cream. Pierce 2 or 3 small holes in the flat side of each choux pastry finger and fill with chocolate pastry cream. Spread a layer of chocolate glaze on the top of the éclairs using a spatula; set aside to dry before serving.

Mini Muffins topped with Milk Chocolate Mousse

MAKES **15** MUFFINS

DIFFICULTY ★ ★ ★

PREPARE: 40 minutes

COOK: 10 – 15 minutes

REFRIGERATE: overnight plus 10 minutes

Chocolate-Chip Muffins

$^1/_2$ cup + 4 tbsp unsalted butter

1 scant cup flour, sifted

1 $^1/_3$ cups almond flour/meal, sifted

1 $^1/_4$ cups superfine sugar

7 egg whites (7 oz)

2 tbsp mild honey

$^1/_2$ cup chocolate chips

Milk Chocolate Mousse

7 $^1/_2$ oz milk chocolate

1 $^1/_3$ cups ml heavy whipping cream

$^1/_2$ vanilla pod, split

Decoration

Milk chocolate

◇ See p.319: Making a paper pastry bag.

◇ The recipe must be started the day ahead. You will need a silicone mini-muffin mold producing 15 muffins 1 $^1/_4$ x 1 $^3/_4$ in.

Chocolate-chip Muffins: Heat the unsalted butter until it turns golden brown and the milk solids color and stick to the bottom of the saucepan. Remove from the heat immediately and strain through a fine-mesh wire strainer; set aside to cool. Tip the sifted flour and almond flour/meal into a large bowl. Add the sugar, egg whites, and honey and whisk until creamy. Blend in the strained butter a little at a time until the mixture increases in volume; fold in the chocolate chips and refrigerate overnight. On the day of serving, preheat the oven to 350°F. Fill the muffin imprints to the $^3/_4$ mark, using a pastry bag or spoon, and bake for 10– 15 minutes, or until the point of a knife inserted in the center of a muffin comes out clean. Cool for several minutes before turning out onto a wire rack.

Milk Chocolate Mousse: Chop the chocolate and melt over a slowly simmering bain-marie until the temperature registers approximately 115°F on a candy thermometer. Using the point of a knife, scrape the seeds from the vanilla pod into the cream. Beat the cream until firm peaks cling to the whisk. Whisking quickly, add about a third of the whipped cream to the hot chocolate to lighten it. Pour the mixture over the remaining cream and fold in gently with the whisk or a spatula to evenly blend the ingredients. Fit a pastry bag with fluted tip and fill with the milk chocolate mousse; pipe rosettes of mousse on each muffin; refrigerate for 10 minutes.

Decoration: Melt the chocolate over a bain-marie; cool. Fill a small paper pastry bag with the cooled chocolate, folding the top over until the chocolate is squeezed into the nose. Snip off the tip and streak the muffins with fine lines of chocolate.

CHEF'S TIP: You can also use bittersweet or white chocolate to make the mousse and for the decoration.

Chocolate-Orange Financiers

MAKES 12

DIFFICULTY ★ ★ ★

PREPARE: 30 minutes

COOK: 10 – 15 minutes

REFRIGERATE: Overnight

Chocolate-Orange Financiers

5 tbsp unsalted butter

$1/4$ cup candied orange peel

$6^1/2$ tbsp flour, sifted

1 cup confectioners' sugar, sifted

$1/2$ cup almonds flour/meal, sifted

4 egg whites

3 tbsp chocolate chips

Ganache

4 oz bittersweet chocolate

$1/2$ cup heavy whipping cream

4 tsp unsalted butter

◇ This recipe must be started one day ahead. You will need 12 "financier" molds or mini loaf pans measuring 2 x 4 in.

Chocolate-Orange Financiers: Heat the unsalted butter until it turns golden brown and the milk solids color and stick to the bottom of the saucepan. Remove from the heat immediately and strain through a fine-mesh wire strainer; set aside to cool. Finely dice the candied orange peel. Tip the sifted flour, confectioners' sugar, and almond flour/meal into a large bowl. Add the egg whites and whisk until creamy. Blend in the strained butter a little at a time until the mixture increases in volume; fold in the chocolate chips and the diced candied orange peel. Refrigerate overnight.

On the day of serving, preheat the oven to 350°F. Brush 12 small rectangular financier molds or mini loaf pans with unsalted butter, dust with flour, and tap out the excess.

Using a pastry bag or spoon, fill the molds to the $3/4$ mark and bake for 10– 15 minutes, or until the point of a knife inserted in the center of a financier comes out clean. Cool for several minutes before turning out onto a wire rack.

Chocolate Ganache: Chop the chocolate and place in a bowl. Heat the cream until simmering and pour it over the chocolate, stir until smooth; blend in the unsalted butter. Fit a pastry bag with a plain round tip and fill with the chocolate ganache; decorate the tops of the financiers. Serve three per person.

Florentines

MAKES **40**

DIFFICULTY ★ ★ ★

PREPARE: 45 minutes

COOK: 30 minutes

COOL: 30 minutes

1³/₄ oz mixed candied fruit

5 tbsp candied orange peel

3 tbsp candied cherries

1¹/₄ cups sliced almonds

¹/₄ cup flour, sifted

¹/₂ cup heavy whipping
  cream

Scant ¹/₂ cup superfine
  sugar

2 tbsp mild honey

10¹/₂ oz bittersweet
  chocolate

◇ See p.315: Tempering
chocolate.

Preheat the oven to 325°F. Butter a baking sheet.

Finely chop the mixed candied fruit, orange peel, and cherries and place in a bowl; add the sliced almonds. Tip the flour into the bowl and stir carefully by hand to separate the pieces of candied fruit.

Heat the cream, sugar, and honey until simmering; stir over low heat for 2–3 minutes, or until the sugar dissolves. Using a wooden spoon, carefully blend the hot cream mixture into the candied fruit and flour. (If desired, the Florentine mixture could be kept refrigerated for 2 days.)

Using a teaspoon, put small mounds of the mixture on the baking sheet placing them well apart. Flatten with the back of the spoon into thin 1¹/₄-in discs. Transfer to the oven and when the discs start to bubble, remove and cool for about 30 minutes. Lower the oven temperature to 325°F and bake the discs for another 10 minutes. Cool and transfer to wire rack.

Temper the chocolate: Coarsely chop the chocolate. Place two-thirds (7 oz) of the chopped chocolate in a bowl; melt over a bain-marie until the temperature reaches 115°F on a candy thermometer. Remove the bowl from the heat and add the remaining chocolate, stirring until the temperature drops to 75°F. Return the bowl to the bain-marie, stir gently and reheat the chocolate to 90°F.

Using a pastry brush, apply a layer of tempered chocolate to the flat side of each Florentine; tap each one on the work surface to release any air bubbles in the chocolate. Spread with a second layer, using a spatula to remove any excess chocolate. Harden the Florentines at room temperature.

CHEF'S TIP: Make sure that you spread the dough out thinly on the baking sheet otherwise the Florentines will be not be easy to eat when cooked.

Chocolate-Cinnamon Melting Moments

MAKES 45

DIFFICULTY ★ ★ ★

PREPARE: 15 minutes

REFRIGERATE: 45–60 minutes

COOK: 12–15 minutes

Chocolate Dough

$^1/_2$ cup + $4^1/_2$ tbsp soft unsalted butter

1 scant cup confectioners' sugar

1 egg yolk

$1^2/_3$ cups flour, sifted

2 tbsp unsweetened cocoa powder, sifted

Cinnamon Dough

$^1/_2$ cup + 3 tbsp soft unsalted butter

$^2/_3$ cup confectioners' sugar

$^1/_2$ tsp vanilla extract

$^1/_2$ tsp cinnamon

1 egg yolk

$1^2/_3$ cups flour, sifted

Decoration

2 egg whites, beaten

1 cup shredded coconut

Chocolate Dough: Beat the unsalted butter with the confectioners' sugar until smooth and creamy. Add the egg yolk then the sifted flour and cocoa powder; mix until smooth. Refrigerate the dough for 15–20 minutes.

Cinnamon Dough: Beat the unsalted butter with the confectioners' sugar until smooth and creamy. Blend in the vanilla extract and cinnamon powder. Add the egg yolk then the sifted flour and mix until smooth. Refrigerate the dough for 15–20 minutes.

Roll out the chocolate dough to a thickness of $^1/_2$ in. Form the cinnamon dough by hand into a $1^1/_4$-in diameter cylinder, and wrap the chocolate dough around it, retaining the cylinder shape; refrigerate for 15–20 minutes.

Preheat the oven to 325°F. Butter 2 baking sheets.

Brush the chocolate-cinnamon dough cylinder with egg white and roll in the shredded coconut. Using a sharp knife dipped in hot water and wiped dry between each slice, cut the dough into $^1/_2$-in thick slices. Transfer to the buttered baking sheets and bake for 12–15 minutes, or until firm but springy. Cool on a wire rack.

Mini Chocolate Macaroons

MAKES **30**

DIFFICULTY ★ ★ ★

PREPARE: 30 minutes

REST: 20 – 30 minutes

COOK: 10 – 15 minutes

REFRIGERATE: 24 hours

Macaroon Batter

1 1/4 cups almond flour/meal, sifted

1 2/3 cups confectioners' sugar, sifted

6 tbsp unsweetened cocoa powder, sifted

5 egg whites (5 1/2 oz)

6 tbsp superfine sugar

Ganache

5 1/2 oz bittersweet chocolate

3/4 cup heavy whipping cream

1 tbsp mild honey

◇ This recipe must be prepared a day before serving.

Macaroons: Tip the sifted almond flour, confectioners' sugar, and cocoa powder into a bowl; set aside. In a separate bowl, whisk the egg whites until frothy. Add 2 tbsp of the sugar a little at a time, whisking until the egg whites are smooth and shiny. Gradually add the remaining sugar, whisking until stiff peaks form. Slowly fold in one-quarter of the almond flour mixture: cut straight down to the bottom of the bowl with a spatula, and lift up the contents, bringing the spatula up the side of the bowl while giving it a quarter turn. Add the remainder of the almond flour mixture in the same manner, in three separate batches. Stop folding as soon as the mixture is smooth and shiny. Fit a pastry bag with a 1/4-in plain round tip and fill with the macaroon batter. Cover a baking sheet with parchment paper; pipe 60 small, 3/4-in rounds of batter on it. Set aside at room temperature for 20– 30 minutes.

Preheat the oven to 325°F.

Bake the macaroons for 5– 7 minutes then lower the oven temperature to 250°F and continue baking for a further 5– 7 minutes, or until set. Remove from the baking sheet and cool on a wire rack; refrigerate when the rounded part of the macaroon is hard.

Ganache: Chop the chocolate and place in a bowl. Heat the cream and honey slowly until simmering. Pour half of the hot liquid over the chocolate and whisk to combine, add the remainder little by little, whisking gently; set aside until cold.

Spread the flat side of 30 macaroons with ganache and sandwich with the remaining halves. Refrigerate for 24 hours, when the centers will become moist.

CHEF'S TIP: Use a raspberry jam or chocolate-hazelnut spread as an alternative filling. Macaroons can be frozen after being baked.

Chocolate Macaroons

MAKES **8**

DIFFICULTY ★ ★ ★

PREPARE: 30 minutes

REST: 20 – 30 minutes

COOK: 18 minutes

REFRIGERATE: 24 hours

Chocolate Macaroon Batter

2 cups almond flour/meal, sifted

2 1/4 cups confectioners' sugar, sifted

6 tbsp unsweetened cocoa powder, sifted

5 egg whites (5 1/2 oz)

2 tbsp superfine sugar

Sea salt crystals or fleur de sel

Ganache

5 1/2 oz bittersweet chocolate

2 egg yolks

1/2 cup superfine sugar

6 1/2 tbsp heavy whipping cream

1 vanilla pod, split

◇ This recipe must be prepared a day before serving.

Chocolate Macaroons: Tip the sifted almond flour, confectioners' sugar, and cocoa powder into a bowl; set aside. In a separate bowl, whisk the egg whites until frothy. Add 1 tbsp of the sugar a little at a time, whisking until the egg whites are smooth and shiny. Gradually add the remaining sugar, whisking until stiff peaks form. Slowly fold in one-quarter of the almond flour mixture: cut straight down to the bottom of the bowl with a spatula, and lift up the contents, bringing the spatula up the side of the bowl while giving it a quarter turn. Add the remainder of the almond flour mixture in the same manner, in three separate batches. Stop folding as soon as the mixture is smooth and shiny. Fit a pastry bag with a plain round tip and fill with the macaroon batter. Cover a baking sheet with parchment paper; pipe 16 2-in rounds of batter on it. Set aside at room temperature for 20– 30 minutes.

Preheat the oven to 325°F. Sprinkle a few sea salt flakes on the rounds of batter. Bake for 9 minutes then lower the oven temperature to 250°F and continue baking for a further 9 minutes, or until set. Remove from the baking sheet and cool on a wire rack; refrigerate when the rounded part of the macaroon is hard.

Ganache: Chop the chocolate and place in a bowl. Beat the egg yolks and the sugar until pale yellow and creamy. Put the whipping cream into a saucepan. Using the point of a knife, scrape the seeds from the vanilla pod into cream; add the pod and heat until simmering. Quickly whisk a third of the hot cream into the egg yolks-sugar mixture; pour into the remaining hot cream. Stirring constantly with a wooden spoon, cook over low heat until the cream thickens and coats the back of the spoon. (Do not allow to boil!) Remove from the heat immediately. Strain over the chopped chocolate; stir until smooth. Set aside until cold; stir from time to time.

Fit a pastry bag with a plain round tip, fill with the ganache; carefully pipe balls of ganache onto the flat side of 8 macarons; top with the remaining halves. Refrigerate for 24 hours until the centers will become moist.

Marbled Chocolate-Lemon Madeleines

MAKES **48** MADELEINES

DIFFICULTY ★ ★ ★

PREPARE: 30 minutes

REFRIGERATE: Overnight

COOK: 10 – 12 minutes

Chocolate Batter

6 tbsp unsalted butter

2 eggs

$^2/_3$ cup superfine sugar

2 tbsp milk

1 $^1/_4$ cups flour, sifted

$^1/_3$ cup unsweetened cocoa powder, sifted

1 tsp baking powder, sifted

Lemon Batter

6 tbsp unsalted butter

2 eggs

$^2/_3$ cup superfine sugar

2 tbsp milk

1 $^1/_2$ cups flour, sifted

1 tsp baking powder, sifted

Grated zest of 2 lemons

◇ This recipe must be started one day ahead. You will need 4 regular-sized Madeleine sheet molds (12 Madeleines) or you will have to cook 4 batches.

Chocolate Batter: Heat the unsalted butter until it turns golden brown and the milk solids color and stick to the bottom of the saucepan. Remove from the heat immediately and strain through a fine-mesh wire strainer; set aside to cool. Beat the eggs and sugar until pale yellow and creamy. Add the milk then the sifted flour and baking powder; stir to combine. Gradually blend in the strained butter until the batter starts to become foamy and increases in volume. Cover the bowl with plastic wrap; refrigerate overnight.

Lemon Batter: Repeat the preceding step replacing the cocoa powder with the grated lemon zest.

The next day, preheat the oven to 400°F. Brush a Madeleine mold with unsalted butter, dust with flour, and tip out the excess.

Spoon or pipe the chocolate batter into the imprints to the halfway mark. Then, fill with the lemon batter. Bake for 5 minutes, or until the Madeleines start to color; lower the oven temperature to 350°F and continue cooking for 5–7 minutes, or until firm. Remove from the oven, turn out immediately, and cool on a wire rack.

If you are using a single mold, you will have enough dough for four batches.

CHEF'S TIP: For a little variation, you could cook the batters separately and have all chocolate or all lemon madeleines.

Chocolate-Dipped Honey Madeleines

MAKES **24** MADELEINES
DIFFICULTY ★ ★ ★
PREPARE: 45 minutes
REFRIGERATE: Overnight
COOK: 10 – 12 minutes

6 tbsp unsalted butter
2 eggs
6 tbsp mild honey
2 tbsp milk
1 1/3 cups flour, sifted
1 tsp baking powder, sifted
7 oz bittersweet chocolate

◇ This recipe must be started one day ahead. You will need 2 regular-sized Madeleine sheet molds (12 Madeleines) or you will have to cook 2 batches.

Heat the unsalted butter until it turns golden brown and the milk solids color and stick to the bottom of the saucepan. Remove from the heat immediately and strain through a fine-mesh wire strainer; set aside to cool.

Beat the egg yolks and the honey. Add the milk then the sifted flour and baking powder; stir to combine. Gradually blend in the strained butter until the batter starts to become foamy and increases in volume. Cover the bowl with plastic wrap; refrigerate overnight.

The next day, preheat the oven to 400°F. Brush the mold with unsalted butter, dust with flour, and tip out the excess.

Fill the imprints with the batter using a spoon or pastry bag. Bake for 5 minutes, or until the Madeleines start to color; lower the oven temperature to 350°F and continue cooking for 5– 7 minutes, or until firm. Remove from the oven, turn out immediately and cool on a wire rack.

If you are using only one mold, you'll have enough for a second batch.

Temper the chocolate: Coarsely chop the chocolate. Place two-thirds (5 oz) in a bowl and melt over a simmering bain-marie until the temperature reaches 115°F on a candy thermometer. Remove the bowl from the heat and add the remaining chocolate, stirring until the temperature drops to 75°F. Return the bowl to the bain-marie, stir gently, and reheat the chocolate to 90°F.

Using a fork, dip the lined side of the Madeleines into the chocolate; set aside on parchment paper. Let the chocolate harden at room temperature before serving.

CHEF'S TIP: When buttering the mold, brush it twice with soft, creamy butter, letting it harden between each coat. Dust with flour and refrigerate for a few minutes before filling with the batter. This way, your Madeleines will be much easier to turn out after they are baked.

Chocolate-Orange Bites

MAKES **12**

DIFFICULTY ★ ★ ★

PREPARE: 45 minutes

REFRIGERATE: Overnight + 1 hour

COOK: 25 minutes

Orange Compote
1 orange

$1/4$ cup superfine sugar

$3^1/_2$ tbsp soft brown sugar

2 tbsp mild honey

Chocolate-Orange Batter
$1^3/_4$ oz bittersweet chocolate

4 tbsp soft unsalted butter

1 cup almond flour/meal

6 tbsp superfine sugar

2 eggs, beaten

2 tsp mild honey

2 tsp Cointreau

Decoration
Confectioners' sugar (optional)

◊ This recipe must be started the day ahead. You will need a silicone mini-muffin mold.

Orange Compote: Peel and segment the orange (p.228). Place the orange segments, superfine and soft brown sugars, and honey in a saucepan over low heat. Cook for 25 minutes, or until the orange segments soften and the mixture thickens; cool and refrigerate the compote overnight.

Chocolate-Orange Batter: The next day, chop the chocolate and melt over a bain-marie. Beat the unsalted butter until creamy then add the melted chocolate, a little at a time. Place the almond flour and sugar in the bowl of an electric mixer; beating continuously, gradually add the eggs until the mixture is thick and smooth. Add the honey. Blend in the melted chocolate-butter mixture then the Cointreau. Continue beating until the batter is smooth and velvety; refrigerate for 1 hour.

Preheat the oven to 350°F. Brush the mini-muffin mold with butter.

Fit a pastry bag with a plain round tip and fill with the chocolate-orange batter; pipe a $1/_2$-in layer in the bottom of each imprint. Use a teaspoon to place a little orange compote on the batter; reserve the remainder for decoration. Fill the imprints with more batter to come to the $2/_3$ mark. Bake for 10 minutes, lower the oven temperature to 325°F, and continue baking for another 15 minutes, or until firm but springy to the touch.

Cool the chocolate-orange mini muffins then turn out onto a wire rack. Decorate the top of each with the reserved orange compote. If desired, dust lightly with confectioners' sugar.

Chocolate-Vanilla Napoleons

Chocolate Puff Pastry

3$^1/_2$ tbsp unsalted butter

1$^3/_4$ cups + 2 tbsp flour, sifted

$^1/_3$ cup unsweetened cocoa powder, sifted

$^1/_4$ tsp salt

1 tbsp superfine sugar

$^1/_2$ cup water

1 cup + 2 tbsp cold unsalted butter

Vanilla Pastry Cream

3 cups milk

2 vanilla pods, split

6 egg yolks

1 cup superfine sugar

$^1/_3$ cup cornstarch

3 tbsp flour

Decoration

Unsweetened cocoa powder, sifted

◇ This recipe must be started the day ahead.

Chocolate Puff Pastry: Heat 3$^1/_2$ tbsp butter until it turns golden brown and the milk solids color and stick to the bottom of the saucepan. Remove from the heat immediately and strain through a fine mesh wire strainer; set aside to cool. Tip the sifted flour and cocoa powder, salt, and sugar into a large bowl; make a well in the center. Pour in the water and melted butter;mix with your fingers. Pull the flour gradually into the well, mixing until blended and forms a smooth ball. Cut an "X" into the top to stop the dough shrinking and wrap in plastic wrap; refrigerate for 1 hour. Lightly flour the work surface, place the dough on it; flatten slightly. Roll out into a cross shape, leaving a mound in the center large enough for the butter.

Sandwich the 1 cup + 2 tbsp cold, unsalted butter between 2 sheets of parchment paper and tap with a rolling pin until it is the same consistency as the dough; form into a $^3/_4$-in thick square. Place it on the mound in the center of the dough; fold the extended dough sections up and over, enclosing it completely. Dust the dough and rolling pin lightly with flour then lightly roll the dough to seal in the butter. Dust the work surface with flour and roll out the dough into a 4$^1/_2$ x 14-in rectangle. Fold the top third over the middle then, fold the bottom third over to form a square; make sure all the edges are aligned. Give the dough a 45° turn to the right. Lightly press the rolling pin along the edges to seal then, roll out into a 4$^1/_2$ x 14-in rectangle again, folding as before; refrigerate 30 minutes. Roll and turn the dough twice again, as previously described and refrigerate for another 30 minutes. Roll and fold the dough twice more. (The dough should have been rolled and folded six times.) Refrigerate overnight.

The next day, preheat the oven to 300°F. Butter a 12 x 15-in baking sheet and lightly sprinkle with water. Roll the dough out to a thickness of $^1/_2$ - $^3/_4$ in, cutting it to the same dimensions as the baking sheet. Transfer to the baking sheet, place an oven rack on top, and bake for 45 minutes or until it puffs, becomes crisp, and browns. Cool the puff pastry on a wire rack.

Vanilla Pastry Cream: Using the ingredients listed, follow the instructions on p.296; refrigerate 25 minutes.

Cut the puff pastry into 3 rectangles measuring 4 x 15-in. Spread the pastry cream onto 1 rectangle, place another rectangle on top and repeat with the pastry cream; finish with the remaining rectangle. Use a serrated knife and gently cut into 6– 8 portions; dust with sifted cocoa powder.

Mini Chocolate Éclairs

MAKES **20** MINI ÉCLAIRS

DIFFICULTY ★ ★ ★

PREPARE: 1 hour

COOK: 18 minutes

REFRIGERATE: 25 minutes

Choux Pastry Dough

$^1/_2$ cup water

3$^1/_2$ tbsp unsalted butter

$^1/_2$ tsp salt

$^1/_2$ tsp superfine sugar

Scant $^2/_3$ cup flour, sifted

2 eggs

1 beaten egg for glazing

Chocolate Pastry Cream

2$^3/_4$ oz bittersweet
  chocolate

1 cup milk

1 vanilla pod, split

2 egg yolks

$^1/_3$ cup superfine sugar

2$^1/_2$ tbsp cornstarch

Chocolate Glaze

1$^3/_4$ oz bittersweet
  chocolate

6$^1/_2$ tbsp confectioners'
  sugar

2 tsp water

◇ See p.254: The best way
to fill éclairs.

Preheat the oven to 350°F. Butter a baking sheet.

Choux Pastry Dough: Using the ingredients listed, follow the instructions on p.232. When the dough is ready to be used, fit a pastry bag with a plain round tip, and spoon in the dough. Pipe fingers of dough, 2– 2$^1/_2$ in long, on the baking sheet; brush the tops with the egg glaze. Transfer to the oven and bake for 8 minutes without opening the door. Then lower the oven temperature to 325°F and continue baking for another 8– 10 minutes, or until the choux pastry fingers are golden and sound hollow when tapped. Cool on a wire rack.

Chocolate Pastry Cream: Finely chop the chocolate and place in a bowl. Pour the milk into a saucepan. Using the point of a knife, scrape the seeds from the vanilla pod into the milk, add the pod, and bring to the boil; remove from the heat. Beat the eggs and sugar until pale yellow, thick, and creamy; add the cornstarch. Discard the vanilla pod. Whisking continuously, add half the hot milk into the eggs-sugar-flour mixture; whisk in the remaining milk. Return the mixture to the saucepan and cook over low heat, whisking continuously until the cream thickens then; boil for 1 minute while continuing to whisk. Remove from the heat and pour the pastry cream over the chopped chocolate; stir until smooth. Cover the surface of the chocolate pastry cream with plastic wrap; set aside to cool then refrigerate for 25 minutes.

Chocolate Glaze: Melt the chocolate over a bain-marie. Combine the confectioners' sugar and water and blend into to the melted chocolate. Heat until the temperature of the mixture registers 100°F on a candy thermometer.

Fit a pastry bag with a plain round tip and fill it with pastry cream. Pierce two or three small holes in the flat side of each choux pastry finger and fill with chocolate pastry cream. Spread a layer of chocolate glaze on the top using a spatula; set aside to dry before serving the éclairs.

Chocolate Butter Cookies with Lemon Cream

MAKES **20–30** COOKIES

DIFFICULTY ★ ★ ★

PREPARE: 55 minutes

REFRIGERATE: Overnight

COOK: 15–20 minutes

Chocolate Butter Cookies

$^1/_2$ cup + 6$^1/_2$ tbsp unsalted butter

1 scant cup superfine sugar

$^1/_4$ tsp sea salt crystals or fleur de sel

5 egg yolks

2 cups flour, sifted

3 tsp baking powder, sifted

$^1/_3$ cup unsweetened cocoa powder, sifted

Lemon Cream

2 sheets or 1$^1/_2$ tsp gelatin

4 eggs

1 scant cup superfine sugar

$^2/_3$ cup lemon juice

10$^1/_2$ oz soft unsalted butter

7 oz raspberries

7 oz strawberries

◇ This recipe must be started the day ahead.

Chocolate Butter Cookies Place the unsalted butter, sugar, and sea salt flakes in a large bowl and beat until creamy. Add the egg yolks, one at a time, beating after each addition. Blend in the sifted flour, baking and cocoa powders, and form the dough into a ball. Wrap in plastic wrap and refrigerate overnight.

Lemon Cream: On the day of serving, soften the gelatin in water. Beat the eggs. Heat the sugar and lemon juice over a bain-marie then whisk in the beaten eggs. Whisk briskly for 10–15 minutes, or until thickened. (If using, squeeze the excess water from the gelatin sheets.) Remove the lemon juice mixture from the bain-marie, add the softened gelatin; stir to dissolve. Pour the mixture into a separate bowl and blend in half the soft unsalted butter; refrigerate for 15 minutes. Gradually add the remaining butter, whisking until the mixture is smooth and shiny. Fit a pastry bag with a plain round tip and fill with the lemon cream; refrigerate until required.

Preheat the oven to 350°F. Line a baking sheet with parchment paper. Brush a 2$^3/_4$-in round pastry cutter with butter.

Dust the work surface with flour and roll the dough out to a thickness of $^1/_4$ in. Cut out discs of dough with the pastry cutter and place on the baking sheet using a palette knife; leave sufficient space between each one to allow for spreading during cooking. Bake for 15–20 minutes, or until firm to the touch. Remove from the oven; cool on a wire rack.

Pipe mounds of lemon cream on each of the cookies; refrigerate until required. Serve with fresh raspberries and strawberries.

CHEF'S TIP: If desired, you could replace the lemon juice with grapefruit, lime, or passion fruit juice.

Chocolate-Raspberry Cookies

MAKES 35 COOKIES

DIFFICULTY ★ ★ ★

PREPARE: 1 hour

REFRIGERATE: 40 minutes

COOK: 10 minutes

Cookies

$^1/_2$ cup + 3 tbsp soft salted butter

Scant $^3/_4$ cup confectioners' sugar

3 egg yolks

1$^3/_4$ cups flour, sifted

1 tsp baking powder, sifted

Chocolate Mousse

5$^1/_4$ oz dark (55-70%) chocolate

1 cup heavy whipping cream

6 tbsp superfine sugar

4 egg yolks

Decoration

Raspberry jam

2 cups raspberries

Cookies: Place the salted butter and confectioners' sugar in a large bowl and beat until creamy. Add the egg yolks, one at a time, beating after each addition. Blend in the sifted flour and baking powder. Form the dough into a ball and wrap in plastic wrap; refrigerate 20 minutes.

Preheat the oven to 350°F. Line a baking sheet with parchment paper.

Brush a 2$^1/_2$-in round pastry cutter with butter. Dust the work surface with flour and roll the dough out to a thickness of $^1/_{16}$ in. Cut out discs of dough using the pastry cutter and place on the baking sheet using a palette knife; leave sufficient space between each one to allow for spreading during cooking. Bake for 10 minutes, or until firm to the touch. Remove from the oven; cool on a wire rack.

Chocolate Mousse: Chop the chocolate and melt over a bain-marie; remove from the heat. Whisk the whipping cream with the sugar until firm peaks cling to the whisk. Quickly beat one-third of the cream and the egg yolks into the melted chocolate. Fold in the remaining cream with a spatula. Fit a pastry bag with a fluted tip and fill with the chocolate mousse; refrigerate for about 20 minutes.

Using a teaspoon, spread a little raspberry jam on each cookie, pipe with a rosette of chocolate mousse and top with a raspberry. Refrigerate the cookies until required.

CHEF'S TIP: In place of the raspberry jam, you could use a seedless raspberry jelly.

Chocolate Cookies

MAKES 35 COOKIES

DIFFICULTY ★ ★ ★

PREPARE: 30 minutes

REFRIGERATE: 20 minutes

COOK: 15 minutes

$1/2$ cup + 6 tbsp salted
  butter, chilled

$1^3/4$ oz bittersweet
  chocolate

$1^2/3$ cups flour, sifted

$1/3$ cup unsweetened cocoa
  powder, sifted

6 tbsp soft brown sugar

1 egg yolk

Preheat the oven to 350°F. Line a baking sheet with parchment paper.

Cut the chilled salted butter into small cubes. Finely chop the chocolate. Tip the sifted flour, cocoa powder, and brown sugar into a large bowl. Add the butter cubes rubbing them into the dry ingredients with your fingertips until the mixture resembles fine breadcrumbs. Blend in the egg yolk and the chopped chocolate.

Divide the dough in two even portions. Roll each one into a $1^1/4$-in diameter cylinder. Refrigerate for 20 minutes. Cut the dough into $1/2$-in thick slices and place on the baking sheet; leave sufficient space between each one to allow for spreading during cooking. Bake for about 15 minutes, or until firm to the touch; cool on a wire rack.

CHEF'S ADVICE: For a sweeter cookie, use half bittersweet and half white chocolate.

Chocolate-Mascarpone Semolina Fritters

MAKES 12

DIFFICULTY ★ ★ ★

PREPARE: 2½ hours

REFRIGERATE: 2 hours

INFUSE: 30 minutes

COOK: 45 minutes

Chocolate-Mascarpone Filling

3½ oz bittersweet chocolate

3½ oz mascarpone

Semolina

1¼ cups milk

1 vanilla pod, split

2½ tbsp semolina

2 tbsp superfine sugar

2–3 drops bitter almond extract

Almond flour/meal

Coating

1 cup blanched almonds

⅔ cup breadcrumbs

2 eggs, beaten

Vegetable oil for frying

Superfine sugar

Chocolate-Mascarpone Filling: Melt the chocolate over a bain-marie. When cooled, blend in the mascarpone. Refrigerate the mixture until firm enough to be rolled into 12 small balls, then refrigerate again for 1 hour.

Semolina: Pour the milk into a saucepan. Using the point of a knife, scrape the seeds from the vanilla pod into the milk; add the pod and heat until almost simmering. Remove from the heat, cover and infuse for 30 minutes. Discard the vanilla pod and bring the milk to the boil. Remove the saucepan from the heat and, stirring continuously, add the semolina in a thin, steady stream. Continue stirring and add the sugar and bitter almond extract; bring the mixture to the boil. Cook over low heat for about 20 minutes, stirring often to stop the semolina sticking. Pour the mixture, in an even layer, into a jelly roll pan or shallow gratin dish; set aside until cold.

Divide the semolina in 12 portions. Cover each chocolate-mascarpone ball with a layer of cooked semolina and roll in almond flour/meal to stop the semolina balls sticking to the fingers or hands.

Coating: Coarsely chop the blanched almonds and combine with the breadcrumbs. Dip the semolina balls into the beaten egg then roll in the almond-breadcrumb mixture; refrigerate for at least 30 minutes.

Pour the vegetable oil into a deep fat fryer (or heavy-bottomed saucepan), to a depth of approximately 3 in; heat to 400°F. Use tongs to immerse 3 or 4 balls in the hot oil then deep fry for 3–5 minutes, or until lightly golden. Drain on paper towels and roll the fritters in sugar. Repeat for the remaining semolina balls; serve.

CHEF'S TIP: To make it easier to coat the chocolate-mascarpone balls with the semolina mixture, they could be frozen for 2 hours.

Chocolate "Tagliatelle" in Orange Salad

SERVES 4

DIFFICULTY ★ ★ ★

PREPARE: 1 hour

REFRIGERATE: 1½ hours

REST: 30 minutes

COOK: 10 minutes

Chocolate "Tagliatelle"

1 ⅔ cups flour, sifted

1 pinch salt

2 eggs

⅓ cup confectioners' sugar

½ cup unsweetened cocoa powder

2– 3 tbsp water

Orange Salad

4 oranges

2 tbsp superfine sugar

2 tbsp grenadine syrup

1 tbsp orange marmalade

2 tbsp Cointreau

6 cups water

1 cup superfine sugar

¼ tsp vanilla extract

Decoration

Mint leaves

Chocolate "Tagliatelle": Tip the sifted flour and salt into a bowl and make a well in the center. Beat the eggs in a separate bowl. Sift the confectioners' sugar and cocoa powder into the beaten eggs, stir to combine, then blend in the water. Pour the mixture into the well and slowly draw in the flour to form a ball. Knead until the dough no longer sticks to the fingers; refrigerate for 1 ½ hours.

Dust the work surface with flour. Divide the dough into three pieces and roll out each one into a ⅛-in thick rectangle. Lightly dust each rectangle with flour and place one on top of the other then cut to form an even rectangle. Roll up the rectangle of dough fairly tightly so it forms a cylinder; use a sharp knife to cut ⅛-in thick slices to obtain "tagliatelle." Spread out a clean dish towel, dust it lightly with flour and place the tagliatelle on it to dry for about 30 minutes.

Orange Salad: Squeeze two of the oranges and put the juice into a saucepan. Add the sugar and bring to the boil. Remove from the heat, stir in the grenadine syrup, orange marmalade, and Cointreau; set aside until cold.

Segment the remaining oranges: Using a very sharp knife, cut a small slice off both ends of the orange. Stand it on a cutting board and, working from top to bottom, cut off the peel and all the pith in wide strips. Hold the peeled orange in the palm of your hand. Insert the knife between the membrane and the flesh, cutting toward the center without cutting the membrane. Then cut on the other side of the segment and ease it out. Continue until all the segments have been removed; repeat for the remaining orange. Transfer the segments to the syrup; refrigerate the orange salad until required.

Bring the water, sugar, and the vanilla extract to the boil. Add the "tagliatelle" and cook for 10 minutes. Drain in a colander then carefully combine with the orange salad. Divide among four rimmed soup dishes and decorate with mint leaves.

Chocolate Tuile Cookies

MAKES 15
DIFFICULTY ★ ★ ★
PREPARE: 35 minutes
COOL: 15– 25 minutes

9 oz bittersweet chocolate
1 1/4 cups sliced almonds,
  toasted

◇ See p.315:
Tempering chocolate.

Cut out five 2 x 12-in rectangles of acetate. Prepare a pastry brush, a rolling pin, and some adhesive tape.

Temper the chocolate: Coarsely chop the bittersweet chocolate. Place two-thirds (6 oz) of the chopped chocolate in a bowl, melt over a bain-marie until the temperature reaches 115°F on a candy thermometer. Remove the bowl from the heat and add the remaining chocolate, stirring until the temperature drops to 75°F. Return the bowl to the bain-marie, stir gently and reheat the chocolate to 90°F.

Work quickly and use a pastry brush to form three 3 1/4-in diameter chocolate discs, approximately 1/16-1/8 in thick, on one of the rectangles; sprinkle with toasted almonds. Immediately place the acetate rectangle on the rolling pin, gently curling the chocolate discs around the pin; secure the acetate with adhesive tape. Repeat the operation four more times, placing the acetate rectangles one on top of the other, as soon as they are prepared. Cool at room temperature for 15– 25 minutes, or until the chocolate hardens. Lift off the rectangles one by one and gently remove the chocolate discs. Place in an airtight container and store in a cool location (50°F maximum).

CHEF'S TIP: Chocolate is easier to work with when the weather is mild. You could also make the tuiles using either white or milk chocolate but be sure to follow the tempering instructions given on p.315.

Chocolate-Hazelnut Tuile Cookies

MAKES 30

DIFFICULTY ★ ★ ★

PREPARE: 30 minutes

REFRIGERATE: 20 minutes

COOK: 6–8 minutes

3 1/2 tbsp soft unsalted butter

1 scant cup confectioners' sugar

2 egg whites

1/3 cup flour, sifted

2 tbsp unsweetened cocoa powder, sifted

1 1/2 cups hazelnuts, toasted and chopped

Preheat the oven to 350°F. Line a baking sheet with parchment paper. Lightly brush a rolling pin with unsalted butter or oil.

Beat the unsalted butter and confectioners' sugar until creamy. Add the egg whites little by little, mixing well after each addition. Then, blend in the sifted flour and cocoa powder.

Use a spoon to thinly spread out the mixture on the baking sheet forming 2 1/2-in diameter discs. Leave sufficient space between each one to allow for spreading during cooking. Sprinkle with the chopped hazelnuts and bake for 6–8 minutes, or until lightly crisp around the edge.

Loosen the tuiles from the baking sheet (using a metal scraper), and working very quickly (the tuiles may shatter if allowed to harden), curl them over the rolling pin while still warm and pliable. When firm, slip off and cool completely on a wire rack. Repeat until all the tuiles have been formed.

CHEF'S ADVICE: Pastry chefs often have among their tools, a triangular metal paint scraper which makes lifting tuiles off the baking sheet much easier. To prevent the tuiles becoming too hard to fashion, you may prefer to make them in batches.

Delicious mouthfuls

The best way to make praline paste

The following will produce about 1 cup praline paste. Any paste greater than the quantity necessary for the recipe of your choice can be stored in a glass jar in a cool, dry location for 3 weeks. Before using, stir well.

① Heat 2 tbsp of water and ¾ cup of sugar in a medium saucepan over low heat, stirring until the sugar dissolves completely; increase the heat and boil for 2 minutes without stirring. Stir in ⅔ cup almonds and ⅔ cup hazelnuts using a wooden spoon. Remove from the heat and continue stirring until the sugar crystalizes covering the nuts with a white powder. Return the saucepan to the heat until the sugar melts and the nuts turn golden brown.

② Spread the caramelized nuts on an oiled baking sheet; set aside until cold.

③ Break the praline in pieces, place in a food processor and grind, first to a powder then, to a creamy paste. To avoid overworking the food processor, stop the food processor often and mix with a spatula or grind the praline in several batches.

The best way to temper chocolate

The following steps will ensure a glossy and crisp finish. If you are tempering milk chocolate, melt to 110°F, cool to 75°F, and reheat to 85°F. If you are tempering white chocolate, melt to 100°F, cool to 70°F ,and reheat to 80°F.

(1) Coarsely chop 7 oz bittersweet (preferably couverture) chocolate or the amount specified in your choice of recipe (see pages 326 and 356). Place ²/₃ of the chocolate in a bowl; melt over a bain-marie of gently simmering water. The bottom of the bowl should not touch the water; or shine and smoothness may be lost.

(2) Heat until the temperature reaches 115°F on a candy thermometer. Remove the bowl from the heat and stir in the remaining chocolate; stir with a spatula from time to time.

(3) As soon as the temperature cools to 75°F, return the bowl to the bain-marie and reheat, stirring gently until the chocolate reaches 90°C. When the chocolate is smooth and shiny, it is ready to be used for chocolate curls or as a coating.

The best way to mold chocolates

Temper the chocolate, prepare the ganache, and use the mold(s) indicated in the recipe of your choice (for example, p.332).

(1) Place a sheet of acetate on the work surface. Hold the mold at an angle over the plastic and using a small ladle, fill the imprints with tempered chocolate.

(2) Tap the mold on the work surface to release any air bubbles in the chocolate then invert it, tipping out the excess. Use a metal scraper to remove the residual chocolate from the top of the mold. The surface of the mold should be clean and the chocolate should only line the bottom and side of the imprints (i.e. there is space in the center). Set the mold aside at room temperature for 30 minutes, or until the chocolate hardens.

(3) Fit a pastry bag with a small round tip and fill with ganache. Place the tip in the center of each imprint and fill to the ¾ mark with ganache, without touching the hardened chocolate edge. Then, refrigerate for 20 minutes until hardened.

(4) Change the acetate sheet on the work surface. Hold the mold at an angle and. using a small ladle. pour tempered chocolate over the mold completely covering the ganache-filled imprints.

(5) Use the spatula to scrape the surface of the mold covering and sealing the imprints with the chocolate; refrigerate 20 minutes until the chocolate is hardened.

(6) Once the chocolate has hardened, invert the mold and lightly tap it on the work surface to turn out the chocolates.

The best way to coat candies with chocolate

Prepare a ganache, shape it into small balls, and refrigerate until hardened as indicated in the recipe of your choice (pp. 336, 364, or 372).

① Remove the ganache balls from the refrigerator and bring them to room temperature (ideally between 64–70°F). Put unsweetened cocoa powder into a large, flat, high-sided container. Temper a sufficient quantity of chocolate (p.315).

② Slide a regular or chocolate fork (ringed or pronged) under the ganache ball and dip the ball carefully into the tempered chocolate. Then lift the ball up, letting the excess chocolate drip into the bowl. Gently shake the fork, wiping the base several times on the side of the bowl to remove the residual chocolate and obtain a smooth coating.

③ Using the fork, roll the chocolate in the cocoa powder. Set aside to firm at room temperature. When the chocolates have hardened, place in a wire mesh strainer and shake gently to remove excess cocoa.

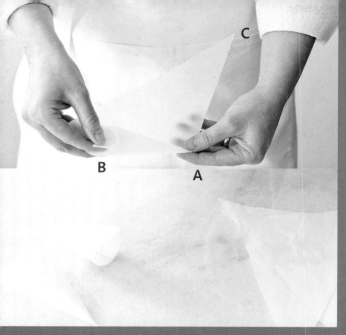

The best way to make a small paper pastry bag for decorating

Use for the quantity of chocolate specified in the recipe of your choice (p.322).

(1) Cut a 10-in square of parchment paper into 2 triangles and discard one. The right angle is "A" and the other two angles are "B" and "C". Hold the parchment paper as shown. Curl the point of "B" around until it meets the point of "A" and forms a cone. Wrap the opposite point "C" around to meet the other two points and tighten the cone. Pull all three points together tightly to create a sharp tip and fold the flap inside, creasing it firmly to hold the bag in shape.

(2) Using a spoon, fill the pastry bag with warm melted chocolate

(3) Roll and fold over the top of the bag until the chocolate is squeezed into the nose of the cone. The paper should be taut around the chocolate. Just before using, snip off the tip. For fine lines of piping, cut close to the tip.

Chocolate Almond Treats

MAKES 20

DIFFICULTY ★ ★ ★

PREPARE: 45 minutes

REST: 30 minutes

7 oz yellow almond paste
20 blanched almonds,
 toasted

Chocolate Coating
10$^1/_2$ oz bittersweet
 chocolate

◇ See p.315: Tempering
chocolate.

Roll the almond paste into a $^3/_4$-in diameter rope. Cut the rope into 20 equal pieces. Wearing rubber gloves, roll the pieces by hand to form ovals. Lightly press a toasted almond into each oval.

Chocolate Coating: Temper the chocolate: Coarsely chop the chocolate. Place two-thirds (7 oz) in a bowl and melt over a simmering bain-marie until the temperature reaches 115°F on a candy thermometer. Remove the bowl from the heat and add the remaining chocolate stirring until the temperature cools to 75°F. Return the bowl to the bain-marie and, stirring gently, reheat the chocolate to 90°F.

Line a baking sheet with parchment paper. Insert a toothpick into each almond paste oval.

Dip the bottom of the ovals into the tempered chocolate to come to the $^3/_4$ mark and place on the baking sheet. Set aside at room temperature for 30 minutes, or until the chocolate hardens.

Remove the toothpicks. Store in an airtight container at 54°F maximum; consume within 15 days.

CHEF'S TIP: It's possible to change the color of the paste, if you prefer, by using a plain almond paste and adding food coloring to obtain the color of your choice.

Annabella Bonbons

MAKES 30
DIFFICULTY ★ ★ ★
MACERATE: Overnight
PREPARE: 1½ hours

¼ cup raisins
4 tsp rum
5½ oz almond paste
Confectioners' sugar

Chocolate Coating

10½ oz white chocolate

Decoration

1¾ oz bittersweet
  chocolate

◊ This recipe must be
started the day before.
◊ See p.319: Making a paper
pastry bag

Macerate the raisins in the rum overnight.

The next day, combine the macerated raisins and the almond paste. Dust the work surface with confectioners' sugar. Wearing rubber gloves, divide the almond paste into two equal parts and form each one into a rope. Cut the rope into pieces ½ in thick. Roll by hand into balls and place on a plate.

Chocolate Coating: Temper the white chocolate: Coarsely chop the chocolate. Place two-thirds (7 oz) of the chopped chocolate in a bowl; melt over a simmering bain-marie until the temperature reaches 100°F on a candy thermometer. Remove the bowl from the heat and add the remaining chocolate, stirring until the temperature cools to 70°F. Return the bowl to the bain-marie and, gently stirring reheat the chocolate to 80°F.

Make a small paper pastry bag using parchment paper. Melt the bittersweet chocolate over a bain-marie; cool. Wearing rubber gloves, dip the almond paste balls into the tempered white chocolate, shake gently to remove the excess, and set on parchment paper to harden. Fill the paper pastry bag with the melted bittersweet chocolate. Roll and fold over the top of the bag until the chocolate is squeezed into the nose of the cone. The parchment should be taut around the chocolate. Snip off the end close to the tip and streak the white chocolate with fine lines of bittersweet chocolate.

CHEF'S TIP: You could also use a teaspoon dipped in bittersweet chocolate to streak the white chocolates. When serving, play with colors. Here we have accompanied the Annabella Bonbons with Plain Chocolate Truffles (p. 364), rolled into log shapes before dipping into cocoa powder.

Soft Chocolate Caramels

MAKES **25**

DIFFICULTY ★ ★ ★

PREPARE: 30 minutes

REFRIGERATE: 2 hours

3 oz bittersweet chocolate

1 cup heavy whipping
  cream

1 1/4 cups superfine sugar

3 1/2 tbsp mild honey

2 tbsp unsalted butter

Chop the chocolate and place in a bowl.

Heat the cream until simmering and set aside. Place 1/4 cup of the sugar in a separate saucepan, stir from time to time with a wooden spoon and cook until it turns golden. To stop the sugar cooking, add the cream, a little at a time, stirring with the wooden spoon (the mixture will bubble violently). Add the remaining sugar and continue stirring until the mixture is thick and creamy; be careful not to let the mixture burn.

Moisten a wooden spoon and use it to blend the honey into the caramel. Return the mixture to the heat and cook until it registers 240°F on a candy thermometer; remove from the heat. Stir in a little chopped chocolate, gradually add the remainder, then blend in the unsalted butter.

Place a 7-in square dessert frame on a sheet of parchment paper and pour in the chocolate caramel; refrigerate for 2 hours.

Slide the point of a knife around the wall of the frame and lift it off. Cut the caramel as desired.

CHEF'S TIP: If you do not have a dessert frame, use a 7-in square cake pan lined with plastic wrap. Let the edges of the plastic wrap hang over the sides of the pan, so that you can turn out the hardened caramel easily.

Chocolate Coated Cherries

MAKES 30

DIFFICULTY ★ ★ ★

DRAIN: Overnight

PREPARE: 30 minutes

REST: 30 minutes

30 stemmed Morello or
  Montmorency cherries, in
  fruit brandy

Chocolate Coating

12 oz bittersweet chocolate

◊ See p.315: Tempering
chocolate

◊ This recipe must be
started the night before.

Drain and set the cherries aside to dry overnight

Chocolate Coating: Temper the chocolate: Coarsely chop the chocolate.
Place two-thirds (8 oz) of the chopped chocolate in a bowl; melt over a
simmering bain-marie until the temperature reaches 115°F on a candy
thermometer. Remove the bowl from the heat and add the remaining
chocolate stirring until the temperature cools to 75°F. Return the bowl
to the bain-marie and, stirring gently, reheat the chocolate to 90°F.

Holding the stem, dip each cherry into the tempered chocolate and
shake gently to remove the excess; place on parchment paper. Set
aside to harden at room temperature for 30 minutes.

CHEF'S TIP: To ensure that the chocolate coating is smooth and shiny, the
cherries must be dry and at room temperature when dipped.

Chocolate-Orange Truffles

MAKES **30** TRUFFLES

DIFFICULTY ★ ★ ★

PREPARE: 1 hour 20 minutes

DRY: Overnight

Orange-Almond Filling
$1/_4$ cup candied orange peel
7 oz almond paste
1 tbsp Kirsch
Confectioners' sugar

Chocolate Coating
12 oz bittersweet chocolate

◇ See p.315: Tempering chocolate.
◇ This recipe must be started the day ahead.

Orange-Almond Filling: Finely chop the candied orange peel, combine with the almond paste and Kirsch; mix until smooth. Dust the work surface with confectioners' sugar. Wearing rubber gloves, divide the mixture in two equal parts and form each one into a long rope. Cut each rope in 15 equal pieces. Roll by hand into balls and place on a plate. Set aside to dry out overnight.

The next day, cover a baking sheet with parchment paper and set out a wire rack.

Chocolate Coating: Temper the chocolate: Coarsely chop the chocolate and place two-thirds (8 oz) in a bowl; melt over a simmering bain-marie until the temperature reaches 115°F on a candy thermometer. Remove the bowl from the heat and add the remaining chocolate stirring until the temperature cools to 75°F. Return the bowl to the bain-marie and, stirring gently, reheat the chocolate to 90°F.

Wearing rubber gloves, dip the balls one by one, into the tempered chocolate; set on the parchment paper to harden. Then coat with chocolate again, shaking gently to remove the excess and place on the rack. When the chocolate starts to firm, roll the balls on the rack to form "spikes." Place on the baking sheet to harden at room temperature for 20 minutes. Store the chocolates in an airtight container.

Chocolate-Pistachio Truffles

MAKES 40 TRUFFLES

DIFFICULTY ★ ★ ★

PREPARE: 1 hour 20 minutes

DRY: Overnight

Pistachio-Almond Filling

1 tbsp water

2 tbsp superfine sugar

1 tsp mild honey

1/4 cup shelled pistachios

7 oz almond paste

4 tsp soft unsalted butter

1/2 tbsp rum

Confectioners' sugar, sifted

Chocolate Coating

14 oz bittersweet chocolate

◊ See p.315: Tempering chocolate.
◊ This recipe must be started the day ahead.

Pistachio-Almond Filling: Bring the water, sugar, and honey to the boil to make a syrup; set aside. Put the pistachios into a blender or food processor and grind to a fine powder; add the syrup and continue mixing to obtain a thin paste. Combine the pistachio paste with the almond paste, soft unsalted butter, and rum. Dust the work surface with sifted confectioners' sugar. Wearing rubber gloves, divide the mixture in two equal parts and form each one into a rope about 12-in long. Cut each rope into 20 equal pieces. Roll by hand into balls and place on a plate. Set aside to dry out overnight.

The next day, cover a baking sheet with parchment paper and set out a wire rack.

Chocolate Coating: Temper the chocolate: Coarsely chop the chocolate and place two-thirds (9 1/4 oz) in a bowl; melt over a slowly simmering bain-marie until the temperature reaches 115°F on a candy thermometer. Remove the bowl from the heat and add the remaining chocolate, stirring until the temperature cools to 75°F. Return the bowl to the bain-marie and, gently stirring, reheat the chocolate to 90°F.

Wearing rubber gloves dip the balls, one by one, into the tempered chocolate; set on the parchment paper to harden. Then coat with chocolate again, shaking gently to remove the excess and place on the rack. When the chocolate starts to harden, roll the balls on the rack to form small "spikes" Place on the baking sheet to harden at room temperature for 20 minutes. Store the chocolate-pistachio truffles in an airtight container.

Banana Ganache Chocolates

MAKES **30**

DIFFICULTY ★ ★ ★

PREPARE: 1 hour

COOK: 10 minutes

REFRIGERATE: 40 minutes

REST: 30 minutes

Banana Ganache

2¹/₂ tbsp mild honey

2 tsp unsalted butter

¹/₂ banana

2¹/₄ oz milk chocolate

1¹/₄ oz bittersweet
chocolate

3¹/₂ tbsp heavy whipping
cream

Chocolate Coating

14 oz bittersweet chocolate

◊ See p.316: Molding
chocolates.

Banana Ganache: Heat the honey and unsalted butter in a saucepan. Crush the banana, add to the honey-butter mixture and cook to a smooth purée. Coarsely chop the milk and bittersweet chocolates and place in a bowl. Heat the cream to simmering, pour over the chopped chocolate and stir until smooth. Combine the banana purée mixture with the chocolate mixture and set aside until thickened.

Chocolate Coating: Temper the bittersweet chocolate: Coarsely chop the chocolate and place two-thirds (9¹/₄ oz) in a bowl; melt over a slowly simmering bain-marie until the temperature reaches 115°F on a candy thermometer. Remove the bowl from the heat and add the remaining chocolate, stirring until the temperature cools to 75°F. Return the bowl to the bain-marie and, stirring gently, reheat the chocolate to 90°F.

Hold a polycarbonate chocolate mold containing 30 imprints at an angle over a sheet of acetate and using a small ladle, fill the imprints with tempered chocolate. Tap the mold on the work surface to release the air bubbles and invert to tip out the excess. Remove the chocolate from the surface of the mold using a metal scraper: Only the base and walls of the imprints should be chocolate coated. Set aside at room temperature for 30 minutes, or until the chocolate hardens. Fit a pastry bag with a small round tip and fill with banana ganache. Place the tip in the center of each imprint and fill to the ²/₃ mark, without touching the molded chocolate edge; refrigerate 20 minutes, or until firm. Hold the mold at an angle again and ladle the tempered chocolate over the ganache-filled imprints. Smooth with the spatula to evenly cover and seal the imprints, scraping the excess chocolate from the surface of the mold; refrigerate 20 minutes. When the chocolate is hard, invert the mold and lightly tap it on the work surface to turn out the banana ganache chocolates.

CHEF'S TIP: To give the ganache a more intense flavor, flame the banana with rum in the honey and butter mixture before crushing it.

Lemon Tea Chocolates

MAKES **50**

DIFFICULTY ★ ★ ★

PREPARE: 1 hour

INFUSE: 15 minutes

REFRIGERATE: 50 minutes

Lemon Tea Ganache

3¹/₂ tbsp water

2 lemon teabags

Juice of 2 lemons

8¹/₂ oz milk chocolate

3 oz bittersweet chocolate

2 egg yolks

¹/₂ cup superfine sugar

3¹/₂ tbsp whipping cream

Chocolate Coating

14 oz bittersweet chocolate

Confectioners' sugar

Grated zest of 3 lemons

◇ See p.318: Dipping and coating chocolates.

◇ See p.315: Tempering chocolate.

Lemon Tea Ganache: Bring the water to the boil, add the lemon teabags and infuse for 15 minutes. Pour about 2 tbsp of the infused tea into a bowl, add the lemon juice, and set aside. Finely chop the milk and bittersweet chocolates and place in a bowl. Beat the egg yolks and ¹/₄ cup of the sugar. Put the whipping cream, lemon tea, and the remaining sugar in a saucepan; heat until simmering and, whisking quickly, pour into the egg yolk and sugar mixture. Return the mixture to the saucepan and cook over low heat, stirring continuously with a wooden spoon, until the cream thickens and coats the back of the spoon. (Do not allow to boil!) Remove from the heat immediately and strain over the chopped chocolate; stir until smooth. Refrigerate for 30 minutes, or until firm.

Line a baking sheet with parchment paper. Use a teaspoon or a pastry bag fitted with a small round tip to form 50 mounds of ganache on the parchment; refrigerate until firm.

Coating: Temper the bittersweet chocolate: Coarsely chop the bittersweet chocolate and place two-thirds (9¹/₄ oz) in a bowl; melt over a simmering bain-marie until the temperature reaches 115°F on a candy thermometer. Remove the bowl from the heat and add the remaining chocolate, stirring until the temperature cools to 75°F. Return the bowl to the bain-marie, and stirring gently. reheat the chocolate to 90°F.

Sift the confectioners' sugar into a flat container and stir in the lemon zest. Remove the ganache balls from the refrigerator and bring to room temperature. Using a regular or a chocolate fork (ringed or pronged), dip the ganache balls one by one into the tempered chocolate. Tap the fork on the side of the bowl and shake gently to remove any excess chocolate. Roll the chocolates in the confectioners' sugar and lemon and place on a rack to harden. Then, place in a strainer and shake gently to remove the excess confectioners' sugar; store in an airtight container.

Matcha Green Tea Chocolates

MAKES **50**

DIFFICULTY ★ ★ ★

PREPARE: 1 hour

REFRIGERATE: 50 minutes

Matcha Green Tea Ganache

8¹/₂ oz milk chocolate

3 oz bittersweet chocolate

2 egg yolks

¹/₂ cup superfine sugar

¹/₂ cup heavy whipping
  cream

¹/₄ tsp powdered matcha
  green tea

Chocolate Coating

14 oz bittersweet chocolate

Unsweetened cocoa
  powder

◊ See p.315: Tempering
chocolate.

Matcha Green Tea Ganache: Finely chop the milk and bittersweet chocolates and place in a bowl. In a separate bowl, beat the egg yolks and sugar until pale yellow and creamy. Put the cream and powdered matcha green tea into a saucepan and heat until simmering. Whisking quickly, pour a little into the egg yolk and sugar mixture. Return to the saucepan and cook the mixture over low heat, stirring continuously with a wooden spoon, until the cream thickens and coats the back of a spoon. (Do not allow to boil!) Remove from the heat immediately and strain over the chopped chocolate; stir until smooth. Refrigerate for 30 minutes, or until firm.

Line a baking sheet with parchment paper. Use a teaspoon or a pastry bag fitted with a round tip to form 50 mounds of ganache on the parchment; refrigerate until firm.

Chocolate Coating: Temper the bittersweet chocolate: Coarsely chop the bittersweet chocolate and place two-thirds (9¹/₄ oz) in a bowl; melt over a simmering bain-marie until the temperature reaches 115°F on a candy thermometer. Remove the bowl from the heat and add the remaining chocolate, stirring until the temperature cools to 75°C. Return the bowl to the bain-marie and, stirring gently, reheat the chocolate to 90°F.

Sift the cocoa powder into a flat container. Remove the ganache balls from the refrigerator and bring to room temperature. Using a regular or a chocolate fork (ringed or pronged), dip the ganache balls one by one, into the tempered chocolate. Tap the fork on the side of the bowl and shake gently to remove any excess chocolate. Roll the chocolates in cocoa powder and set aside to harden. Then, place in a wire mesh strainer and shake gently to remove the excess cocoa; store in an airtight container.

Chocolate Rum and Raisin Bites

MAKES 20

DIFFICULTY ★ ★ ★

MACERATE: Overnight

PREPARE: 30 minutes

REFRIGERATE: 2 hours

$^1/_4$ cup raisins

$3^1/_2$ tbsp rum

$^3/_4$ cup + 2 tbsp superfine
  sugar

4 tbsp glucose (or mild
  honey)

$^2/_3$ cup heavy whipping
  cream

1 tbsp unsalted butter

$2^3/_4$ oz bittersweet
  chocolate

◇ See p.314: Making praline
paste

◇ This recipe must be
started the night before.

Macerate the raisins overnight in rum.

The next day, line an 8 x $6^1/_4$-in cake pan with parchment paper. Put the superfine sugar, glucose (or honey), whipping cream, and unsalted butter into a saucepan. Heat the mixture until the temperature registers 250°F on a candy thermometer; remove from the heat. Drain the raisins and add to the sugar mixture; cool to 140°F without stirring.

Coarsely chop the chocolate and melt over a bain-marie; remove from the heat. When the sugar mixture has cooled, blend in the melted chocolate. Stir slowly until the mixture thickens and becomes opaque (if you stir too quickly, crystals could form). Pour a uniform layer into the prepared cake pan. Refrigerate for 2 hours, or until firm.

Turn out the chocolate and, using a knife dipped in hot water, cut into $1^1/_2$-in squares; store in an airtight container at room temperature.

CHEF'S TIP: Glucose is a liquid sugar, which does not crystalize and makes preparations such as this one smooth and moist. If it's not available in your local supermarket, you can purchase it from specialist cooking stores or on the internet.

Crunchy Praline Chocolates

MAKES **20**

DIFFICULTY ★ ★ ★

PREPARE: 1¼ hours

COOL: 10 minutes

Crunchy Praline Filling

2 tbsp water

¾ cup superfine sugar

⅔ cup blanched almonds

⅔ cup blanched hazelnuts

2¾ oz milk chocolate

1⅔ cups Frosties®, lightly
  crushed

Caramelized Almonds

2 tbsp water

1 tbsp superfine sugar

⅓ cup blanched almonds

1 tsp unsalted butter

Chocolate Coating

14 oz milk chocolate

Crunchy Praline Filling: Put the water and sugar into a saucepan over low heat, stirring until the sugar dissolves. Increase the heat and boil for 2 minutes without stirring; stir in the blanched nuts using a wooden spoon. Remove from the heat, and continue stirring until the sugar crystalizes, covering the nuts with a white powder. Return the saucepan to low heat until the sugar melts and the nuts turn golden brown. Immediately spread on an oiled baking sheet; set aside until cold. Break the praline in pieces, place in a food processor and grind, first to a powder then, to a creamy paste. It will be necessary to stop the food processor often, and mix with a spatula. (Or, to avoid overworking the food processor, grind the praline in several batches.) Place the praline paste in a bowl. Melt the milk chocolate over a bain-marie, pour it over the praline paste, and add the crushed Frosties®. Spread the mixture in a 7 x 5½-in cake pan using a spatula; refrigerate until required.

Caramelized Almonds: Put the sugar and water into a small saucepan over low heat, stirring until the sugar is completely dissolved. Remove from the heat; add the almonds, and stir until the syrup crystalizes, covering the nuts with a white powder. Return the saucepan to low heat and cook until the sugar melts and the nuts turn golden; incorporate the unsalted butter. Spread on parchment paper, roll with a spatula to separate and cool the caramelized almonds.

Chocolate Coating: Temper the milk chocolate (see p.315).

Turn out the praline filling and cut into ¾ x 1¼-in rectangles using a knife dipped in hot water. Use a fork to dip the rectangles, one by one, into the tempered milk chocolate. Then, shake gently and scrape on the side of the bowl to remove the excess. Transfer to parchment paper. Dip the bases of the caramelized almonds, one by one, into the melted chocolate and place each on a crunchy praline chocolate.

CHEF'S ADVICE: If you do not have a 7 x 5½-in cake pan, use a rectangular plastic container of the same dimensions.

Chocolate-Dipped Fruit

SERVES 4–6

DIFFICULTY ★ ★ ★

PREPARE: 20 minutes

REFRIGERATE: 15 minutes

18 strawberries
2 satsumas or clementines
6¼ oz bittersweet
  chocolate, chopped
1 tbsp vegetable oil

Cover a baking sheet with parchment paper. Wash and dry the strawberries, keeping them whole. Peel and separate the satsuma or clementine segments; dry with kitchen paper.

Melt the bittersweet chocolate slowly over a simmering bain-marie. Add the vegetable oil and stir until smooth; remove from the heat. Place the bowl on a folded dish towel to keep the chocolate warm.

Holding the strawberries by their stems dip them, one by one, into the chocolate so the chocolate covers half or three-quarters of the berry. Carefully wipe off the excess on the side of the bowl and transfer to the baking sheet. Repeat the operation for the satsuma segments.

Refrigerate the dipped fruit for 15 minutes. Serve at room temperature to enhance the fruit flavor and allow the chocolate to soften.

CHEF'S ADVICE: When you are dipping the fruit, if the chocolate becomes too thick, reheat the bain-marie and place the bowl of chocolate over it, being careful not to cook the chocolate. All types of fruit can be used for this recipe. The important thing to remember is that the surface of the fruit must be dry before dipping.

White Chocolate-Pistachio Fudge

MAKES 36 PIECES

DIFFICULTY ★ ★ ★

PREPARE: 20 minutes

REFRIGERATE: 2 hours

7 oz white chocolate

4 tsp unsalted butter

$^2/_3$ cup whipping cream

2$^1/_2$ tbsp mild honey

$^1/_2$ cup + 2 tbsp superfine sugar

Scant $^2/_3$ cup chopped pistachios

Line a 7-in square cake pan with parchment paper.

Chop the white chocolate and place in a bowl with the unsalted butter. Heat the whipping cream, honey, and sugar until the temperature of the mixture registers 240°F on a candy thermometer. Pour the mixture over the chopped chocolate and butter; stir until smooth. Then blend in the chopped pistachios.

Pour the white chocolate-pistachio fudge mixture into the prepared cake pan and refrigerate for 2 hours. When the fudge is firm, cut into 1$^1/_4$-in squares; serve.

CHEF'S TIP: The fudge can be kept for one week in an airtight container lined with parchment to stop it sticking. Store at room temperature in a cool dark place.

Creamy Chocolate-Caramel Parcels

MAKES 10 PARCELS

DIFFICULTY ★ ★ ★

PREPARE: 30 minutes

COOK: 6-8 minutes

REFRIGERATE: 15 minutes

10¹/₂ oz bittersweet
  chocolate
1¹/₂ cups heavy whipping
  cream
¹/₂ cup milk
1¹/₂ cups superfine sugar
6¹/₂ tbsp salted butter
6¹/₂ tbsp unsalted butter
¹/₄ cup unsalted butter
Filo pastry sheets

Line an 8-in square cake pan with plastic wrap.

Chop the chocolate and place in a bowl. Heat the whipping cream and milk until simmering; set aside. In a separate saucepan, cook ¹/₂ cup of the sugar, stirring from time to time with a wooden spoon until it becomes an amber-colored caramel. Stop the sugar cooking by stirring in a little of the creamy milk (the mixture will bubble violently!); add the remainder of the creamy milk a little at a time. Then add the rest of the sugar, continue stirring, and cook until smooth; be careful not to let it burn. Cook until the temperature of the mixture registers 237°F on a candy thermometer; remove from the heat. Stir in a little chopped chocolate, adding the remainder gradually. Blend in the salted butter and the 6¹/₂ tbsp of unsalted butter.

Pour the mixture into the prepared cake pan and refrigerate for at least 15 minutes, or until completely cold.

Preheat the oven to 400°F. Line 2 baking sheets with parchment paper. Melt the ¹/₄ cup unsalted butter. Cut the filo into 10 rectangles (8 x 6 in); cover with a damp dish towel so they do not dry out.

Divide the cold caramel chocolate in 10 equal portions; form into "logs" (about 1¹/₂ x 4 in). Place one "log" on each filo pastry rectangle, and wrap to form a parcel similar to a wrapped candy. Place wooden clothes pegs dipped in water at each end of the filling to enclose it and brush the parcel with the melted butter. Place on the baking sheets, transfer to the oven and cook for 6–8 minutes, or until lightly colored. Serve hot.

CHEF'S TIP: For this recipe, French chefs use feuilles de brick, which are paper thin discs of pastry, often used in Moroccan and Tunisian cooking. They can be purchased through the Internet.

Chocolate Caramel-Coated Chestnuts

MAKES 12

DIFFICULTY ★ ★ ★

DRAIN: Overnight

PREPARE: 30 minutes

COOL: 15 minutes

12 whole canned chestnuts
  in syrup

1³/₄ oz bittersweet
  chocolate

1¹/₄ cups superfine sugar

4 tbsp water

2¹/₂ tbsp mild honey

◇ This recipe must be
started the day ahead.

Place a rack over a bowl and drain the chestnuts overnight.

The next day, chop the bittersweet chocolate. Line a baking sheet with parchment paper.

Straighten 12 paper clips, leaving a hook at one end. Insert the straight part of the paper clips into the drained chestnuts.

Place the sugar, water and honey in a saucepan and cook until the temperature of the mixture registers 240°F on a candy thermometer; remove from the heat. Add the chopped chocolate gradually; stir until smooth.

Cover a work surface with parchment paper and position an 8-in wire rack above it. Dip the chestnuts into the chocolate caramel and hook them onto the rack for about 15 minutes until cold. When cooling, the caramel will drip forming a tail.

Chocolate Fruit and Nut Wafers

MAKES **30** WAFERS

DIFFICULTY ★ ★ ★

PREPARE: 1 hour

REST: 30 minutes

18 oz bittersweet chocolate

$^1\!/_2$ cup hazelnuts

$^1\!/_2$ cup sliced dried apricots

$^1\!/_2$ cup chopped pistachios

$^1\!/_2$ cup dried cranberries

◇ See p.315: Tempering chocolate.

Line a baking sheet with parchment paper.

Temper the bittersweet chocolate: Coarsely chop the bittersweet chocolate and place two-thirds (12 oz) in a bowl; melt over a simmering bain-marie until the temperature reaches 115°F on a candy thermometer. Remove the bowl from the heat and add the remaining chocolate, stirring until the temperature cools to 75°F. Return the bowl to the bain-marie and, gently stirring reheat the chocolate to 90°F.

Fit a pastry bag with a $^1\!/_4$-in round tip and fill with the tempered chocolate. Pipe discs of chocolate, of about $1\,^1\!/_4$-in diameter, on the baking sheet.

Before the chocolate starts to harden, arrange the nuts and dried fruits on each disc. Set the wafers aside for about 30 minutes, or until the chocolate is hard; store in an airtight container.

CHEF'S ADVICE: You can use other types of dried fruit, such as dried figs, on the wafers. In the traditional French (normally Christmas) confection, known as mendicants, the dried fruits and nuts represent the four monastic orders of the Dominicans (raisins), Augustinians (hazelnuts), Franciscans (figs), and Carmelites (almonds).

Milk Chocolate Rolls

MAKES 30 ROLLS
DIFFICULTY ★ ★ ★
PREPARE: 1 hour
REFRIGERATE: 20 minutes

Milk Chocolate Ganache
7 oz milk chocolate
$^1/_3$ cup heavy whipping
  cream
4 tsp mild honey
4 tsp praline paste (p.314)

Milk Chocolate Coating
12 oz milk chocolate

Decoration
Confectioners' sugar

◊ See p.318: Dipping and
coating chocolates.

Line a baking sheet with parchment paper.

Milk Chocolate Ganache: Chop the milk chocolate and place in a bowl. Heat the whipping cream and honey until simmering and pour over the chopped chocolate. Stir gently with a spatula until smooth then blend in the praline paste; set aside until cold. Fit a pastry bag with a $^1/_2$-in round tip and fill with the cold ganache. Pipe two long ropes of ganache on the baking sheet; refrigerate for 20 minutes. Dip a knife in hot water, dry it, and cut each rope into 15 pieces, each 1 $^1/_4$ in long.

Milk Chocolate Coating: Temper the chocolate: Coarsely chop the chocolate and place two-thirds (8 oz) in a bowl; melt over a simmering bain-marie until the temperature reaches 110°F on a candy thermometer. Remove the bowl from the heat and add the remaining chocolate, stirring until the temperature cools to 75°F. Return the bowl to the bain-marie and, stirring gently, reheat the chocolate to 85°F.

Sift the confectioners' sugar into a flat container. Using a fork, dip the ganache pieces, one by one, into the tempered milk chocolate. Shake gently and scrape the fork on the side of the bowl to remove the excess chocolate. Roll in the confectioners' sugar; set aside until hardened. Then, place the rolls in a wire mesh strainer and shake gently to remove the excess confectioners' sugar.

Store in an airtight container at 54°F maximum; consume within 15 days.

CHEF'S ADVICE: If desired, replace the praline paste with 4 tsp chocolate hazelnut spread.

Chocolate Nougats

MAKES 50

DIFFICULTY ★ ★ ★

PREPARE: 45 minutes

COOK: 15 minutes

REFRIGERATE: 2 hours

2$\frac{1}{2}$ cups hazelnuts

2 cups candied red cherries

10$\frac{1}{2}$ oz bittersweet
  chocolate

Italian Meringue

1 scant cup mild honey

2 egg whites

1 pinch salt

1 tbsp superfine sugar

Sugar Paste

1 cup + 6$\frac{1}{2}$ tbsp superfine
  sugar

6$\frac{1}{2}$ tbsp water

2$\frac{1}{2}$ tbsp mild honey

Preheat the oven to 275°F.

Place the hazelnuts on a baking sheet, transfer to the oven and toast for 15 minutes. Chop the candied cherries. Finely chop the chocolate and melt over a simmering bain-marie; stir from time to time. Set the toasted hazelnuts, chopped cherries, and melted chocolate aside.

Italian Meringue: Place the honey in a saucepan and heat until the temperature registers between 245°F on a candy thermometer. While the honey is heating, put the egg whites and salt into a metal bowl and beat with an electric mixer until foamy. Beating continuously, gradually pour the boiling honey down the side of the bowl into the egg whites. Continue beating until the Italian meringue becomes very firm and cold.

Line a baking sheet with parchment paper.

Sugar Paste: Combine the sugar, water, and honey in a saucepan, stirring over low heat until the sugar dissolves. Increase the heat and cook until the mixture registers 300°F on a candy thermometer.

Beat the sugar paste gradually into the meringue. Continue beating and rotate the bowl, heating it with a blow torch to dry out the mixture. Add the melted chocolate, chopped cherries, and hazelnuts, mixing with a spatula to combine the ingredients. Pour a layer of the chocolate nougat, $\frac{5}{8}$ in thick, onto the prepared baking sheet; refrigerate for 2 hours.

Remove from the refrigerator and cut the chocolate nougat in small squares or rectangles. They can be kept for 2 or 3 weeks in an airtight container.

CHEF'S TIP: If you do not have a blow torch, use a hair dryer to dry the Italian meringue mixture. Also, the pieces of nougat could be coated with tempered bittersweet chocolate (p.315).

Gold-Flecked Palettes

MAKES 30

DIFFICULTY ★ ★ ★

PREPARE: 1 hour approx

REFRIGERATE: 1 hour

Ganache
6¼ oz bittersweet
  chocolate
6 tbsp heavy whipping
  cream
1 tbsp mild honey
2½ tbsp soft unsalted
  butter

Chocolate Coating
14 oz bittersweet chocolate

Decoration
Edible gold flakes or dust

◇ See p.315: Tempering
chocolate.

Line a 7-in square baking sheet or cake pan with parchment paper.

Ganache: Chop the bittersweet chocolate and place in a bowl. Heat the whipping cream and honey until simmering, pour over the chopped chocolate and stir gently until smooth using a spatula; blend in the soft unsalted butter. Pour the ganache into the cake pan, in a layer approximately ⅜ in thick; refrigerate for at least 1 hour. When cold, turn the ganache out onto a clean work surface and using a knife, cut it into 1¼-in squares.

Chocolate Coating: Temper the bittersweet chocolate: Coarsely chop the chocolate and place two-thirds (9 oz) in a bowl; melt over a simmering bain-marie until the temperature reaches 115°F on a candy thermometer. Remove the bowl from the heat and add the remaining chocolate, stirring until the temperature cools to 75°F. Return the bowl to the bain-marie, and, stirring gently, reheat the chocolate to 90°F.

Using a fork, dip the ganache pieces, one by one, into the tempered chocolate. Shake gently and scrape the fork on the side of the bowl to remove any excess chocolate. Place on a sheet of plastic wrap for 30 minutes, or until almost hardened. When still slightly soft, remove the chocolates from the plastic wrap, turn them over and decorate with the edible gold flakes or dust (if the chocolate is too hard, the gold will not adhere!).

Store the chocolates in an airtight container, in a cool place (54°F maximum); consume within 10 days.

CHEF'S ADVICE: If you do not have a 7-in square cake pan, use the top of a plastic container with the same dimensions but be sure to line it with parchment paper. For round palettes, use a 1¼-in round cutter.

Chocolate Praline Truffles

MAKES **30**

DIFFICULTY ★ ★ ★

PREPARE: 1 hour

Praline Ganache

1 cup + 3 tbsp chopped
 almonds

2¹/₄ oz dark (55-70%)
 chocolate

¹/₂ cup praline paste

Chocolate Coating

9 oz bittersweet chocolate

◊ See p.314: Making praline paste
◊ See p.315: Tempering chocolate.

Praline Ganache: Place the chopped almonds in a non-stick frying pan over low heat and toast until fragrant and evenly golden brown. Chop the chocolate and melt over a bain-marie; remove from the heat. Blend in the praline paste and the 3 tbsp of the chopped toasted almonds. Set the mixture aside until it can be rolled easily. Wearing rubber gloves, divide the mixture in two equal portions and form into long ropes of the same length. Cut each rope into 15 equal pieces; roll by hand into balls and place on a plate.

Chocolate Coating: Temper the chocolate: Coarsely chop the bittersweet chocolate and place two-thirds (6 oz) in a bowl; melt over a simmering bain-marie until the temperature reaches 115°F on a candy thermometer. Remove the bowl from the heat and add the remaining chocolate, stirring until the temperature cools to 75°F. Return the bowl to the bain-marie and, stirring gently, reheat the chocolate to 90°F.

Wearing rubber gloves, dip the ganache balls, one by one, into the tempered chocolate, shaking gently to remove any excess; set on parchment paper to harden. When the chocolate starts to harden, gently roll each ball in the remaining chopped toasted almonds; set aside. The truffles will keep for two weeks stored in an airtight container, in a cool place (54°F maximum).

Crunchy Almond Wafers

MAKES **30** WAFERS

DIFFICULTY ★ ★ ★

PREPARE: 1½ hours

Caramelized Almond Sticks

4 tbsp water

³/₄ cup superfine sugar

2 cups slivered almonds

Chocolate Coating

5¹/₂ oz bittersweet
  chocolate

◊ See p.315: Tempering
chocolate.

Caramelized Almond Sticks: Heat the water and sugar, stirring to dissolve the sugar; bring to the boil and cook for about 5 minutes (do not stir!) until the syrup registers 245°F on a candy thermometer. Remove from the heat, add the slivered almonds, and stir until the sugar crystalizes and coats the nuts with a white powder. Return the saucepan to low heat until the sugar melts and coats the almonds with a golden brown caramel. Remove from the heat immediately and spread on parchment paper; roll to cool then place in a bowl.

Chocolate Coating: Temper the bittersweet chocolate: Coarsely chop the bittersweet chocolate and place two-thirds (3¹/₂ oz) in a bowl; melt over a simmering bain-marie until the temperature reaches 115°F on a candy thermometer. Remove the bowl from the heat and add the remaining chocolate, stirring until the temperature cools to 75°F. Return the bowl to the bain-marie and, stirring gently, reheat the chocolate to 90°F.

Line a baking sheet with parchment paper. As soon as the chocolate reaches 90°F, pour it over the caramelized almonds. Use a tablespoon to make small piles of the mixture on the parchment. Harden at room temperature for 30 minutes.

CHEF'S TIP: The almonds could be replaced with pine nuts.

Hazelnut Clusters

MAKES 25

DIFFICULTY ★ ★ ★

PREPARE: 1½ hours

Caramelized Hazelnuts

3 tbsp water

¹/₂ cup superfine sugar

²/₃ cup hazelnuts

1 tsp unsalted butter

Milk Chocolate Coating

10¹/₂ oz milk chocolate

◊ See p.315: Tempering chocolate.

Caramelized Hazelnuts: Bring the water and sugar to the boil, swirling the saucepan to dissolve the sugar; cook for about 5 minutes or until the syrup registers 245°F on a candy thermometer. Remove from the heat, add the hazelnuts, and stir until the sugar crystalizes, coating the hazelnuts with a white powder. Return the saucepan to low heat until the sugar melts and coats the hazelnuts with a golden brown caramel; add the butter. Remove from the heat immediately and spread on parchment paper. Using a fork, immediately arrange the hazelnuts into groups of three bonded by the caramel; set aside to harden for about 10 minutes.

Milk Chocolate Coating: Temper the milk chocolate: Coarsely chop the chocolate and place two-thirds (7 oz) in a bowl; melt over a simmering bain-marie until the temperature reaches 110°F on a candy thermometer. Remove the bowl from the heat and add the remaining chocolate, stirring until the temperature cools to 75°F. Return the bowl to the bain-marie and, stirring gently, reheat the chocolate to 85°F.

Using a fork, dip the hazelnut clusters into the tempered chocolate. Shake gently to remove any excess chocolate and place on parchment paper. Set aside to harden for 30 minutes before serving.

Plain Chocolate Truffles

MAKES 50 TRUFFLES

DIFFICULTY ★ ★ ★

PREPARE: 40 minutes

REFRIGERATE: 50 minutes

Ganache

10¹/₂ oz bittersweet
  chocolate

6¹/₂ tbsp heavy whipping
  cream

1 tsp vanilla extract

Coating

Unsweetened cocoa
  powder

Ganache: Finely chop the chocolate and place in a bowl. Heat the whipping cream until simmering and pour over the chopped chocolate; add the vanilla extract. Whisk lightly until the mixture is smooth and thick.

Line a baking sheet with parchment paper. Using a teaspoon or a pastry bag fitted with a round tip, make small balls of ganache on the paper; refrigerate for 50 minutes.

Coating: Sift the cocoa powder into a flat container. Wearing rubber gloves, use a fork to roll the balls in the cocoa powder, coating them evenly. Then place in a wire mesh strainer and shake gently to remove any excess cocoa; put each truffle into a small paper baking case.

Place in an airtight container and store in a cool place (54°F maximum). Consume the chocolate truffles within 15 days.

CHEF'S TIP: You can keep the truffles refrigerated for 1 week on a plate filled with cocoa powder, before rolling them completely in cocoa and placing in paper baking cases. Children will like this recipe, too, because it contains no alcohol.

Lemon Truffles

MAKES **50 TRUFFLES**

DIFFICULTY ★ ★ ★

PREPARE: 1 hour

REFRIGERATE: 50 minutes

Lemon Ganache

8$\frac{1}{2}$ oz milk chocolate

3 oz bittersweet chocolate

2 egg yolks

$\frac{1}{2}$ cup superfine sugar

6$\frac{1}{2}$ tbsp heavy whipping
  cream

Zests of 2 lemons, finely
  chopped

Coating

14 oz bittersweet chocolate

Confectioners' sugar

◊ See p.315: Tempering
chocolate.

Lemon Ganache: Finely chop the milk and bittersweet chocolates and place in a bowl. In a separate bowl, beat the egg yolks and sugar until pale yellow and creamy. Heat the whipping cream until simmering; whisking quickly, pour a little into the egg yolk and sugar mixture. Return to the saucepan and cook the mixture over low heat for 2 minutes, stirring continuously with a wooden spoon, until the cream thickens and coats the back of a spoon. (Do not allow to boil!) Remove from the heat immediately and strain over the chopped chocolate; stir until smooth and thick. Stir in the chopped lemon zest; refrigerate for 30 minutes or until firm.

Line a baking sheet with parchment paper. Using a teaspoon or a pastry bag fitted with a round tip, make small balls of lemon ganache on the baking sheet; refrigerate for 20 minutes.

Coating: Temper the chocolate: Coarsely chop the bittersweet chocolate and place two-thirds (9$\frac{1}{4}$ oz) in a bowl; melt over a simmering bain-marie until the temperature reaches 115°F on a candy thermometer. Remove the bowl from the heat and add the remaining chocolate, stirring until the temperature cools to 75°F. Return the bowl to the bain-marie and, stirring gently, reheat the chocolate to 90°F.

Sift the confectioners' sugar into a flat container. When the ganache balls are firm, remove from the refrigerator. Wearing rubber gloves, dip the ganache balls, one by one, into the tempered chocolate, shaking gently to remove any excess. Roll the lemon truffles in confectioners' sugar and set aside to harden at room temperature. Then place in a wire mesh strainer and shake gently to remove any excess confectioners' sugar.

Consume the lemon truffles within 7 days; store in an airtight container, in a cool place (54°F maximum).

Cointreau Truffles

MAKES **50 TRUFFLES**

DIFFICULTY ★ ★ ★

PREPARE: 1 hour

REFRIGERATE: 1 hour approx.

Two-Chocolate Ganache
5$^1/_2$ oz milk chocolate

5$^1/_2$ oz bittersweet
chocolate

$^2/_3$ cup heavy whipping
cream

2$^1/_2$ tbsp mild honey

2 tbsp Cointreau

Chocolate Coating
18 oz bittersweet chocolate

1$^1/_4$ cups unsweetened
cocoa powder

◊ See p.318: Dipping and
coating chocolates.

Line a baking sheet with parchment paper.

Two-Chocolate Ganache: Chop the milk and bittersweet chocolates and place in a bowl. Heat the whipping cream and honey until simmering and pour over the chopped chocolate, stir until smooth; add the Cointreau. Refrigerate the ganache for 20 minutes. Fit a pastry bag with a plain round tip. When the ganache is completely cold, remove from the refrigerator and gently stir. Pour it into the pastry bag and pipe 50 mounds on the baking sheet; refrigerate for 20 minutes. Wearing rubber gloves, roll the ganache by hand to form round balls; refrigerate again for 20 minutes.

Chocolate Coating: Temper the chocolate: Coarsely chop the bittersweet chocolate and place two-thirds (12 oz) in a bowl; melt over a simmering bain-marie until the temperature reaches 115°F on a candy thermometer. Remove the bowl from the heat and add the remaining chocolate, stirring until the temperature cools to 75°F. Return the bowl to the bain-marie and, stirring gently, reheat the chocolate to 90°F.

Sift the cocoa powder into a flat container. Slide a fork under the ganache balls and carefully dip, one by one, into the tempered chocolate; shake gently to remove any excess. Using the fork, roll in the cocoa powder. Set aside to firm at room temperature. When firm, place in a wire mesh strainer and shake gently to remove any excess cocoa.

The truffles will keep about 15 days stored in an airtight container in a cool place (54°F maximum).

CHEF'S TIP: You can replace the Cointreau with a different liqueur or alcohol, using the same quantity. If you have left-over tempered chocolate, use it to make a sauce.

Rum Truffles

MAKES 30 TRUFFLES

DIFFICULTY ★ ★ ★

PREPARE: 1 hour

REFRIGERATE: 30 minutes

Chocolate-Rum Ganache

6 oz bittersweet chocolate

$^2/_3$ cup heavy whipping
  cream

1 tbsp soft unsalted butter

1 tsp rum

Chocolate Coating

18 oz bittersweet chocolate

1$^1/_4$ cups unsweetened
  cocoa powder

Line a baking sheet with parchment paper.

Chocolate-Rum Ganache: Chop the chocolate and place in a bowl. Heat the whipping cream until simmering and pour over the chopped chocolate, let it melt for a couple of seconds then, stir until smooth; blend in the soft unsalted butter and rum. Refrigerate the ganache for 10 minutes. Fit a pastry bag with a plain round tip. When the ganache is cold, remove from the refrigerator and gently stir with a spatula. Pour it into the pastry bag and pipe 30 small mounds on the baking sheet; refrigerate for 20 minutes. Wearing rubber gloves, roll the ganache by hand to form round balls; refrigerate until required.

Chocolate Coating: Temper the chocolate: Coarsely chop the bittersweet chocolate and place two-thirds (12 oz) in a bowl; melt over a simmering bain-marie until the temperature reaches 115°F on a candy thermometer. Remove the bowl from the heat and add the remaining chocolate, stirring until the temperature cools to 75°F. Return the bowl to the bain-marie and, stirring gently, reheat the chocolate to 90°F.

Sift the unsweetened cocoa powder into a flat container. Slide a fork under each ganache ball and carefully dip, one by one, into the tempered chocolate; shake gently to remove any excess. Use a teaspoon to roll the rum truffles in the cocoa powder. Set aside to firm at room temperature for 30 minutes. When firm, place in a fine mesh wire strainer and shake gently to remove any excess cocoa.

The truffles will keep about 15 days stored in an airtight container in a cool place (54°F maximum).

Mini Mocha Truffles

MAKES 45-50 TRUFFLES
DIFFICULTY ★ ★ ★
PREPARE: 1 hour
REFRIGERATE: 1 hour approx.

Two-Chocolate Ganache
4¹/₂ oz milk chocolate
6¹/₂ oz bittersweet
  chocolate
³/₄ cup heavy whipping
  cream
2 tbsp mild honey
3 tbsp instant coffee
³/₄ cup superfine sugar

Chocolate Coating
14 oz bittersweet chocolate
³/₄ cup chopped almonds,
  toasted

◇ See p.318: Dipping and
coating chocolates.

Two-Chocolate Ganache: Coarsely chop the milk and bittersweet chocolates and place in a bowl. Heat the whipping cream, honey, and coffee until simmering. Put the sugar in a separate saucepan and cook until it becomes a golden brown caramel color. Slowly add the hot cream mixture to stop the sugar cooking (be careful, the mixture will sputter violently). Return to the heat until simmering. Pour the caramel cream over the chopped chocolate and gently stir until smooth; cool. Refrigerate for 30 minutes. When the ganache is completely cold, remove from the refrigerator and gently stir with a spatula. Fit a pastry bag with a small round tip and fill with the ganache. Pipe 45–50 tiny mounds on the prepared baking sheet; refrigerate for 20 minutes. Wearing rubber gloves, roll the ganache mounds by hand to form balls; refrigerate again for 10–15 minutes.

Chocolate Coating: Temper the chocolate: Coarsely chop the bittersweet chocolate and place two-thirds (9¹/₄ oz) in a bowl; melt over a simmering bain-marie until the temperature reaches 115°F on a candy thermometer. Remove the bowl from the heat and add the remaining chocolate, stirring until the temperature cools to 75°F. Return the bowl to the bain-marie and, stirring gently, reheat the chocolate to 90°F.

Slide a fork under each ganache ball and carefully dip, one by one, into the tempered chocolate; shake gently to remove any excess. Place on parchment paper to harden. As soon as the chocolate starts to harden, roll the truffles in the chopped toasted almonds.

The mocha truffles will keep about 15 days; store in an airtight container in a cool place (54°C maximum).

CHEF'S ADVICE: The almonds could be replaced with crushed Frosties®.

GLOSSARY

Bain-marie: A hot water bath. Can be bought as a specialist piece of equipment or improvised by sitting a bowl containing the ingredient(s) in a larger pan of simmering water. Used for cooking or warming food (especially delicate sauces), melting chocolate, and for making a Génoise sponge or sabayon, which must not be put on direct heat.

Bake: To cook food uncovered in an oven at a required temperature.

Baking powder: A dry chemical raising agent used to increase volume and lighten the texture of baked goods such as cakes.

Boil: To heat a liquid until bubbles break on the surface. To boil a foodstuff is to cook it in boiling liquid (usually water). The boiling point of water is 212°F but varies for other liquids.

Beat: A technique to mix ingredients by hand with a fork, spoon, whisk, or beater in a quick, circular motion until the ingredients are smooth and evenly blended. Also used for aerating soufflé and ingredients needing to rise during cooking.

Beurre en pomade: Softened (not melted) butter, beaten until it becomes creamy and smooth.

Beurre noisette: Nut-brown butter, which is obtained by heating butter until it liquefies and turns golden brown, and the milk solids color and stick to the bottom of the saucepan.

Biscuit: One of the basic French cakes — a fine, light sponge made with butter, sugar, and egg yolks, to which stiffly beaten egg whites (or baking powder) have been added.

Brûlée: A sugar topping melted under a hot broiler until it caramelizes. When cool, a crisp crust forms.

Butter/oil: To lightly coat a baking dish or other container with soft or melted butter or oil, using a pastry brush, to prevent foods sticking.

Caramel: Sugar melted and cooked to 356°F. The sugar changes from a light golden to a dark brown syrup during the cooking process. When cooled, it is very brittle and breaks easily.

Caramelize: To coat food or line a mold with caramel. Sugar can also be caramelized when sprinkled on a dessert and melted under a hot broiler (see brûlée).

Chantilly cream: Whipped cream with the addition of confectioners' sugar.

Chill: To place food in a refrigerator or a bath of iced water or crushed ice to make or keep it cool or firm.

Chinois: A conical metal strainer..

Chop: To cut food into small pieces using a knife or food processor.

Churn/freeze: The process of converting a liquid mixture into ice cream or sorbet using an ice cream or sorbet machine.

Clarified butter: A process of gently melting butter in which the whey (or milk solids) sinks to the bottom of pan and the impurities float to the top of the liquefied butter. Clarified, butter can be kept refrigerated for longer than non-clarified butter without becoming rancid; it also burns less quickly when heated.

Coat: To completely cover an ingredient with another, such as chocolate.

Cocoa nibs: Roasted cocoa beans separated from their husks and broken into small bits. Also known as chocolate nibs .

Compote: A preparation of fresh or dried fruit cooked in sugar syrup until soft.

Cookie or bar: A small sweet pastry or cake.

Core: To remove the central core from fruit such apples and pears.

Coulis: A strained, smooth purée of sweetened fruit combined with a small amount of lemon juice.

Couverture chocolate: A very high quality chocolate containing extra cocoa butter. The higher percentage of cocoa butter combined with proper tempering gives the chocolate more sheen, firmer «snap» when broken, and a creamy mellow flavor. The total «percentage» cited on many brands of chocolate is based on a combination of cocoa butter in relation to cocoa solids (cacao). To be properly labeled as «couverture», the percentage of cocoa butter must be between 32% and 39%, and the total percentage of the combined cocoa butter plus cocoa solids must be at least 54%. It is used by professionals for dipping, coating, molding, and garnishing.

Cream: To beat ingredients together until they have blended into a light, fluffy and smooth consistency. The term is usually applied to incorporating a fat, such as butter, into sugar.

Cream, whipped: Whipping cream whisked until firm peaks cling to the whisk.

Crème anglaise: A vanilla custard cream sauce made with milk, eggs, and sugar and served with a variety of desserts. The vanilla can be replaced with other flavors such as chocolate and pistachio. It is the base preparation for ice cream.

Crème pâtissière: A thick pastry cream made with milk, egg yolks, sugar, and flour and traditionally flavored with vanilla. Used as the base preparation in many desserts and also as a filling for éclairs.

Crush: To reduce a solid ingredient to small pieces using a food processor or a rolling pin.

Crystalized: Describes fruit or flower petals, generally used for decoration, that have been coated in lightly beaten egg white then sugar.

Dessert or tart ring: A metal circle of various diameters and heights used for assembling desserts. Pastry chefs prefer this tool over the traditional round mold.

Détrempe: A flour-and-water mixture, which is the first step in the preparation of puff pastry.

Dice: To cut food into small cubes.

Dough: A thick, malleable paste made from flour and water that is soft, yet firm enough to hold its form.

Dropping consistency: Describes the consistency of a preparation dropped by the spoonful on to a baking sheet, which holds its shape once dropped.

Dust: To lightly sprinkle food or a work surface with a powdery ingredient such as flour, cocoa powder, or confectioners' sugar.

Enrich: To add cream, egg yolks, or butter to a preparation giving it a richer texture or flavor.

Flour: To dredge or sprinkle pans with flour, usually over a thin layer of butter, to prevent food sticking.

Fold: To blend a light ingredient with a heavier one. Usually, the lighter is placed on the heavier one. The two are combined using a spatula or metal spoon in a figure-of-eight motion, to retain air in the mixture.

Fritter: Food coated in batter and deep-fried. The batter coating varies according to the food.

Fry: To cook food in hot fat. Deep-fried foods are submerged in fat. Sautéed or pan-fried foods are cooked in a small amount of fat—just enough to coat the bottom of the pan and prevent sticking.

Ganache: A mixture obtained by pouring hot cream over chopped chocolate. It is used for garnishing desserts and as a filling for cakes and chocolates.

Gelatine: A colorless solid, in powder or leaf form, used as a gelling agent. When added to hot liquid it becomes viscous and when cold, solidifies.

Génoise: One of the basic French cakes. It is a whisked yellow sponge made with eggs, sugar, and flour.

Glaze: 1. To coat the surface of dessert with a thin, sweet liquid such as ganache, or icing that will set to a smooth, glossy finish. 2. To brush uncooked dough with beaten egg to give it a sheen when cooked.

Grind: To reduce dry foods to a powder or into tiny grains using either a pestle and mortar or a food processor.

Hull: To remove the stalk and core from fruit such as strawberries.

Ice-Bath: To immerse the base of a hot pan of ingredients in a bowl of water and ice cubes to rapidly stop the cooking process.

Imbibe: To use a flavored syrup or liqueur to soak a cake, adding flavor and increasing moisture.

Infuse: To steep herbs, spices, or citrus zests, etc. in a hot liquid giving the liquid flavor and aroma.

Julienne: To cut fruit, citrus peel, or vegetables into very fine shreds or strips.

Knead: To manipulate dough by hand pushing it and pulling it across the work surface to thoroughly blend ingredients.

Line: 1. To cover a baking sheet or the inside of a mold with parchment paper to prevent the finished product from sticking during cooking. 2. To cover the interior wall and/or bottom of a tart or flan tin with pastry dough before baking or adding a filling.

Macerate: To soak and flavor food, usually fruit, in sugar syrup, liqueur, or alcohol.

Marbling: A decorative effect achieved by partially mixing cake batters or chocolates of different colors.

Meringue: A whisked egg white and sugar mixture. There are 3 types. French: egg whites into which sugar is beaten progressively until stiff peaks form. Italian: whisked egg whites with a cooked sugar syrup added. Swiss: egg whites and sugar whisked over a bain-marie until firm.

Mix: The technique of combining two or more ingredients.

Mold: 1. To shape a dessert by placing a soft, supple preparation in a mold to set into that shape either by chilling or using a setting agent such as gelatin. 2. A container available in a variety of shapes and sizes.

Mousse: A preparation with a light, airy texture, obtained by the addition of whisked egg whites.

Nap: To lightly coat a dessert with a coulis or cream.

Parchment paper: A non-stick paper that is particularly useful for lining baking pans and sheets.

Paste: Food ground to a fine texture and moistened slightly to make a stiff spreadable mixture.

Pastry cutter: A metal or plastic tool in a variety of shapes and sizes used to cut pastry dough into even shapes.

Pâte: A pastry mixture such as pâte sucrée (sweet pastry), pâte brisée (shortcrust pastry), or pâte sablé (shortbread pastry).

Pâton: Uncooked puff pastry dough.

Pinch: A very small quantity of an ingredient such as salt or sugar taken using the thumb and the forefinger.

Pith: The bitter white layer of skin between the colored outer skin (the zest) and flesh of citrus fruit.

Poach: To immerse food and cook it in a slowly simmering liquid such as water or a sugar syrup.

Praline: Almonds and/or hazelnuts cooked in boiling sugar until caramelized. The mixture is then cooled and ground to a powder. If it is ground further, it becomes praline paste.

Prick: To make small holes in pastry dough with fork to prevent air pockets forming during baking.

Purée: Cooked or raw fruit or vegetables processed in an electric blender or food mill to obtain a pulp, which is then strained. It can be used as a sauce or as a base for other preparations.

Quenelles: Ovals of a soft preparation such as ice cream or whipped cream, shaped with two spoons and often used decoratively.

Reduce: To boil a liquid at a high heat in an uncovered pan, evaporating it and concentrating the flavor.

Ribbon: When a beaten egg-and-sugar mixture falls from a spoon or whisk in a smooth, unbroken flow, it is said to be at ribbon consistency.

Sift: To pass dry ingredients such as flour or confectioners' sugar through a sifter or strainer, to add air and remove lumps.

Simmer: To maintain a liquid just below boiling point, so that the surface bubbles gently. The term also refers to cooking food gently in a liquid (see poaching).

Skim: To remove impurities or foam from the surface of a preparation using a ladle or large spoon.

Slice: To cut an item such as fruit using a knife or slicer into thin or fine, even slices.

Soufflé: A light, airy preparation based on whisked egg whites. Cooked versions rise.

Strain: To pass a liquid through a strainer to remove any solids.

Sweat: To gently cook fruit or vegetables in a little butter or oil without coloring to bring out the flavor.

Syrup: A liquid made by heating sugar and water. Syrups have a variety of uses depending on the ratio of sugar to water and the temperature to which they are heated.

Temper: To heat, cool, and reheat chocolate to three precise temperatures (p. 315), giving it a glossy, streak-free, and crisp finish.

Tip: Piping tips are hollow and conical and made from steel or plastic. They can be plain or fluted and used in a piping bag to pipe cream, choux paste, or meringue.

Turn/fold: A technique used to blend the butter into puff pastry dough.

Vanilla essence/extract: Products made from pure vanilla to obtain a reliable flavor, which can be used to replace a vanilla pod.

Well: A large hollow made in the center of a quantity of flour, either in a bowl or on the work surface, to hold liquid ingredients.

Whisk: A technique using a wire whisk or electric mixer, to rapidly beat ingredients incorporating as much air as possible into a preparation.

Zest: The colored outer skin of citrus fruit (without the pith).

INDEX

INDEX OF FRENCH RECIPE NAMES

ACKNOWLEDGEMENTS

Le Cordon Bleu wishes to thank its Chef teams located in nearly 20 countries and 40 schools around the globe. Thanks to their know-how and creativity, we have been able to write this book.

We wish to express our gratitude to the Paris school and its chefs: Patrick Terrien, Nicolas Bernardé (MOF), Marc Chalopin, Didier Chantefort, Philippe Clergue, Xavier Cotte, Jean-François Deguignet, Patrick Lebouc, Franck Poupard, Bruno Stril, Marc Thivet, Jean-Jacques Tranchant

The London school (Great Britain): Chefs Yann Barraud, Eric Bédiat, Christophe Bidault, Stuart Conibear, Jérôme Drouart, Franck Jeandon, Loïc Malfait, Julie Walsh, Jonathan Warner The Tokyo school (Japan): Chefs Olivier Oddos, Marc Bonard, Dominique Gros, Hiroyuki Honda, Kenji Hori, Patrick Lemesle, Katsutoshi Yokoyama

The Kobe school (Japan): Chefs Chefs Bruno Lederf (MOF), Thierry Guignard, Nakamura Minoru, Kawamichi Tsuyoshi, Cyril Veniat

The Ottawa school (Canada): Chefs Phillipe Guiet, Armando Baisas, Jean Marc Baque, Marc Berger, Herve Chabert, Christian Faure (MOF), Benoit Gelinotte, Nicholas Jordan, Thierry Laroche, Gilles Penot, Christopher Price, Daniel Verati

The Seoul school (South Korea): Chefs Philippe Bachmann, Laurent Beltoise, Franck Colombie, Jean Pierre Gestin

The Lima school (Peru) : Chefs Cecilia Aragaki Uechi, Jaques Benoit, Gabriela Espinosa Anaya, Gregor Funche Krümdiek, César Gago Salazar, Gloria Hinostroza de Molina, Pierre Marchand Gómez-Sáanchez, José Meza Maldonado, Andrea Monge, Samuel Moreau, Fernando Oré Lund, Maríe del Pilar Alvarez de Ruesta, Daniel Punchín León, Olivier Rousseau, Mariella Vargas Loret de Mola

The Mexico City school (Mexico): Chefs Patrick Martin (Vice-President), Denis Delaval, Arnaud Gueripillon, Christian Leroy, Raul Martinez, Carlos Santos

The Bangkok school (Thailand): Chefs Fabrice Danniel, Arnaud Lindivat, Cedric Maton, Bruno Souquières, Pruek Sumpantaworavoot

The Australian schools under the responsibility of Chefs Hervé Boutin (MOF) and George Winter

The American schools under the aegis of Paul Ryan and Brian Williams

And, the Pierre Deux-French Country ® team for the use of their table arts accessories highlighting the French art de vivre

The publication of the book would not have been possible without the professionalism, enthusiasm and continual follow-up by the coordination and administrative teams, nor without the photographer or the recipe testers under the leadership of Chef Walter: Sylvie Alarcon, Catherine Baschet, Kaye Baudinette, Isabelle Beaudin, Guillemette Bouche, Emilie Burgat, Robyn Cahill, Marie-Anne Dufeu, Mélanie Hergon, Christian Lalonde (Photolux Studio), Leanne Mallard, Sandra Messier, Kathy Shaw, Lynne Westney

Our special thanks to Larousse's Isabelle Jeuge-Maynard (Chairman of the Board, CEO) and Ghislaine Stora (Deputy Chief Executive Officer) and their team ; Brigitte Courtillet, Anne Charlotte Diverres, Camille Durette, Véronique de Finance-Cordonnier, Colette Hanicotte, Aude Mantoux

NOTES

NOTES